VGM Professional Careers Series

CAREERS
IN HEALTH CARE

BARBARA SWANSON

VGM Career Horizons
a division of *NTC Publishing Group*
Lincolnwood, Illinois USA

Cover photo credit:
Courtesy of the National Cancer Institute.

Library of Congress Cataloging-in-Publication Data
Swanson, Barbara Mardinly.
    Careers in health care / Barbara M. Swanson.
        p.   cm.
    Includes bibliographical references.
    ISBN 0-8442-4198-9 (hard) — ISBN 0-8442-4199-7 (soft)
      1. Allied health personnel—United States—Vocational guidance.
    2. Medical personnel—United States—Vocational guidance.
    I. Title.
    R697.A4S93   1994   94-29089
    610.69—dc20   CIP

1996 Printing

Published by VGM Career Horizons, a division of NTC Publishing Group
4255 West Touhy Avenue
Lincolnwood (Chicago), Illinois 60646-1975, U.S.A.
© 1995 by NTC Publishing Group. All rights reserved.
No part of this book may be reproduced, stored in a retrieval system,
or transmitted in any form or by any means,
electronic, mechanical, photocopying, recording or otherwise,
without the prior permission of NTC Publishing Group.
Manufactured in the United States of America.

6 7 8 9 0 VP 9 8 7 6 5 4 3

DEDICATION

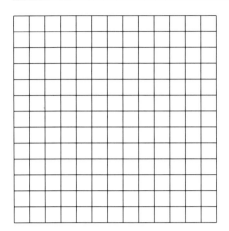

This book is dedicated, with love
and thanks, to my three terrific
sons, John, Jeff, and Matt, and
to my amazing husband, Bob,

and

it is dedicated to the memory of
Richard J. Smith, M.D.

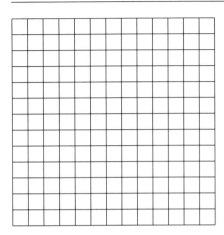

CONTENTS

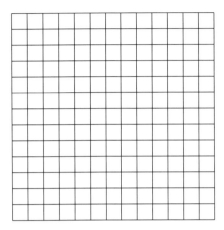

ABOUT THE AUTHOR

Barbara Mardinly Swanson is a professional writer with a lifelong interest in health care and extensive knowledge of the American health care system and the services it provides. It was her abiding respect for medical professionals that motivated her to write this book.

Previous books by Barbara Swanson include *Tax Shelters: A Guide for Investors and Their Advisors* (Dow Jones-Irwin, 1982), which she co-authored with her husband, Robert E. Swanson. Her essays and poetry have appeared nationally. A graduate of Smith College, the author lives in Ridgewood, New Jersey, with her husband. They have three sons, John, Jeff, and Matt.

PREFACE

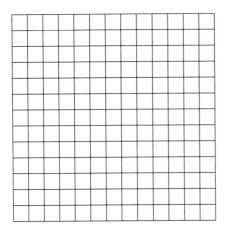

This book was written because, more than ever, students, parents, teachers, guidance counselors, new graduates, men and women seeking new careers, and individuals reentering the work force want, need, and deserve correct, complete, current, and readable information about the myriad exciting career options that exist in the health field today. In addition to the noble profession of physician, there are dozens of other vital and challenging ways to contribute in the health field, and it is on these professions that *Careers in Health Care* focuses.

For each career covered in this book, the following questions have been carefully researched and answered: What is the theory behind the work? What does the work entail? What is the workday like? How many men and women are in the profession? What education and training are necessary? What certification and licensure requirements exist? What personal qualities and abilities are important to success and satisfaction? What salaries and promotions may be anticipated? What, if any, drawbacks are inherent in the work? And, finally, what does the future of the profession look like?

To the hundreds of health care professionals I interviewed in the course of researching this material who so generously and graciously shared their knowledge and time, including the good people of the American Medical Association, and to the folks at the U.S. Department of Labor, goes my sincere appreciation. And special thanks go to Roy Pollack, M.D.; Celia Ores, M.D.; David Ores, M.D.; Youngick Lee, M.D.; Lonna Yegen, M.D.; James J. Pedicano, M.D.; Goldie Alfasi-Siffert, Ph.D.; Rose Mardinly; George Mardinly; Arthur J. Geiringer, Jr.; and the late Robert H. Ringewald, M.D.; for their guidance and encouragement.

Barbara Mardinly Swanson

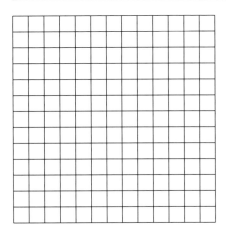

INTRODUCTION

From television, movies, or perhaps from personal experience, we've all glimpsed the drama of the modern hospital—the fast pace of the emergency room, the methodical intensity of the operating room, the dozen pairs of educated hands setting to work to provide essential care. In a hospital, there are many educated people working together to improve lives, to save lives.

Every medical recovery and every medical discovery is the product of teamwork. There are no nonessential jobs in health and medicine. And not all of the drama in modern medicine and health care takes place in the operating room. There is drama—and challenge and satisfaction, too—in the occupational therapy room of a community rehabilitation clinic, in a rural home where a nurse-midwife is helping to deliver a baby, or in a laboratory looking through an electron microscope.

There is room in the health field for almost every ability, talent, and interest. Are you artistically inclined? Then you might consider a career as an art therapist or as a medical illustrator. Are you mechanically orientated? Biomedical engineering might offer the challenges you seek. Do you enjoy working with your hands? Manual arts therapy calls for such dexterity, and so do careers in orthotics, prosthetics, and dental and ophthalmic laboratory technology. Are you interested in music? Or dance? Or gardening? Then you may find your place in music therapy or dance therapy or horticultural therapy. Do you like to write? Americans today are thirsty for medical and health-related information, and opportunities in medical writing are booming. Does photography interest you? Biological photography is a fascinating field. If you have ever considered becoming a librarian, health sciences librarianship might be the perfect specialty for you. If you love working with children, a career as a child life specialist can offer very special rewards. If you would like to work in the exciting atmosphere of a hospital but do not want direct patient care responsibility, a position as a dietitian or as a technician in the laboratory might be ideal. If you do want patient contact but do not plan to become a physician, you might consider becoming a nurse, or a surgical technologist, or an extracorporeal perfusionist, or a physician assistant. Are sports your love? The demand for certified athletic trainers is growing fast. The options go on and on—there is even a place for magicians in medicine.

The possibilities are great and growing greater every day as new medical technologies and techniques are developed. Last year, Americans spent one trillion dollars on health care—that is 15 percent of the nation's total output of goods and services. The demand for medical services has never been greater, and the opportunities for serving are more diverse and, in most cases, more plentiful than ever before. Simultaneously, scrutiny of medical services has never been greater, as the health care reform movement emphasizes cost containment in addition to successful medical outcomes.

The men and women who bring their intellect, talent, and dedication to the health care field do very important work in our society. Good luck as you seek your special place among them on the health care team.

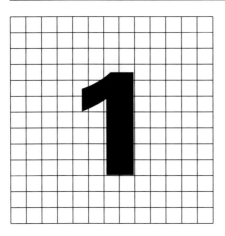

ANESTHESIOLOGISTS' ASSISTANT

Anesthesiologists' assistants (AAs) are health care professionals who have successfully completed an accredited program of academic and clinical training and are qualified to work under the supervision of an anesthesiologist (a physician with special residency training in anesthesiology). AAs assist in administering anesthetics to patients undergoing surgery.

Anesthesiologists' assistants are to anesthesiologists what primary care physician assistants are to primary care physicians (i.e. family practioners, pediatricians, etc.) and surgeon assistants are to surgeons—that is, they are *dependent* practitioners participating in a medical care team. Specific responsibilities may vary from site to site depending on the particular practice guidelines in individual hospitals and individual states. Although some AAs may participate in the pre-anesthetic evaluation, more commonly they are involved in assisting the anesthesiologist in reviewing the data available from the surgical and medical teams. In collaboration with the anesthesiologist, they participate in the induction and maintenance of anesthesia and in monitoring the patient's status during the surgical procedure. It has been the general plan that the anesthesiologist has been available in the hospital (although not necessarily always present in the room) during all portions of the case. As a general rule, both the AA and the anesthesiologist are present at the beginning and the end of the case and at the time of major changes in the patient's status. In some instances, AAs also assist the anesthesiologist in the intensive care unit and in pain clinic work.

SETTING, SALARIES, STATISTICS

Anesthesiologists' assistants work wherever anesthesiologists work: in hospitals, clinics, outpatient surgical facilities, and academic settings. They

1

practice in all states that accept physician assistant practice. The greatest concentration of AAs is in the two states that currently have educational programs—Georgia and Ohio. There are only approximately 400 AAs at this time. Men and women are equally represented in this profession.

Salaries for anesthesiologists' assistants begin in the $55,000 to $65,000 range.

HOW TO BECOME AN ANESTHESIOLOGISTS' ASSISTANT

Formal educational requirements for this field are only about ten years old. A master's degree specifically in anesthesiologists' assisting is required, and this degree is offered by only two universities at this time: Emory and Case Western, which established their programs only twenty years ago. Both of these programs are accredited by the Commission for the Accreditation of Allied Health Education Programs (CAAHEP), which accredits most allied health education programs in the United States and which, on July 1, 1994, became the successor to the American Medical Association's Committee on Allied Health Education and Accreditation (CAHEA). CAAHEP is an independent body in which the AMA participates as one sponsor among many. Last year, thirty-five men and women graduated from these programs.

Applicants to a program must have premedical undergraduate backgrounds, but may have college degrees in one of several areas. Typically, they are degrees in biology or chemistry or a related allied health area such as respiratory therapy, nursing, or medical technology. The age of students entering these programs ranges from those who are immediately out of college to those who have been out of college and have been working in other areas for ten to fifteen years. Over the years, approximately ten to fifteen percent of the graduates of the two programs have gone on for further graduate medical education, and the overwhelming majority of those who have gone to medical school have done residencies in anesthesiology.

As of July 1992, a national certification examination for anesthesiologists' assistants has been available. This examination is given by the National Commission on the Certification of Anesthesiologists' Assistants (NCCAA) in collaboration with the National Board of Medical Examiners, which is the group that also assists with the national examination for primary care physician assistants and surgeon assistants.

THE FUTURE

Recent graduates are much in demand, and it appears that employment in this still relatively new profession will remain stable.

For information about anesthesiologists' assistants, write to:

Anesthesiologists' Assistant Program
Emory University
617 Woodruff Memorial Building
P.O. Box AK
Atlanta, Georgia 30322

Anesthesiologists' Assistant Program
Case Western University
2074 Abbington Road
Cleveland, Ohio 44106

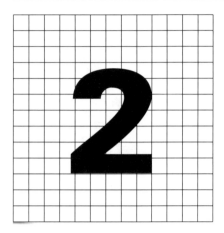

ART THERAPIST

"One picture is worth more than ten thousand words" goes the Chinese proverb. For psychiatric patients whose inner turmoil has rendered them non-verbal, the pictures, patterns, and doodles they create in an art therapy session can speak volumes. Art therapy is the use of art activities as a device for non-verbal expression and communication, leading to the resolution of emotional conflicts, self-understanding, and personal growth for a wide variety of mentally and physically impaired patients. It is used as a medium for interpretation and rehabilitation with patients who are unable or unwilling to speak, as well as with those who are verbal but who use words as a defense or cover-up.

Like the other creative arts therapies (dance therapy, music therapy, psychodrama, and poetry therapy), art therapy is effective because the patient's emotions are directly tapped and the visual expressions of the emotions—the pictures, sculptures, montages created—are often more telling than words. The feelings that are aroused and expressed when patients draw a picture of their home, or family, or themselves are often more direct, more honest, and more revealing than a verbal description of their house or family or themselves can be. The colors used, the spatial arrangement of the figures included, the detail or lack of it, and the perspective, proportions, and technique are more than just the aesthetic elements of the drawing—they are reflections of how patients see the world. The patients are really drawing a map of their subconscious feelings, desires, and fears. The patients' abilities, personalities, interests, concerns—the very nature of their emotional distress and progress—can be revealed in the artwork they create.

Art therapists are human service providers who, by virtue of their graduate-level education and extensive training in both art and psychology, are experts at involving a wide variety of patients in art activities that can help to uncover problems and bring about improvement. They may act as primary therapist or as adjunctive within the treatment team, depending on the needs of the institution and the treatment objectives of the patient.

Art therapists treat individuals, families, and groups. The vast majority (75 percent) of all patients seen by art therapists are emotionally disturbed, and individuals with physical disabilities are the second largest group (6 percent). Art therapy is also used effectively with people with mental retardation, AIDS, autism, Alzheimer's Disease, learning disabilities, hearing impairment, sight impairment, brain damage, multiple disabilities, alcohol and drug abuse, as well as individuals who have experienced sexual abuse, the elderly, and prison inmates. A recent survey conducted by the American Art Therapy Association (AATA) revealed that approximately 43 percent of all art therapy patients are adults, 28 percent are adolescents, 22 percent are children, 6.5 percent are elderly, and 1.5 percent are infants.

Art therapists plan art activities, maintain and distribute various arts and crafts materials, provide instruction in a variety of artistic techniques, and observe and record what takes place during the art therapy session. Again, the emphasis is not on the quality of the artwork produced but on the patient's well-being. Usually, the art therapist will confer with other members of the medical health team to make the diagnosis, devise a treatment plan, and assess progress.

Art therapy offers other potential benefits. When administered to a group of patients (as when a group mural is being created), it provides an important social—and potentially socializing—opportunity. In addition, creating art can provide relaxation, pleasure, and a sense of satisfaction for anyone; but these benefits can be especially important to a patient who feels confused, victimized, or who has a low self-image.

Art therapy emerged as a profession in the 1930s. At the turn of the century, artwork found on hospital walls and on scraps of paper found in patients' rooms piqued the curiosity of psychiatrists who collected and studied them, hoping to gain insight into the patients and their illnesses. Since then, art therapy has developed into an effective and important method of diagnosis and rehabilitation.

SETTINGS, SALARIES, STATISTICS

Art therapists work in psychiatric centers; clinics; community centers; nursing homes; drug and alcohol treatment centers; schools; halfway houses; group homes; women's shelters; prisons; development centers; residential treatment centers; general hospitals; colleges; universities; other clinical, educational, and rehabilitative settings; and in private practice. Of these settings, long- and short-term psychiatric hospitals employ the most art therapists. Community mental health centers are the second-largest employer, residential treatment centers rate third, and private practice ranks fourth. The northeastern section of the United States has the highest concentration of art therapy practitioners. Both full-time and part-time opportunities are available. Between 5,000 and 6,000 art therapists are practicing today. Approximately 1,900 of them are registered art therapists, which means that they are art therapists who have satisfied the education, experience, and other requirements of the AATA. Approximately 85 percent of all art therapists are female.

Salaries vary widely depending on credentials, employer, and state. Starting salaries are usually comparable to those paid to public school teachers holding a master's degree—in the high teens. Experienced registered art therapists earn an average of approximately $34,000 per year. Some therapists earn twice that amount. Art therapists who are in private practice tend to earn the most.

HOW TO BECOME AN ART THERAPIST

The entry level for art therapists is at the graduate level—that is, a minimum of a bachelor's degree is prerequisite—and to practice professionally, a master's degree or its equivalent is required.

A master's-degree program in art therapy typically includes courses in normal and pathological art expression, art therapy with children and adolescents, therapeutic art in special education, the nature of creativity, art therapy and the aging process, enhancing learning skills through the use of art, art therapy with stroke patients and other adults with communications problems, creative art therapy for the developmentally disabled, normal and abnormal psychological development, clinical diagnosis and treatment issues, psychological intervening and therapeutic counseling, defense mechanisms of the ego, dynamics of group process, theories of personality, and systems of psychotherapy. Studio fieldwork experience in a variety of clinical settings is also required. These programs are usually two years in length, with the first year dedicated to introductory courses and the second offering the candidate the option to specialize.

As an undergraduate, a candidate should major or minor in the creative or commercial arts or in art education. At many schools, an art portfolio or slides of the student's artwork must be submitted. In addition, undergraduate courses in the behavioral and social sciences are usually required.

There are approximately 130 training programs in art therapy offered by universities, clinical programs, and institutes in the United States. Twenty-seven colleges and universities offer art therapy graduate training programs that are approved by the AATA. Among these programs, the name of the degree awarded and its specific curriculum varies: some award a master of art therapy degree (MAT or MA in art therapy); others confer a master of arts in clinical art therapy, master of professional study (MPS) in art therapy, or master of creative arts therapy (MCAT)—in art therapy. The AATA has also approved two clinical training programs and one institute program.

There are approximately 100 other, non-AATA-approved training programs offered by hospitals, universities, and institutes. These programs exist at every level: undergraduate, graduate-level certificate/diploma, master's, and doctorate.

In addition to artistic talent, personal qualities that are important to success in this career include strong listening and verbal communication skills, analytical ability, patience, compassion, and the genuine desire to work with and help individuals who are impaired.

The American Art Therapy Association (AATA), which is the professional certifying organization for art therapy education programs and art therapists, offers certification to art therapists who satisfy their educational, internship, and paid-work-experience requirements as well as provide a portfolio of slides of their artwork and several letters of recommendation. The AATA has assigned professional quality credit (PQC) values to the different education and experience alternatives available in art therapy, and to be designated an art therapist, registered (or ATR), one must accumulate a minimum of twelve PQCs. While registration is not necessary for employment, it does tend to enhance salaries and the number of job opportunities available. In the past decade, the number of art therapists applying for registration has risen dramatically, an indication both of the increasing popularity of art therapy and of the increasing demand for this credential. State licensure is required only if an art therapist works in a public school.

THE FUTURE

Opportunities in art therapy are expected to grow. Recognition of this therapy and of the other creative arts therapies as valid, effective, and important primary, parallel, or adjunctive therapies for a widening patient population has resulted in the creation of more art therapy programs throughout the country. As the result of hearings before the United States Special Committee on Aging in June of 1992, at which expert testimony was presented attesting to the benefits of the creative arts therapies when they are used in older populations, art therapy, along with dance/movement therapy (see Chapter 11) and music therapy (see Chapter 32) was included and defined in legislation when amendments to the Older Americans Act became law. This federal recognition has meant that more older Americans are receiving the benefits of art therapy and that federal, state, and agency grant monies are available for research.

For more information about art therapists, write to the:

American Art Therapy Association, Inc.
1202 Allanson Road
Mundelein, Illinois 60060

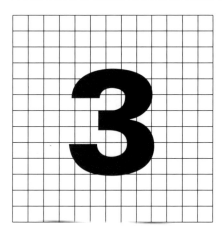

BIOLOGICAL PHOTOGRAPHER

also known as
Medical Photographer
Biophotographer
Biological/Biomedical
 Communicator
Forensic Photographer
Scientific Photographer

Biophotography is the use of photography in documenting things that are living or have lived. *Biological photographers* are highly skilled scientific professionals who are responsible for the production of still and motion pictures of subjects for the health professions and the natural sciences. The prints, motion pictures, digitalized images, videotapes, and transparencies they produce are used for educational purposes, in patient records, in research, and as illustrations in publications. Biophotography is used to capture and record a wide variety of medical events and subjects: the absence, presence, extent, and progress of a patient's condition; an entire surgical procedure (shot under sterile conditions); the intricacies of a highly magnified tissue specimen. Biophotography is equally effective in providing views of fleeting phenomena or of events that unfold slowly. Ours is a very visually oriented age. Doctors, researchers, students, patients, and the general population want to *see* what happens and how it happens. Today, as technologies converge and biological photographers use computers to capture, generate, and manipulate images, ever new visual vistas are opening. The marriage of the biological photographer's artistic abilities with state-of-the-art computer hardware and software has given us "new eyes" with which to view biological form and function. Biophotography is a vital tool in health and medical education, patient treatment, and research, and biological photographers must have a thorough knowledge of photographic procedures and technology as well as a basic understanding of the biological sciences.

Biological photographers can specialize in one or more of several fields: ophthalmic photography (photographing disorders and injuries of the eye), photomicrography (photographs taken through a microscope), cinematography, dental photography, and autopsy/specimen photography.

Biological photography is a creative, diverse, usually people-oriented profession that, increasingly, is proving invaluable in the understanding and communication of medical events.

SETTINGS, SALARIES, STATISTICS

Biological photographers are employed by public and private hospitals, medical schools, universities, libraries, museums, federal health organizations, research institutions, dental facilities, veterinary facilities, natural science facilities, private medical and pharmaceutical companies, advertising agencies, and publishing companies. Some biological photographers freelance.

It is difficult to estimate the number of people in this field. The Biological Photographic Association, Inc. (BPA), the professional association for biological photographers, reports a membership of approximately 1,000 men and women, but not all biological photographers are members, and a complete tally may be ten times that number. There are more men than women in this field.

It is also difficult to pinpoint salaries. Full-time biological photographers who have a minimum of three years of experience in professional photography and life science or a bachelor's degree begin at about $18,000 annually, but the limit on an individual's earnings is a function of many variables, including talent, experience, employer, and luck. The most successful biological photographers earn incomes in the $40,000 to $60,000 per-year range. Some major department heads earn as much as $85,000 annually.

In institutions having large biocommunications (art, television, printing, instructional design, and photography) departments employing as many as twenty-five biological photographers, advancement from an entry-level position (sometimes known as a photographic technician) through photography positions to management and administration positions is possible. Government agencies that employ biological photographers usually have career ladders with steps leading to greater responsibility and authority and higher salary.

HOW TO BECOME A BIOLOGICAL PHOTOGRAPHER

Students contemplating a career in biological photography should anticipate two or four years of post–high school education. Because biophotography has become so vital and integral a part of the health care system, on-the-job training is no longer always adequate. Over the last several years, there has been a trend among employers to seek qualified biological photographers from the colleges offering associate's and bachelor's degrees in this specialty. Several schools across the country offer full or partial degree programs specifically in biological photography. Training and education are also offered by the Biological Photographic Association, which conducts seminars and hands-on workshops and presents a week-long program of intensive training every June. In addition, on-the-job training is sometimes available at the photo departments of teaching hospitals.

Certification and registration in this field are available through the Board of Registry of the Biological Photographic Association, which has established criteria for competency. The BPA administers a three-part certification examination and maintains a registry of certified biological photographers. Upon successful completion of the certification requirements, a biophotographer may use the designation RBP (for registered biological photographer) after his or her name. Membership in the Biological Photographic Association is not required for certification by the BPA.

The certification process consists of three separate examinations: written, practical, and oral. The written part of the examination is four hours in length and is multiple choice. It is designed to test basic and specialized theoretical photography knowledge of photographic optics, biological terminology, planning and producing, materials and processes, photographic chemistry, applied light and filters, applied camera and lighting techniques, audio-visual technique, color, videography, cinematography, photomacrography, and photomicrography.

In the practical part of the examination, the candidate is expected to produce to specifications a number of prints and transparencies on a variety of assignments. In the oral examination, the candidate is expected to give a ten-minute presentation on one of four preannounced broad fields. Candidates must successfully satisfy all three parts of the examination program within five years. Upon satisfying the certification requirements, a biological photographer becomes a registered biological photographer and may use the initials RBP after his or her name. This designation is widely accepted (and in many instances required) as a demonstration of competency.

The BPA provides a Jobs Hotline, which is a continuously updated, prerecorded telephone message listing and describing job openings in the United States and foreign countries for biological photographers. Listening to the often exciting job opportunities being described offers interesting and useful insight into just what biological photographers do.

Personal qualities that are important to a successful and satisfying career in biophotography include precision, patience, a "good eye," manual dexterity, a genuine interest in medicine, the ability to work in sometimes stressful medical settings, and the ability to develop a rapport that will put at ease patients who are to be photographed. Also, because photographic assignments may from day to day vary in subject matter, locale, and technique, biological photographers should be adaptable.

THE FUTURE

The job picture for biological photographers is very favorable. The rapid growth of the American health care industry is causing rapid growth in biophotography. Over the past several decades, biophotography has become a vital component of the educational and research efforts of major medical, dental, and veterinary schools; the various major health- and life-related activities and societies; agricultural research stations; fisheries and wildlife departments; museums and zoological societies; and health-related businesses. With that growth has come a critical demand for skilled professional biological photographers. The clarity, precision, rapid availability, and unique perspective offered by photography (and its many related special visual techniques) make it an essential tool in seeing, recording, and communicating medical subjects. As the health and medical information explosion continues and as advances in photographic technique open new vistas, the need for the services of professional biological photographers should grow.

For more information about biological photographers, contact the:

Biological Photographic Association, Inc.
c/o Mr. Bill Just
1819 Peachtree Street N.W., Suite 712
Atlanta, Georgia 30309

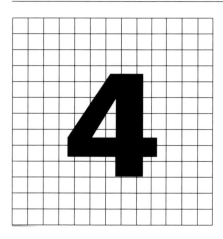

BIOMEDICAL COMMUNICATOR

also known as
Medical Writer

For students who find the fields of medicine and health fascinating and who also like to write or edit, the biomedical communications field can be an interesting career alternative. *Biomedical communications* is a loosely defined term that encompasses everything from writing an in-plain-English question-and-answer personal health column for the general readership of a local newspaper, to writing the package inserts listing contraindications and side effects that accompany pharmaceuticals, to writing the highly technical and precise educational materials from which medical students learn. In between are dozens of other medical writing and/or editing opportunities: writing medical and health news for television and radio; producing public relations copy (informational brochures, in-house newsletters, press releases, magazine articles, and exhibits) for hospitals, clinics, medical schools, and medical societies; preparing highly technical instructional manuals for the operation and maintenance of sophisticated new diagnostic and treatment equipment; developing computer software; writing advertising copy for pharmaceutical and medical/surgical equipment companies; documenting and reporting new discoveries for the medical industries; and writing scripts for public service announcements and health education films. In this wide range of medical writing opportunities, there is also the need for a wide range of competencies and talents—from proofreading for misspelled words and misplaced periods to managing all phases of the production of a new medical periodical.

While many medical research reports, medical textbooks, and other very technical pieces are written by physicians, nurses, scientists, and other health care practitioners, much of what people in the health field and people in general read on the subjects of health and medicine is written and edited by biomedical communicators who have no advance training in a health care discipline. These medical writers are individuals with a talent for understanding, analyzing, interpreting, and then clearly and accurately reporting what is often very complicated information. A top-quality biomedical communicator not only has the intellectual capacity to understand highly technical material, he or she has a strong interest in (if not fascination with) things medical.

When a medical writer writes for a medical audience (to describe a new treatment in a textbook or medical journal, for example), he or she must be comprehensive and meticulously correct. When a biomedical communicator's audience is the general population (as when the copy is being prepared for the mass media—a newspaper column on health or a TV public service message), he or she is an explainer—distilling from a large body of information that which is critical, new, and interesting and putting the complex medical concepts and long medical words into understandable, readable terms without sacrificing accuracy. When a biomedical communicator writes advertising copy or public relations materials, he or she must understand the psychology of selling.

SETTINGS, SALARIES, STATISTICS

Biomedical communicators work for newspapers, magazines, the medical press, textbook publishers, pharmaceutical and medical equipment companies, laboratories, hospitals, clinics, volunteer health agencies, medical schools, medical associations, government agencies, and in television, radio, and advertising.

Most biomedical communicators work full time, but there are also part-time and freelance opportunities that offer the advantage of job flexibility. It is difficult to state salaries in this field because of the wide variety of employment situations involved. Annual salaries for college graduates begin around $25,000, and experienced writers/editors earn an average of $40,000 annually. Many seasoned medical writers earn $50,000 to $85,000. Widely read medical columnists and authors receiving royalties from books on popular medical subjects earn far more.

It is also difficult to estimate the number of men and women engaged in medical writing/editing because the work often overlaps into other forms of technical writing and because so much of the writing is done on a freelance basis by medical and nonmedical personnel. The American Medical Writers Association (AMWA) is a national professional organization for biomedical communicators that offers writing and editing workshops and seminars. AMWA also regularly compiles and publishes a job market sheet listing job openings in the field. AMWA's membership is 2,800 men and women. This figure includes copy and journal editors, advertising writers, freelance science writers and editors, television and film producers, abstractors, translators, public relations people, librarians, and medical illustrators as well as physicians, dentists, nurses, and other medical personnel who write. The total number of people engaged in biomedical communication is certainly higher. In the advertising end of medical writing alone, there are over one thousand job opportunities. Last year, the approximately 200 pharmaceutical and medical/surgical equipment companies doing business in the United States spent over $350 million just on printed advertising. Creating that $350 million worth of copy were medical writers and medical copy editors at approximately one hundred advertising agencies. In response to the public's growing interest in medical and health topics, the mass media (television, radio, magazines, and newspapers) are hiring increasing numbers of medical writers. *The New York Times,* for example, has on its staff ten full-time and two part-time science writers who cover complex medical material, as well as various other reporters from other desks who are also equipped to cover health and science.

HOW TO BECOME A MEDICAL WRITER

To become a medical writer, the minimum of a bachelor's degree is usually required, and, in some cases, a graduate degree in technical writing is necessary for employment. Some employers prefer candidates who have majored in English, journalism, or the liberal arts and minored in a science, while others want writers who have majored in a science, minored in English, and who write effectively. In fact, of those writers presently in the field, 30 percent were English majors as undergraduates, and another 18 percent were technical communications or journalism majors. Less than 10 percent majored in the sciences. In addition, it is almost essential that students entering the field be proficient with a computer or word processor.

In the past decade, many colleges and universities have instituted undergraduate courses in medical and technical writing and scientific communication. While not usually required for employment at this time, such courses do provide background and teach certain technical competencies that can be assets. There are also approximately a dozen universities that offer master's degree programs in technical writing, and such advanced study often enhances advancement.

Since 1979, AMWA has offered a continuing medical education program called the Core Curriculum that is designed to improve skills in six major areas of biomedical communications: audiovisual, editing/writing, freelance, pharmaceutical, public relations/advertising, and teaching. Courses in basic skills are also offered. Upon successful completion of one of these prescribed courses of study, a certificate is awarded to AMWA members. In 1989, AMWA also began offering an Advanced Curriculum to individuals who already have earned Core Curriculum certification or taken certain qualifying core courses or who have at least five years of experience in biomedical communications. An Advanced Certificate is awarded upon the successful completion of eight in-depth advanced courses. Courses are offered at AMWA's annual conference and at regional and chapter workshop meetings. AMWA reports that writers with certificates from their Core Curriculum and Advanced Curriculum education programs tend to earn more and be more in demand than their peers.

Basically, however, most medical writers learn on the job, using the fundamental journalistic techniques of interviewing and researching. They visit hospitals and laboratories; interview doctors, researchers, and other scientific personnel; read textbooks, reports, and studies; analyze raw data; and then digest what they have learned and put those concepts and statistics into language and format that will be appropriate for the reader.

Writers should maintain a portfolio of writing samples to present with their resumes when applying for a job or assignment.

As for the personal qualities that are important for a successful and satisfying career as a biomedical communicator, perhaps the two most critical are (1) a genuine love for writing and/or editing and the temperament to wrestle with a concept until it is in language that accurately, clearly, and appropriately communicates the message, and (2) a genuine and abiding curiosity about medical and scientific topics. A talent for interviewing, a knack for researching and digging for facts, the ability to relate well to others, and a healthy respect for deadlines are also essential.

THE FUTURE

This is certainly a fascinating time to be a biomedical communicator. Almost daily, new research findings and medical and surgical breakthroughs are changing health care worldwide. Worldwide, too, there is also a growing demand for medical, health, and science information. Our country's very sophisticated and specialized medical establishment has its own growing demands for more research literature, instructional materials, and public relations materials. The general public, today, is more interested in and knowledgeable of medical, health, and fitness subjects; and its thirst for more and better information is reflected in the expanding medical coverage in the mass media. There is even a cable television network devoted entirely to health subjects. Technology, too, is generating new demands. Each new piece of equipment and each new pharmaceutical calls for medical writing and editing, and growth here in recent years has been great. For example, the amount spent on pharmaceutical advertising has grown radically in the past five years (with last year's figure being 25 percent higher than that for the year before) because so many new pharmaceuticals are being introduced annually. So, again, opportunities for biomedical communicators are growing.

In realistically appraising the job market for biomedical communicators, however, it must be noted that there is heavy competition for most openings. Therefore, it is prudent for students to acquire the best possible academic credentials in science and English; to develop strong interview skills and a clear, accurate, and adaptable writing style; and to pick up experience writing for school and local newspapers.

For more information about medical writing, contact the:

American Medical Writers Association
9650 Rockville Pike
Bethesda, Maryland 20814-3998

The Society for Technical Communication
815 Fifteenth Street, N.W., Suite 506
Washington, DC 20005

BIOMEDICAL ENGINEER

including
Bioengineer
Medical Engineer
Clinical Engineer

As the Alliance for Engineering in Medicine and Biology says in its educational literature, "The primitive man or woman who carved the first rough crutch from a stick helped begin the development of what has become modern biomedical engineering." Modern biomedical engineering formally began with a challenge forty years ago by the National Institutes of Health (NIH). The NIH asked: "What can engineering contribute to the biological sciences?" The answer has been a long and amazing list of lifesaving and life-enhancing inventions that have changed the way we live. *Biomedical engineers* develop concepts and convert the ideas of physicians, rehabilitation therapists, and biologists into usable devices, instruments, materials, procedures, treatments, and techniques that improve the quality of patients' lives.

Biomedical engineering encompasses almost the full range of engineering specialties—electrical, mechanical, clinical, aerospace, chemical, computer science, agricultural, and civil engineering—as they are applied to improving health care. Biomedical engineers work as members of health and research teams, applying the principles and technologies of these various disciplines to the understanding, defining, and solving of medical and biological problems.

The artificial heart that, in 1982, was implanted in Dr. Barney Clark, the heart-lung machine, the artificial kidney, nuclear magnetic resonance, respiratory and cardiac pacemakers, defibrillators, the artificial lung, surgical lasers, electrical muscle stimulators and battery powered artificial limbs, plastic heart valves, plastic and metal joints, CT scanners, and ultrasound are among the lifesaving and life-enhancing inventions that biomedical engineers have developed or helped to develop. The revolutionary, tiny hearing aid worn by former President Ronald Reagan is the product of biomedical engineering's progress in biophysical acoustics and microcircuitry. Today, as

NASA proceeds toward the realization of manned space stations, a major challenge for biomedical engineers is the maintenance of humans in space.

Some biomedical engineers specialize in applying computerization to medicine. Computers are used primarily in medical imaging (CT and MRI scans). They are also used to monitor patients in the operating room and intensive care room, to improve and expedite laboratory testing, to process medical data, and in numerous other medical situations. Future applications seem almost limitless.

Some biomedical engineers are engaged in the analyzing and testing of different materials (stainless steel, silicon, various plastics) to determine whether they will be accepted or rejected when used in the body in artificial organs and grafts. Others design and build systems to modernize laboratory, hospital, and clinical procedures. Some biomedical engineers who work in hospitals and other institutions apply their knowledge of medicine and engineering to monitoring the accurate and safe performance of the instruments, devices, and machinery in use, and sometimes they teach hospital personnel how to use new equipment.

Under the broad title *biomedical engineer*, there are four commonly recognized specialties: bioengineering, medical engineering, clinical engineering, and rehabilitation engineering. *Bioengineers* apply engineering principles to understanding the structure, function, and pathology of the human body. They also apply engineering concepts and technology to advance the understanding of biological nonmedical systems, such as maintaining and improving the quality of the environment and protecting human, animal, and plant life from toxicants and pollutants. This latter application is sometimes referred to as bioenvironmental engineering. *Medical engineers* use engineering concepts and technologies to develop instrumentation, biomaterials, diagnostic and therapeutic devices, computer systems, artificial organs, joints, and other equipment needed in biology and medicine. *Clinical engineers* use engineering concepts and technologies to improve and manage patient-oriented health care delivery systems in hospitals and clinics (selecting, maintaining, and testing medical instruments and machines and training personnel in their use; ensuring that systems do not interact in ways that may be detrimental to patients and hospital staff). *Rehabilitation engineers* apply engineering science and design to problems caused by disability (orthopedic devices, systems to electrically stimulate paralyzed muscles, augmentative communications apparati).

Biomedical engineering can be a very challenging and satisfying profession for men and women who are interested and talented in engineering as well as medicine and who want to contribute to the improvement of health care without necessarily having direct contact with and responsibility for patients. Although a biomedical engineer may never actually meet the patients he or she helps, the ideas he or she develops and the inventions he or she creates touch those patients' lives in very important ways.

SETTINGS, SALARIES, STATISTICS

Biomedical engineers are employed in a wide variety of settings: in hospitals; research foundations; medical, industrial, academic, and government laboratories; undersea and space programs; industry (over 4,500 companies make medical devices); universities; and private consulting firms. The Department of Veterans Affairs, National Institutes of Health, NASA, the Department of Defense, and the Environmental Protection Agency all employ biomedical engineers. Most job opportunities are in or near major cities.

There are approximately 6,000 biomedical engineers in the United States. Although the majority of them are men, a steadily increasing number of women are entering this profession. In 1993, of the 756 graduates of bachelor's degree programs in biomedical engineering, 32 percent were women.

Because of the wide variety of work settings available to biomedical engineers and the variety of credentials encompassed by this job title, there is significant variety in salaries. Annual starting salaries for biomedical engineers holding bachelor of science degrees range from $29,000 to $34,000, those with master's degrees begin in the $35,000 to $41,000 range, and biomedical engineers with Ph.D.s start at between $42,000 and $57,000 per year. Highly skilled, experienced clinical engineers who have management responsibilities can earn significantly more. Teaching positions tend to pay less, as do jobs in state medical institutions and hospitals.

Like other professionals, biomedical engineers work hours that can be highly variable. Biomedical engineers who work in research or on the production side, especially, may put in long, irregular hours as projects reach critical phases. Biomedical engineers who install and calibrate biomedical equipment and medical engineers who act as sales representatives for companies that manufacture biomedical equipment usually must travel to some extent.

HOW TO BECOME A BIOMEDICAL ENGINEER

Although a bachelor's degree in biomedical engineering from one of the twenty programs accredited by the Accreditation Board for Engineering and Technology (ABET) is considered entry level in this profession, a graduate degree in biomedical engineering (a master's or, preferably, a doctorate) is highly recommended and, in many settings, necessary for employment. A doctorate degree is almost always necessary for university and college teaching positions and for top research positions in industry and government laboratories. Among the courses typically offered by a four-year undergraduate program are biomedical engineering systems and design, biomedical computers, engineering biophysics, bioinstrumentation, biomechanics, biomaterials, biothermodyamics, biotransport, and artificial organs.

For graduate study there are 88 university programs in the U.S. to choose from at this time.

Another route to a career in biomedical engineering is to concentrate only on the traditional engineering disciplines as an undergraduate and then to go on to do biomedical engineering work at the graduate level(s). Also, many universities offer ABET accredited degrees in traditional engineering disciplines (mechanical, chemical, etc.) with specialties or options in biomedical engineering.

In high school, prospective biomedical engineering students should concentrate on mathematics (typically, advanced algebra and trigonometry or precalculus is the minimum requirement for acceptance into an engineering discipline, with high school calculus preferred), chemistry, biology, physics, and English. Proficiency in a foreign language is strongly recommended. Courses in computer science are becoming increasingly necessary. Engineering schools look for a good scholastic average, and while solid college entrance examination scores are important for acceptance to many of these schools, some do not weigh these tests heavily

In addition to the obvious aptitudes necessary for this career—mathematical ability, analytic thinking, inventiveness, logic in thought process (which is learnable), and science ability—there are other, personal qualities that can contribute to success and satisfaction as a biomedical engineer. They include patience, perseverance, and, because biomedical projects are almost always team efforts, the important ability to communicate verbally and in writing and to cooperate with a wide variety of coworkers. Biomedical engineers must have or learn that very special kind of creativity that can cross disciplines to come up with the best answers. From the various physical and medical sciences, biomedical engineers adopt, adapt, merge, and synthesize theories, principles, technologies, and materials in their efforts to analyze situations and solve problems.

A career in biomedical engineering can offer very stimulating, exciting challenges that entail a minimum of repetition and a maximum of innovative thinking.

Of the biomedical engineering specialties, only clinical engineers have a special, voluntary certification process. Biomedical engineers who are clinical engineers may be certified by the International Certification Commission for Clinical Engineering and Biomedical Technology. This certifying body was created in May of 1983. For the ten years prior to May 1983, two competing organizations, the Board of Examiners for Clinical Engineering Certification and the American Board of Clinical Engineering, offered certification. The International Certification Commission represents the merging of these two groups.

To qualify for certification, a candidate must hold a degree in engineering or in biomedical engineering, provide proof of at least three years' experience working as a clinical engineer in a hospital, and pass an examination that consists of a five-hour written test and an oral test. Certification has evolved for clinical engineers because of the life-and-death importance of their work in hospitals. Certification demonstrates that an engineer possesses specialized knowledge of hospital systems.

Licensing as a professional engineer is encouraged and, for some employment situations, absolutely required by law.

THE FUTURE

At present, the demand for qualified biomedical engineers far exceeds the supply, and a huge shortfall of biomedical engineers (and other types of engineers) is expected by 2000. Several factors are at work here. Many of the original biomedical engineers are reaching retirement age. They are not being replaced in adequate numbers because the student pool is smaller now. Also, demand for rehabilitation engineers, especially, should be great as more types of disabilities caused by illness and accident are helped and as the older population expands and lives longer. But perhaps the strongest factor creating this shortage is the current trend on the part of hospitals to replace service-contractors who maintain equipment with on-staff, in-house biomedical engineers, as part of critical cost containment measures. Last year $1.5 billion were available for biomedical instrumentation alone. There is a great awareness of the value of this work. Some undergraduate programs of biomedical engineering are recruiting all the way down at the junior high school level so that the United States will have the man and woman power to continue this important and exciting work.

For more information about what biomedical engineers do, the various educational options in this field, and a list of colleges and universities offering biomedical engineering degree programs, write to the:

Biomedical Engineering Society
P.O. Box 2399
Culver City, California 90231

Association for the Advancement of Medical Instrumentation
3330 Washington Boulevard, Suite 400
Arlington, Virginia 22201-4598

Accreditation Board for Engineering and Technology (ABET)
345 East Forty-seventh Street
New York, New York 10017

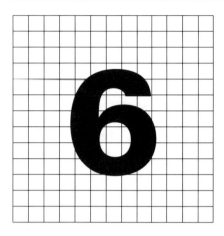

BIOMEDICAL EQUIPMENT TECHNICIAN

also known as
BMET
Biomedical Engineering Technician
Biomedical Electronic Technician

including
BMET I—or Jr. BMET
BMET II
SR. BMET III—or Sr. BMET
BMET Supervisor

Breakthroughs in biomedical engineering are radically improving the ways disease and injury are diagnosed and treated. The application of the various engineering disciplines and technologies to health and medical problems happily has resulted in thousands of pieces of biomedical equipment that save lives once lost; alleviate discomfort; and earlier, more accurately, less painfully, and less dangerously diagnose medical conditions. CT scanners, dialysis machines, incubators, inhalators, x-ray machinery, transducers, magnetic resonance imagers (MRI), electrocardiographs (EKGs), and electroencephalographs (EEGs) are but a few of those important pieces of sophisticated biomedical equipment to which doctors, nurses, and other health care personnel turn when diagnosing and treating patients. The number of new biomedical inventions, their complexity, and their success seem to be increasing each year. But modern medicine's sophisticated biomedical equipment is life enhancing or life extending only if it is available, accurate, safe, and correctly used. The health care professionals responsible for the safe use of high-tech biomedical equipment are called *biomedical equipment technicians* (BMETs).

A biomedical equipment technician is a person knowledgeable in the theory of operation; the underlying physiologic principles; and the practical, safe, clinical application of biomedical equipment. His or her capabilities may include the installation, calibration, inspection, preventative maintenance, and repair of general biomedical and related technical equipment. He or she might also be involved in the operation or supervision of equipment and in equipment control, safety, and maintenance. When biomedical equipment does fail, it is the biomedical equipment technician who is responsible for correcting the problem as quickly as possible. Biomedical equipment technicians teach hospital personnel how to use the various pieces of biomedical equipment, and they also assist doctors, nurses, and researchers in conducting experiments and procedures. Their work is crucial to the safety and correct treatment of the patient and is important, too, to the safety of the health care personnel handling the equipment.

There are actually four levels of biomedical equipment technicians. A BMET I (or Jr. BMET) works at the entry level, performing skilled work of routine difficulty under close supervision. He or she primarily carries out preventative maintenance, repair, and safety testing and has the minimum of education and experience required. A BMET II (or BMET) has at least several years of related education or experience and works independently in repair and maintenance programs. A BMET III (or Sr. BMET) has a significant amount of education and/or training, can perform highly skilled work of considerable difficulty, and works with little supervision. The highest level in this occupation, the BMET supervisor, has a significant amount of preparation and supervises others. He or she reports to a department head or to the hospital administration. It should be noted here that these definitions are only general in nature. In reality, the lines between levels are defined by each hospital and tend to be blurred.

SETTINGS, SALARIES, STATISTICS

According to the *Journal of Clinical Engineering*, in 1993 there were between 12,000 and 15,000 BMETs in the United States. They are employed by large hospitals and clinics; university, government, and industrial laboratories; research institutes; biomedical equipment maintenance services; and specific medical instrument manufacturers. Most job openings are in cities—hospitals with budgets large enough to permit the hiring of full-time biomedical equipment technicians are usually located in high-population areas. Some hospitals do not hire their own biomedical equipment technicians but, instead, rely on technicians who are employed by the manufacturers or distributors of their various pieces of biomedical equipment, but, bowing to cost constraints, most are now hiring in-house biomedical equipment technicians, which, in most cases, is a more economical arrangement. There are also biomedical equipment technicians on active duty with the armed forces.

Salaries vary with education, experience, location, and the type of employer. Average starting pay for biomedical equipment technicians who have two-year associate's degrees range from approximately $17,000 to $21,000 annually. Certified biomedical equipment technicians and those with four years of experience average between $24,500 and $31,500 yearly. Well-established technicians average $38,000 per year. Some top biomedical equipment technicians earn as much as $50,000 annually.

Working conditions for biomedical equipment technicians are usually pleasant. Hours are predictable—forty hours per workweek, with evening, weekend, and holiday "on call" duty rotated in for hospital workers. However, the nature of the work means that emergency situations can and do arise, and longer, erratic, and more stressful hours may be required when emergencies occur. Biomedical equipment technicians who work for manufacturers must travel to some degree, and when emergencies develop, this traveling may have to be done without notice.

Biomedical equipment technicians who are employed by hospitals, clinics, and similar institutions may advance from beginning technician to positions of greater responsibility and independence and then on to supervisory positions. A biomedical equipment technician who works for a manufacturer can progress from field service trainee to field service technician and, with experience and success, on to customer service representative and regional service manager. In either case, certification enhances the prospects for promotion.

The vast majority of biomedical equipment technicians are male, but the number of women now entering this field is gradually increasing.

HOW TO BECOME A BIOMEDICAL EQUIPMENT TECHNICIAN

Biomedical equipment technicians train for between one and four years after high school. Nationwide, there are approximately 60 formal biomedical engineering (also called electronic or equipment) technician programs, located in colleges, universities, community colleges, junior colleges, and vocational/technical institutes. Most of these programs offer associate's degrees, but several award bachelor's degrees. In many cases, associate's degree course work may automatically be transferred to a bachelor's program for credit. Almost all of the associate's programs provide fieldwork experience in laboratories or hospitals as part of the training.

The curriculum for a biomedical equipment technician educational program typically includes courses in electronics, computers, mathematics, biology, chemistry, anatomy, physiology, and medical terminology.

An alternative educational route to the training needed for this career is to attend one of the many two-year colleges offering general programs leading to an associate in applied science degree in electronics and then to train on the job in a laboratory or hospital. However, with the growing number of biomedical equipment technicians in the field, it is not as likely that someone without a BMET degree will be employed in a health care setting.

In high school, interested students should take algebra, trigonometry, physics, biology, chemistry, and shop courses. If electronics is offered, it, too, would be beneficial. Because good communication skills are very important to quality performance as a biomedical equipment technician, students should also place emphasis on English and communication courses.

Like biomedical engineers, biomedical equipment technicians must possess both mechanical aptitude and a genuine interest in mechanical, electronic, electrical, and other technical matters. Excellent manual dexterity, vision, eye-hand coordination, and facility with numbers are also essential.

Personal qualities that can contribute to career-long success and satisfaction in this field include an appreciation for precision; the ability to handle emergency situations calmly, quickly, and correctly; and, in the case of those biomedical equipment technicians who work in hospitals and other health care settings, the ability to work among patients. Also very important is the ability to write and speak effectively. BMETs write as well as read correspondence containing crucial detailed information, write operating manuals for hospitals staffers, and routinely give verbal instructions to, and receive feedback from, a wide variety of hospital personnel. The biomedical equipment technician must know how to speak, write, and listen accurately. It is equally important that a biomedical equipment technician know how to relate to his or her various coworkers.

Certification in this field is voluntary, but it does seem to enhance earnings, especially at the entry level. The International Certification Commission (ICC) administers the certification process, which consists of satisfying educational, training, and examination requirements. ICC offers two levels of certification: candidate and full certification (candidate is a step toward full certification), and in both of these levels there are three options: general biomedical equipment, radiological equipment, and clinical equipment. A six-hour competency examination is administered for each option.

To be eligible to take the candidacy certification examination, an individual must have (1) an associate's degree in biomedical equipment technology or (2) an associate's degree in electronic technology plus one year of biomedical equipment technician experience, (3) two years of biomedical equipment technician experience, or, as of May 1994, (4) successfully completed a U.S. military biomedical equipment technician course.

To be eligible to take the General Biomedical Equipment Certification Examination, a person must have a minimum of two years of biomedical equipment technician experience plus an associate's degree in biomedical engineering technology or four years of biomedical engineering technician experience or three years of biomedical equipment technician experience and an associate's degree in electronics technology.

To sit for a certification examination in one of the limited specialty areas of biomedical equipment technology, the requirements are the same as those for the general equipment technician, except that applicants must show that at least 51 percent of their work time is spent in their specialty area.

The General Biomedical Equipment Examination contains questions on anatomy and physiology, electric and electronic fundamentals, medical equipment function and operation, safety in health care facilities, and medical equipment problem solving. Approximately 4,330 BMETs currently are certified at the general level.

The Radiological Equipment Examination covers anatomy and physiology, electric and electronic fundamentals, radiographic instrumentation, safety, and radiographic troubleshooting and management. There are currently 145 BMETs certified in radiological equipment.

The Clinical Laboratory Equipment Specialist Examination covers anatomy and physiology, electric and electronic fundamentals, safety in the health care facility, safety in the clinical laboratory, and clinical laboratory equipment fundamentals. Only 48 individuals are certified at the clinical laboratory level at this time.

THE FUTURE

Biomedical engineering is a rapidly growing field, and as the number of biomedical inventions and their complexity grow, so, too, should the demand for qualified biomedical equipment technicians. As more and more medical institutions recognize the cost effectiveness of regularly maintaining their much-used, often extremely expensive, sophisticated equipment, the hiring of staff biomedical technicians should become more common. Biomedical equipment technicians with the best academic credentials and work experience will be most in demand, but at all levels, opportunities in this profession should continue to expand in the coming decade.

For more information about biomedical equipment technicians, a list of educational programs, and information about certification, contact the:

> Association for the Advancement of
>   Medical Instrumentation (AAMI)
> 3330 Washington Boulevard, Suite 400
> Arlington, Virginia 22201

Also at the same address as the AAMI in Arlington, Virginia, are the International Certification Commission (ICC) and The Society for Biomedical Equipment Technicians (SBET).

> Junior Engineering Technology Society
>   (JETS)
> 1420 King Street, Suite 405
> Alexandria, Virginia 22314

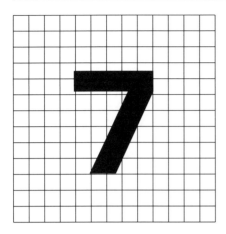

CARDIOVASCULAR TECHNOLOGY PERSONNEL

including
Electrocardiograph Technician
Cardiovascular Technologist

also known as
EKG Technician or Technologist
ECG Technician or Technologist

Cardiovascular technology is the scientific field devoted to recording and studying the function of the heart (cardio) and circulatory (vascular) system. Cardiovascular technology personnel provide supportive services to the physician by gathering and reducing the data necessary to establish a diagnosis and by developing appropriate patient management plans.

Electrocardiograph technician is the entry-level position in the field of cardiovascular technology. EKG technicians work in the laboratory or at the patient's bedside using an electrocardiograph machine to record electromotive variations in the action of the heart muscles. An electrocardiograph picks up minute electrical changes that occur during and between heartbeats. The EKG technician prepares the equipment and explains the procedure to the patient; attaches between three and twelve electrodes (or leads) from the EKG machine to the patient's chest, arms, and legs (applying a gel between the electrodes and the patient's skin to facilitate the passage of electrical impulses); and then, with the machine recording, moves the chest electrodes to specific monitoring positions across the patient's chest. A stylus responds to the electrical impulses, creating a permanent visual record of the heart muscle's action. The electrocardiogram that is produced is then used by the patient's physician in making an evaluation of the patient's heart and circulatory function.

Sophisticated EKG equipment uses computers to read the tracings. Electrocardiograms are routinely ordered before surgery and are often part of physical examinations for insurance and for individuals over a certain age.

Cardiovascular technology provides crucial diagnostic information about the heart's action, the condition of the vascular system, and how certain activities and medications affect these systems. With additional training and class work, an EKG technician may become a *cardiovascular technologist,* specializing in invasive or noninvasive cardiovascular technology. An invasive cardiovascular technologist is a highly specialized diagnostician who, using physiologic analytic equipment and working in an invasive cardiovascular laboratory or hospital coronary care or medical/surgical intensive care unit, carries out tests that require the introduction of various dyes, probes, and medical instruments into the patient's body. Such procedures include cardiac output studies, vessel and chamber pressure recording, cardiac catheterization, angiocardiography, drug response tests, implantation of temporary and permanent pacemakers, and balloon atrial septostomy. In some settings, the title *cardiovascular technologist* is used to describe the individuals who carry out these various procedures. In other settings, more specific titles are used. For example, the technologists who assist cardiovascular surgeons in performing delicate catheterizations (in which a fine tube is inserted through a patient's blood vessel and then "snaked" through to the heart to determine if obstructions exist) may be called *cardiac catheterization assistants* or *technologists.*

Similarly, the job titles for the cardiovascular personnel who carry out the various noninvasive procedures may reflect the specialized nature of the work they perform and the special training it entails. Technologists who conduct echocardiogram tests (in which computerized echocardiograph equipment that uses high-frequency sound waves examines the structure and function of certain portions of the heart) may be called *echocardiogram technicians.* Personnel who conduct twelve to twenty-four-hour-long ambulatory electrocardiogram tests using a Holter monitoring machine are often called *Holter monitor technicians. Stress testing technicians* conduct exercise tests. *Phonocardiograph technicians, vectocardiograph technicians*, and *cardiac Doppler technicians* are other types of noninvasive cardiovascular technologists who perform specific procedures using sophisticated equipment.

All cardiovascular personnel are also trained in advanced life support techniques (CPR, defibrillation, airway management, bag-mask ventilation, preparation and delivery of emergency and support medications) because their patients are often individuals who are at high risk for cardiopulmonary arrest. Among the physicians who typically request cardiovascular function evaluations are adult and pediatric cardiologists, cardiovascular surgeons, internal medicine specialists, and family practice physicians. Cardiovascular technology personnel also interface with other health personnel who have related functions: nurses, extracorporeal perfusionists, diagnostic medical sonographers, radiologic technologists, and nuclear medicine technologists, all of whom may work with components of a diagnostic workup or provide therapeutic care to cardiac patients.

SETTINGS, SALARIES, STATISTICS

Most cardiovascular technology personnel work in hospitals in the invasive and noninvasive laboratory performing cardiac catheterization and cardiac ultrasound, in the emergency room, or at the patient's bedside. A forty-hour workweek, with evening and weekend hours rotated in, is routine. Opportunities for cardiovascular technology personnel also exist in outpatient clinics, comprehensive health centers, health maintenance organizations, health care facilities, and in the private offices of physicians.

These are approximately 26,000 cardiovascular technology personnel in the United States at this time, 21,000 of whom are EKG technicians. The majority of them are female.

Salaries vary widely depending on specific responsibilities, years of experience, educational background, and geographic location. EKG technicians typically earn between $16,500 and $29,000 annually. Specialized cardiovascular technology personnel earn as follows: cardiovascular technologists earn $30,000, on average; salaries for echocardiographic technologists range between $19,000 and $30,000; and cardiac catheterization technologists earn between $18,500 and $32,500.

HOW TO BECOME AN EKG TECHNICIAN OR CARDIOVASCULAR TECHNOLOGIST

Most EKG technicians are trained on the job, and this training, typically provided by an EKG supervisor or a cardiologist, usually takes six weeks. To become an EKG technician, a student must have a high school diploma or its equivalent. In high school, courses in health, biology, and mathematics are helpful. Formal training for EKG technicians is also available. Hospitals, vocational and technical schools, and junior and community colleges offer programs lasting from one semester to two years. Formal classroom programs range from six to eight months for basic EKG procedures. Longer programs, which have both clinical and academic components, prepare technologists to assist with complex procedures such as catheterization and angiography. An associate's degree is awarded upon successful completion of these two-year programs.

For technicians who cannot or choose not to return to the classroom, 12 to 24 months of on-the-job training is usually sufficient to prepare them to perform the more specialized functions.

Education programs in cardiovascular technology are accredited by The Commission for the Accreditation of Allied Health Education Programs (CAAHEP), which on July 1, 1994, succeeded the American Medical Association's Committee on Allied Health Education and Accreditation (CAHEA). (CAAHEP is an independent body in which the AMA participates as one sponsor among many.) There are only four accredited programs at this time and together they graduate about 85 students annually.

There are no licensing requirements for EKG technicians and other cardiovascular personnel, and credentialing, which is available through Cardiovascular Credentialing International (CCI), is voluntary. CCI offers certification for three levels of cardiovascular technologist: invasive, noninvasive, peripheral vascular; and cardiographic exams.

Personal qualities and aptitudes important to effective performance and satisfaction in this occupation include mechanical aptitude, mathematical aptitude (to understand and utilize mathematical and scientific equations in computing calculations from which diagnostic and treatment determinations are made by the physician), presence of mind in emergencies, patience, reliability, and strong written and verbal communication skills. Cardiovascular technology personnel work directly with the patient and, therefore, must be able to relate well to all kinds of people and know how to allay their fears and elicit cooperation so that optimal test results can be obtained.

THE FUTURE

Despite progress in the past decade that has resulted in the death rate from stroke falling by 37 percent and the death rate from heart attack dropping by 25 percent, cardiovascular disease is still the number one killer and cause of disability in America. The American Heart Association estimates that Americans will suffer as many as 1.5 million heart attacks this year. Eighty percent of all patients in hospital settings and 74 percent of all patients in nonhospital settings being seen for suspected heart problems need the evaluative diagnostic testing services provided by cardiovascular technology personnel. Heart disease and stroke and other blood vessel disorders account for more than eleven million physician visits each year. In addition, the noninvasive cardiology procedures that cardiovascular technology personnel assist in or conduct are gaining in popularity because they are so very accurate, they provide new and more specific cardiac information, and they do so with less discomfort, risk, cost, and time lost to the patient. Also, because middle-aged and elderly people are much more likely than young people to have heart and/or blood vessel disease, the coming rapid increase in these population groups should heighten demand for cardiac care and, in turn, for cardiovascular personnel.

Yet, despite these factors that might suggest growth in this profession, ever-present cost containment efforts may actually result in less demand for cardiovascular technology personnel (and especially for technologists) in the coming decade, as hospitals train their on-staff registered nurses, respiratory therapists, and other personnel to perform EKG procedures. However, employment prospects should be stable for those technicians with specialized training.

Three professional organizations that have served cardiovascular personnel—the American Cardiology Technologists Association, the National Alliance of Cardiovascular Technologists, and the National Society for Cardiovascular and Cardiopulmonary Technology—have recently merged and are now the:

American Society of Cardiovascular Professionals
120 Falcon Drive, Unit 3
Fredericksburg, Virginia 22408

Certification information can be obtained from the:

Cardiovascular Credentialing International (CCI)
4456 Corporation Lane, Suite 350
Virginia Beach, Virginia 23463

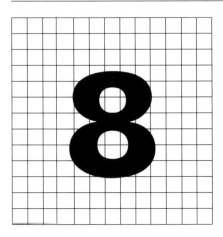

CERTIFIED ATHLETIC TRAINER

Athletic Training, recognized by the American Medical Association in 1990 as an allied health profession, consists primarily of a group of professionals known as *certified athletic trainers* who are health care specialists professionally trained and educated to (1) recognize and evaluate injuries associated with competitive sports; (2) provide immediate treatment and then determine if an injury requires further, specialized care; (3) implement prevention-of-injury programs; (4) plan and implement rehabilitation of injury regimens; (5) educate and counsel athletes concerning health care; and (6) organize and administer an athletic training program, and who have satisfied the requirements of the National Athletic Trainers' Association (NATA), which is the professional association for this career. In most work situations, an athletic trainer works under the supervision of a physician.

More specifically, a certified athletic trainer takes care of athletic trauma (sprains, strains, contusions, etc.); makes protective devices (injury pads, mouthpieces); wraps and pads athletes' injuries; uses a wide range of contemporary therapeutic modalities and rehabilitation equipment; plans and helps athletes with corrective exercise techniques, conditioning, and rehabilitation; and counsels on general health, including nutrition.

An athletic trainer must have a sound knowledge of anatomy, physiology, psychology, hygiene, nutrition, taping, conditioning, prevention of injury methodology, and protective equipment. After the team physician makes a diagnosis of an athlete's injury and prescribes the treatment, it is the athletic trainer who carries out that treatment and who informs the coach of the athlete's physical and emotional progress. Some athletic trainers also purchase and fit the teammates' equipment and make travel arrangements for them. Many of the athletic trainers who work for high schools and higher education institutions also teach classes in related (or other) subjects.

SETTINGS, SALARIES, STATISTICS

About half of all certified athletic trainers work in the athletic programs of colleges and universities; 15 percent work in high schools (where there were over a million athletic injuries last year); about 30 percent work in clinics or in industrial settings; and approximately 5 percent work in professional sports.

There are approximately 9,000 certified athletic trainers, more than 50 percent of whom are male. The number of women in this field is rapidly growing, however, with half of all recent graduates of NATA-college curriculum programs being female.

Salaries vary depending on employer, position, and region. High school teacher-trainers start at between $18,000 and $25,000 per year. In 1993, the median income for all certified athletic trainers was $34,000. Basically, salaries for this career are similar to those for teaching, at the starting level and after five and ten years of experience.

Salary potential and advancement are most often dependent on educational credentials and experience. Today, 70 percent of all athletic trainers hold advanced degrees, and many have doctoral degrees. For these individuals, the possibilities for promotion (and salary increases) are greatest.

The nature of this work requires that athletic trainers work long and often irregular (evening, weekend, holiday) hours. College trainers work an average of 50 hours per week; clinical/industrial trainers work an average of 39 hours each week; high school trainers average about 33 hours weekly (but this excludes time spent on the classroom and teaching responsibilities usually required of athletic trainers in secondary schools); and athletic trainers in professional sports work an average of 57 hours. The average high school or college athletic trainer serves approximately 650 student-athletes each year. Traveling is almost always necessary (especially for athletic trainers employed by professional teams), and emergencies are an inherent part of the work.

HOW TO BECOME AN ATHLETIC TRAINER

As athletic training gains recognition as a profession requiring specialized education and training, certification is becoming increasingly important for employment. The National Athletic Trainers' Association (NATA) is the professional and certifying organization for athletic trainers. To become a certified athletic trainer, or ATC, one must earn a college degree, complete a basic educational program that includes a minimum of 800 hours of clinical experience, and pass a three-part examination measuring basic knowledge, clinical skills, and decision making. To maintain certification, an ATC must earn continuing education units approved by NATA. Apart from certification, some states require athletic trainers to be licensed.

In the United States at this time, there are 97 NATA-approved educational programs for athletic trainers. Of these, 84 are undergraduate programs, and 13 offer graduate degrees.

The undergraduate curriculum typically includes courses in human anatomy; human physiology; the physiology of exercise; applied anatomy and/or kinesiology; psychology; first aid (including CPR); nutrition; adapted physical education; personal, community, and school health; athletic training; physics; pharmacology; histology; pathology; organization and administration of health and physical education; the psychology of coaching; coaching techniques; chemistry; and tests and measurements. Extensive clinical experience is also part of the program.

A graduate athletic training curriculum offers advanced course work in anatomy, physiology, athletic training, pharmacology, nutrition, organization and administration, the physiology of exercise, kinesiology or applied anatomy, statistics, research design, injury and pathology evaluation, school law, sports psychology, kinesiology/biomechanics, therapeutic exercise, therapeutic modalities, clinical experience, and scientific research opportunities.

Personal qualities essential to effectiveness and enjoyment in this career include a genuine interest in athletics and in medicine, the ability to work well under stress, the willingness and stamina to work long and often irregular hours, confidence, cleanliness, common sense, and manual dexterity. In addition, it is important that an athletic trainer be able to relate well to the athletes and to other professionals—team physicians, coaches, and administrators—with whom he or she works. To be effective at this job, an athletic trainer must establish a close and warm rapport with these individuals, and, for this reason, it is important that athletic trainers know how to play as a member of the team working to help the team. Ideally, an athletic trainer is the kind of person who can be a friend to the athletes he or she helps.

In high school, a student interested in a career in athletic training should take biology, chemistry, physics, first aid, health, and general science. Working as a student athletic trainer or manager is also helpful.

THE FUTURE

Growth in this field is expected to be strong. The nationwide interest in athletics, the identification and treatment of sports injuries, and the positive results seen where athletic trainers (and especially where certified athletic trainers) practice are all contributing to increased demand. There is a grass-roots movement among the states to require the hiring of trainers to work in high schools. At this time, athletic trainers are employed at 15 percent of United States high schools, and that number is steadily increasing. Indeed, most new jobs in this field are expected to open up at the high school level and in private and hospital-based sports medicine clinics.

For more information about athletic training and NATA-approved educational programs, write to the:

National Athletic Trainers' Association, Inc.
2952 Stemmons Freeway
Dallas, Texas 75247

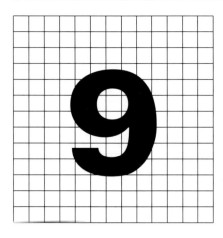

CHILD LIFE SPECIALIST

including
Child Life Assistant
Child Life Administrator

A *child life specialist* is a professional member of a child care team who, through the use of play therapy and other forms of communication, works to alleviate the stress that hospitalization and other health care situations often create for children ages newborn to 21 years and their families. The child life specialist focuses on the emotional and developmental needs of the child.

If you were ever hospitalized as a child and a friendly person who was not in a white hospital uniform invited you down the hall to the children's playroom, that person most likely was a child life specialist. You probably remember how nice it was to play with toys and with that friendly person in a bright, child-sized setting, even though you were still in a large, and perhaps scary, hospital. Perhaps the hospital didn't feel quite so scary afterwards. This, basically, is the concept behind child life work.

It has been well documented and is generally accepted that hospitalization and other medical experiences can be emotionally traumatic to children. Hospitals can be frightening, lonely places for anyone; for a child, and especially for a child in pain, the experience can have permanent, long-lasting, and far-reaching effects. Excessive anxiety and stress related to illness, hospitalization, and other medical encounters can emotionally damage a child or interfere with a child's response to his or her medical treatment. The effects of illness or injury can erode a child's self-esteem. A bad hospital experience can do even more damage to a child's sense of self-worth. In addition, it has been documented that, as compared to the general population, children and adolescents in health care situations are more likely to have experienced excessive social, family, and environmental stress in their lives.

Children are unprepared for the confinement; lack of privacy; separation from home, family, and friends; the sometimes frightening and painful tests and treatments; the suffering; and sometimes the death that they see around them. Children often feel loss of control over what is happening to them. Child life specialists are trained to minimize the stress and anxiety inherent to such situations so that the chances for trauma are reduced. The child life specialist's ultimate goal is to help the child come away from his or her hospitalization or other health situation with a positive growth experience. The child life specialist does so by providing various materials, equipment, play opportunities, and other experiences appropriate to the child's physical condition and developmental needs that encourage the child to vent his or her feelings about what he or she is going through.

Play comes naturally to children, and play therapy is a major tool used by child life specialists to help their patients. Play therapy often involves dolls or puppets that are used by the child to act out the anxiety he or she is experiencing. For example, a child who feels fear and pain and a sense of victimization each time he or she is given an injection may release a lot of hostility playing nurse and giving a doll a "play" injection. For an important moment, instead of being passive, that child is in control. Speaking through a puppet, a child will often express emotions he or she might otherwise repress. From these moments of emotional breakthrough and release, the child life specialist will direct the conversation in ways that can help the child understand his or her feelings. Often, children have frightening misconceptions about what is going to happen to them. Medical terminology makes almost everything sound terrible. Sometimes, a direct, accurate, and easy-to-understand explanation of the situation is all that a child needs. A child life specialist is trained to anticipate and identify common misconceptions and distortions. He or she is an expert at talking to children who knows how, honestly but sensitively, to explain an upcoming operation, treatment, or other medical development to a worried child. The child life specialist is a good listener when a child needs to talk. Other times, the child life specialist is a first-rate storyteller, weaving tales with a message that may relieve anxiety or initiate important communication. Sometimes, the child life specialist becomes a good and trusted friend and, in some cases, a surrogate parent.

A hospital is a big, busy, complex place with a large and what often appears to be a constantly changing cast of characters working in it. The child life specialist's challenge is to humanize and personalize the medical experience for the child. Often the child life specialist serves as the child's advocate in that huge, strange setting. When a child life specialist senses that certain changes in hospital routine might reduce a child's anxieties or just cheer a child, he or she may act as a go-between, asking if it is possible for the nurses to stretch a bedtime or visiting hour; arranging with the dietitian for a special food treat; communicating to therapists, technicians, and physicians a child's particular fear or sensitivity (regarding privacy, a particular position) so that tests, treatments, and examinations may be carried out in ways that will make the child more comfortable.

Often, the child life specialist represents the child and his or her parents in their dealings with members of the health care team. When there are questions or conflicts that have gone unresolved, the child life specialist may act as spokesperson for the child and his or her family. The child life specialist is there for the patient's family in other ways, too, providing comfort and distraction and a cup of coffee to an anxious parent waiting for his or her child to come out of surgery; reassuring siblings with accurate but sensitively presented information about the medical situation; sensitizing the whole family to any special physical and emotional problems that the patient might be facing or might face in the future. Simply put, a child life specialist is the kind of person you like to have in your corner when you are stuck in a stressful, unpleasant, medical situation.

Child life specialists are educated in human growth and development, the effects of stress and trauma, the special needs of children who are chronically ill and/or physically disabled, the preparation of children for hospitalization and medical procedure, basic medical procedures and terminology, the functions and interrelationships of various health care and rehabilitation disciplines, the nature and etiology of illness and disability, group dynamics, the dynamics of the family and the impact that illness has on the family unit, society's attitude toward illness and disability, and the death-and-loss related concerns of patients and their families.

SETTINGS, SALARIES, STATISTICS

Most child life specialists work in hospitals at the patient's bedside, in special playrooms, and in the admissions office where they may offer the child a puppet show or filmstrip or other introduction to the hospital. There are approximately 1,500 child life specialists at this time. Ninety-five percent of them are female. Only 25 percent of all pediatric services have child life programs. There are so few programs because there is still work to do in convincing health administrators of the unique needs of children and because of cost containment pressures. The *Directory of Child Life Activity Programs in North America* lists over 350 existing programs in the United States and Canada.

The growing interest in ambulatory services has resulted in an increasing number of child life specialists working in outpatient facilities. Child life specialists also often work in the community, providing programs and literature designed to acquaint school age children with hospitals.

Starting salaries for child life specialists approximate those for beginning teachers—$17,000 to $19,000—but will vary according to institution and region of the country. Salaries in the Northeastern and Middle Atlantic states tend to be the highest in the nation. Very experienced child life workers earn top salaries in the $24,000 to $41,000 range. Directors of child life programs may earn as much as $58,000.

Child life work goes under many names: child life specialist, child life activity specialist, child life worker, play leader, play specialist, hospital play specialist, play therapist, activity therapist, recreation therapist, and recreation worker; depending on the program, the hospital or clinic, and the region where the child life work is being carried out. *Child life specialist* is a recently recognized health professional title, and it is hoped that in time it will come to represent and encompass all members of this medical profession.

HOW TO BECOME A CHILD LIFE SPECIALIST

There are several routes to a career as a child life specialist. The first is to graduate from a four-year college with a bachelor's degree in child life (or hospitalized child), however, very few colleges offer such programs. A second alternative is for undergraduates majoring in recreational therapy, education, child development, psychology, or art therapy, who can elect a child life practicum prior to or after graduation. The practicum offers first-hand experience in a hospital setting plus classroom study.

In addition, men and women who are in education, recreation, child life development, and similar fields can enter the child life field by adding on-the-job training to their prior work experiences.

A typical child life college program consists of a broad range of liberal arts courses—English, history, science—plus a concentration of courses relating to the healthy child as well as the hospitalized child. Usually in the junior and senior years, students participate in field programs located in hospitals, clinics, day-care centers, preschools, and special education classes. The course work and these supervised experiences should lead to competence in the areas of growth and development, family dynamics, play and activities, interpersonal communication, developmental observation and assessment, the learning process, group process, behavior management, the child's reactions to illness and hospitalization, methods of preventing emotional trauma, interaction with other health care professionals, medical terminology, basic pediatric medicine, and supervisory skills.

A *child life assistant* is a person who carries out certain child life functions under the direct supervision of a child life specialist. Generally, child life assistants have degrees from two-year colleges in appropriately related fields. Currently, only a small number of positions at this level are available.

A *child life administrator* is a child life specialist with additional academic preparation at the master's degree level. This additional education and training prepare the child life administrator to establish child life program objectives; interpret objectives and needs to the child life staff and to the hospital's administration; select, supervise, and evaluate the child life staff; manage budgets; and provide educational resources regarding child life needs to child life students.

It should be noted here that there are many opportunities for child life volunteers who, with training and working closely under the supervision of a child life specialist, can be an important part of the care-giving team.

Personal qualities essential to performance that will be both effective and fulfilling for the childlife specialist include intelligence, excellent communication skills, teaching ability, flexibility, assertiveness and persuasiveness, compassion, sensitivity, a good sense of humor, dedication, the ability to work well as part of a team, and, perhaps especially, optimism. A child life specialist must be able to work with children who are often very sick and dying. A combination of emotional strength and a strong sense of purpose are very important.

Since 1987, the Child Life Certifying Commission, operating as a commission of the Child Life Council, Inc. (CLC), has offered voluntary certification for child life specialists.

At this time, the various states have not established standards or tests to license child life specialists.

THE FUTURE

At present, job opportunities are limited, and it is difficult to estimate how many positions for child life specialists will open in the coming ten to twenty years. Cost containment is an increasingly crucial factor for all health care delivery systems, and often it is such auxiliary support departments of a hospital or clinic that feel the pinch first. In addition, many hospitals have never instituted child life programs for a combination of philosophical and cost containment reasons. Not all hospitals feel that child life specialist programs are essential. Again, only 25 percent of all pediatric services provide child life programs. If, however, a person is open to the possibility of moving and remains flexible, opportunities exist. Also, the educational preparation necessary for child life work is largely transferable and valuable in obtaining positions in related fields such as child and family counseling or working with children in clinics or residential institutions.

Another possible disadvantage of this health profession is that salaries are often low. Salaries in this field do not always coincide with the educational background necessary.

Still, awareness of the unique emotional needs of the hospitalized child is increasing with each year, and with this heightened awareness should come new opportunities for child life specialists.

For more information regarding child life specialists, child life assistants, child life administrators, and child life specialist certification, write to the:

Child Life Council, Inc.
7910 Woodmont Avenue, Suite 310
Bethesda, Maryland 20814

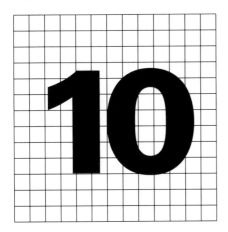

CYTOTECHNOLOGIST

Cytology is the study of the structure and function of cells. *Cytotechnologists* are trained laboratory technologists who work with pathologists (doctors who specialize in structural and functional changes caused by disease) to identify changes in body cells, especially those related to early diagnosis of cancer. Cell specimens are obtained from various body sites: the oral cavity, the female reproductive tract (the most common test run on these cells is the important PAP smear to detect uterine cancer, which is named after the famous American cytologist Dr. George N. Papanicolaou), the lung, or any other body cavity shedding (or exfoliating) cells. Sometimes (in certain situations involving the breast, thyroid gland, lung, or other body part) these cells are collected by fine needle aspiration, which is the drawing off of suspected cells through the use of a syringe or similar instrument inserted through the skin. This relatively noninvasive procedure spares patients surgical procedures that, until recently, were the only means of collecting certain specimens.

The cytotechnologist then places the smears of cell samples on glass slides, adds contrast stain to facilitate viewing, and screens the slides under a microscope. The cytotechnologist is looking for abnormalities in the cellular structure, size, or color; in the patterns of the cytoplasm and nuclei; or other evidence of cellular change that might indicate a benign or malignant condition or other diseases. The cytotechnologist then reports his or her findings to the pathologist.

This is extremely important and exacting work. The cytotechnologist must be thorough and precise and have "expert eyes." Among new advances being developed in cytotechnology is cytometry, which is the use of computers to measure cells.

SETTINGS, SALARIES, STATISTICS

Most cytotechnologists work in the laboratories of hospitals and clinics. Private laboratories and research facilities also employ cytotechnologists, and some cytotechs teach.

There are approximately 8,000 cytotechnologists in the United States. The vast majority, perhaps 90 percent, are women. In 1992 (the most recent year for which figures are available), the median entry-level salary was $27,500.

Advancement in this field may come in the form of promotion to supervisory positions, or an experienced cytotech who has a degree may move on to research and/or teaching. The classifications *cytotechnologist I, II, III* are ascending levels of performance, responsibility, and experience that are sometimes used in position descriptions.

HOW TO BECOME A CYTOTECHNOLOGIST

To become a certified cytotechnologist, a student must graduate from a cytotechnology educational program that is accredited by the Commission for the Accreditation of Allied Health Education Programs (CAAHEP), which on July 1, 1994, replaced the Committee on Allied Health Education and Accreditation (CAHEA) of the American Medical Association. CAAHEP is an independent body in which the AMA participates as one sponsor among many. At this time, nationwide, there are approximately 55 accredited cytotechnology education programs. Students should have a bachelor's degree prior to attending a cytotechnology program, or they should obtain a degree as part of a cytotechnology program. Programs vary in length from one to two years, depending on the amount of college credit required for admission. It is recommended that preparatory college semesters include a minimum of 20 semester hours of biology (general biology, bacteriology, parasitology, physiology, anatomy, histology, embryology, zoology, genetics) and 8 semester hours of chemistry.

More than one-third of the accredited programs require more college credits and/or a longer period of cytologic education and, upon successful completion, award bachelor's degrees. It is anticipated that in the future more schools will offer degree programs for cytotechnology students.

An accredited curriculum will cover the historical background of cytology, cytology as applied in clinical medicine, cytology in the screening of exfoliative tumor cells, and areas of anatomy, histology, embryology, cytochemistry, cytophysiology, endocrinology, and inflammatory disease.

Approximately 300 men and women graduated from accredited cytotech education programs last year. Upon graduation from an accredited cytotech education program, a candidate is eligible to take the certification examination administered by the American Society of Clinical Pathologists. Candidates who pass this examination are entitled to call themselves registered cytotechnologists and to use the initials CT (ASCP), which stands for a cytotechnologist who is certified by the American Society of Clinical Pathologists.

Certification is also available through the International Academy of Cytology (IAC). The IAC does not offer career-entry certification. Rather, it certifies cytotechnologists only after they have received ASCP certification and have accumulated three years of experience. At present, only three states require cytotechnologists to be licensed.

The personal qualities that are important to effectiveness and satisfaction in this job include a keen interest and proficiency in the biological sciences, patience, the ability to concentrate for long periods of time and to work independently, manual dexterity, seriousness, dependability, and concern and appreciation for precision. Essential, too, is a genuine fascination with the diagnostic process. Reading all the facts in a patient's medical record (age, sex, occupation, previous illnesses, previous treatments, family medical history, test results, etc.) and then looking through a microscope at the patient's cells in an attempt to identify the problem is something like piecing together a puzzle. The best cytotechs are those individuals with all of the above abilities and training who find laboratory "detective work" to be intriguing and challenging.

It is highly recommended that cytotechs have good vision and be able to distinguish fine shades of color. Persons who are interested in medicine and who have physical disabilities that prevent them from moving about may find cytotechnology an ideal profession.

THE FUTURE

The job outlook for cytotechnologists is bright. The number of job openings available in the next ten years may increase by as much as 40 percent. Today, demand for trained cytotechnologists is high, and most cytotechs gain employment immediately upon graduation. In some geographic locations, there is presently an acute shortage of cytotechs.

For more information about a career in cytotechnology, write to the:

American Society of Cytology
1015 Chestnut Street, Suite 1518
Philadelphia, Pennsylvania 19107

For certification information, contact the:

Board of Registry
American Society of Clinical Pathologists
P.O. Box 12277
Chicago, Illinois 60612-0277

The International Academy of Cytology
1640 East 50th Street, Suite 20B
Chicago, Illinois 60615-3161

DANCE/MOVEMENT THERAPIST

also known as
Dance Therapist
Movement Therapist
Psychomotor Therapist

For many years the American Dance Therapy Association had as its logo the figure of a person with arms gracefully stretched skyward and head raised, reaching out of an egg-shaped boundary that is drawn all around. This simple symbol very effectively conveyed what dance therapy is all about. Dance therapy is the psychotherapeutic use of movement as a process that furthers the emotional and physical integration of the individual. Dance and movement are used in the diagnosis and treatment of persons suffering from schizophrenia, psychotic depression, personality disorders, brain injury, and learning disabilities, as well as for the visually impaired, the hearing impaired, individuals with physical disabilities, the elderly, adult survivors of violence, sexually and physically abused children, substance abusers, individuals with eating disorders, autistic children, the homeless, and others who experience psychological and/or physical limitations. Over three million people in the United States currently receive dance/movement therapy services.

Fundamental to dance therapy is the concept that the human mind and body constantly interact. Pain or pleasure felt on the skin registers emotionally, and we feel frightened or happy. Conversely, pain—or anxiety, depression, disorganization—felt within, can involuntarily be reflected outwardly in posture, movements, muscle tension, and breathing patterns.

For centuries and in many cultures, the therapeutic value of dance and other forms of body movement has been recognized. To "dance" makes one "feel good." It provides diversion, which, in turn, provides a respite from worries; it eases tensions, recharges energy, and, in general, renews emotional well-being. Most important, dancing and other body movements can communicate feelings perhaps otherwise left unexpressed.

Dance/movement therapy began formally in the United States during World War II, when a dancer/choreographer named Marian Chace, working with psychiatrists created the first program, at St. Elizabeth's Hospital in Washington, D.C., to gain insight into and treat the 750,000 men who were rejected for military service and the additional 750,000 who were discharged, all because of emotional problems, as well as the scores of veterans who were returning home traumatized by war.

Dance/movement therapists are health care professionals trained in both dance and psychology. The job of the dance therapist is to read the outward physical indicators in a patient that might suggest (or, in severe cases, that scream) inward disorder and then to use this same mind/body dynamic to make contact with the patient, working with him or her toward the attainment of greater emotional and/or physical freedom. Dance therapists' goals for their patients are communication, improved self-image, greater confidence in dealing with the environment and with other individuals, and, in general, better integration of the physical, mental, and emotional aspects of the individual, all leading to a better ability to enjoy life. Ideally, the body is exercised to exercise and heal the mind. The mind, in turn, heals the body.

For example, among the most severely emotionally disturbed patients dance therapists treat in institutions are schizophrenics and individuals who suffer from extreme depression. A schizophrenic may manifest the severe personality disorganization he or she is feeling inside by moving in abrupt, fragmented, and disconnected motions. The depressed patient's movements may become limp and slow, or he or she may become altogether immobile. Dance therapy can help to draw these patients out of their psychoses. Group activities that call for touching and rhythmic motion, for example, can promote renewed contact with the environment and interaction with others, thereby breaking the isolation and rebuilding the damaged self-image that often accompany these illnesses. Gradually, mind/body integration can be restored. Drawing on a repertoire of movements led by a dance therapist, the patient may be willing to nonverbally express the fears and impulses he or she is feeling but will not talk about. Emotional pains that have been locked up are gradually communicated through movement experiences. With time, after repeated safe and successful expressions of these highly charged emotions, the patient may progress to the point where verbalization can take place. In some cases, the communication achieved in the dance therapy session is the patient's first step toward recovery.

Children who suffer from a form of emotional illness known as autism are unable to form relationships or to interact with the environment in any meaningful way. They shut out the world and retreat within themselves. Often, their psychological isolation is expressed in bizarre, repetitive movements, such as rhythmic rocking or twirling, that draw their attention further inward and away from the environment. Autistic children may seem lost even to themselves—not speaking, only sitting, expressionless, rocking for hours. Working one-on-one, a dance therapist may try to establish contact with an autistic child nonverbally by mirroring the repetitive movements— creating for him or her a sort of "dance" that is familiar and, therefore, reassuring. It is hoped that an important acknowledgement of another individual—the dance therapist—will take place, and, with time, a relationship that will allow the autistic child to explore his or her emotions and the environment will be forged.

Persons who are developmentally disabled often experience problems with coordination, mobility, communication, and social interaction. A dance therapist can initiate activities that teach them size, direction, and time and spatial relationships that will improve attention span, focus, and motor skills so that developmentally disabled people may care for themselves and eventually work.

Children with brain damage or learning disabilities are also helped. The perceptual and behavioral problems; poor balance and coordination; and disoriented, incomplete body images exhibited by these children can often be relieved through movement activities that stimulate kinesthetic and tactile senses and teach organization.

For the elderly, who often feel social isolation, loss of mobility, and inactivity, a dance therapy session can provide an atmosphere of physical and psychological safety in which a sense of self-worth and revitalization may be restored.

Dance therapists can help individuals who are visually impaired in a variety of ways. The dance therapy studio becomes a safe and familiar space to explore, where the ability to move with assertiveness and confidence can be developed. The postural misalignment and accompanying tensions created by habitually tentative movement can also be relieved. Dance therapy provides the visually impaired patient with a special opportunity to vent deep feelings and fears.

Dance and movement can often counteract feelings of isolation that many individuals with hearing impairment experience, and the "vocabulary" of symbolic movements that a dance therapist can teach a hearing impaired person can expand his or her communicative skills. And, for the individual with physical disabilities, a dance therapist can teach exercises that improve coordination, focus, and endurance.

SETTINGS, SALARIES, STATISTICS

Dance therapists work in psychiatric hospitals, community mental health centers, substance abuse treatment programs, special education settings, nursing homes and senior citizen centers, day-care facilities, rehabilitation settings, correctional facilities, private and group practices, and research centers. However, because interest in this field is relatively new and there are so few dance therapists at this time, and, too, because of recent budget conservatism, most dance therapists can be found working in hospitals and long-term health care facilities in metropolitan areas.

There are dance therapists working throughout the United States, in Canada, Europe, South America, Asia, the Middle East, and Africa.

At this time, there are approximately 700 dance therapists who are certified by the American Dance Therapy Association (ADTA), which is the professional organization for dance therapists. Another approximately 300 men and women are currently providing dance therapy as they work toward certification.

Salaries for dance therapists range from $20,000 to $50,000 per year, depending on training, experience, region of the country, and type of facility.

HOW TO BECOME A DANCE THERAPIST

To work as a dance therapist, a minimum of a master's degree is necessary. At the graduate level, studies include courses in dance/movement therapy theory and practice, psychopathology, human development, observation and research skills, and a supervised internship in a clinical setting. As an undergraduate, a student interested in becoming a dance/movement therapist should pursue a broad liberal arts background with an emphasis in psychology. Extensive training in a variety of dance forms, with courses in theory, improvisation, choreography, and kinesiology (the science of human muscular movement), plus experience teaching dance to healthy children and adults are recommended.

Master's degree programs in dance therapy typically entail two years of study. At this time, there are seven institutions that offer graduate degree programs in dance therapy. The specific degree awarded varies from program to program—some award a master of arts in movement therapy (MMT); others award a master's in dance therapy; still others confer a master of arts in creative arts therapy (MCAT). Twelve institutions offer graduate courses in dance/movement, and another eight offer undergraduate preparation or course work. In addition, there are approximately six other programs nationwide that offer specific training programs and workshops for dance therapists. Approximately thirty institutions have internships in dance therapy.

The American Dance Therapy Association (ADTA) registers dance therapists and has established specific criteria for two different levels of registration. A D.T.R. (dance therapist registered) is a therapist who has a master's degree, which includes 700 hours of supervised clinical internship and who is deemed, by the ADTA, to be fully qualified to work in a professional treatment system. An A.D.T.R. (Academy of Dance Therapists Registered) is a therapist who has met additional requirements, including 3,640 hours of supervised clinical work, and is considered fully qualified to teach, supervise, and engage in private practice. Registration is not required for employment. However, increasingly, this credential is recognized as the standard of competency and proficiency in dance therapy. Registration tends to enhance the quality and quantity of employment opportunities open to a dance therapist. The ADTR also approves graduate programs of dance/movement therapy.

To become a dance therapist, a student should love dance and people. A strong commitment to both is necessary to function in this profession. Strength, flexibility, stamina, and a strong desire to relate to and help others are essential.

At this time, there are no state licensing requirements for dance therapists.

THE FUTURE

Dance/movement therapy is a relatively new and still-small health care profession, and the number of job openings is limited. The economy may play the biggest role in determining the employment outlook for this field. Both the validity and the importance of dance therapy are well recognized. More emotionally and physically impaired Americans are, today, in public and private health care settings that can accommodate the creative arts therapies. And the American population is growing larger and older, and the number of people who could benefit from dance therapy is likely to increase. On June 18, 1992, the Unites States Senate Special Committee on Aging held a hearing on dance/movement therapy. Expert testimony was presented attesting to the benefits of this particular therapy to older people. Later that year, dance/movement therapy, along with music therapy (see Chapter 32), and art therapy (see Chapter 2), was included and defined in federal legislation when amendments to the Older Americans Act became law. This federal recognition has meant that more older Americans are receiving the benefits of dance/movement therapy and that, for the first time, dance/movement therapists can obtain state funds to provide their services. In late 1993, the ADTA received a national grant to study dance/movement therapy's applications with head injury patients, and the National Institutes of Health (NIH) recently awarded the ADTA a study grant, as well. Opportunities exist, and there will be future growth. Exactly how much growth will, in large part, be determined by budget considerations and health care reform.

Dance/movement therapy is important and potentially satisfying work. For students who are interested in dance and who would like to apply their talents to serving others, dance therapy is a very special career possibility.

For more information about dance/movement therapy and a list of dance/movement therapy educational programs, contact the:

American Dance Therapy Association, Inc.
2000 Century Plaza, Suite 108
Columbia, Maryland 21044

DENTAL ASSISTANT

Dr. C. Edmund Kells, who practiced dentistry in New Orleans in the late 1800s, is generally credited with hiring the first dental assistant, whose name, unfortunately, has been lost to time. We do know quite a bit about her, though, because of an article entitled "Management of Dental Practice," which Dr. Kells wrote in 1893. In it, he described his ideal "lady assistant":

> To be a successful assistant, a young lady must be quick, quiet, gentle, attentive without being obtrusive, and intelligent. In your office her duties will be systematically arranged.... While the engine is being used for excavating, she should keep the cavity free from chips with the chip-blower, which will allow the wall to be always in plain sight, and that step in the operation will be much more rapidly completed. Just before being ready for it, she should prepare the filling material, whether it be gold, amalgam or cement, that all will be ready and no delay met with when the same is called for. It should be her duty to see that supplies of all kinds are always on hand; a small stock of everything that is used should be kept in a cabinet reserved for that purpose. The rubber dam should be cut in the sizes used, silk cut into proper lengths and waxed, spunk torn up into various sizes desired, and placed, according to size, into the several compartments reserved for it.... In a little while she will learn to anticipate your wants, and a look or semi-gesture may be frequently used instead of a sentence. That during a protracted sitting she will rapidly perform one duty after another, with scarcely a word from yourself, will be frequently a source of surprise to the patient.... It should be her duty to receive all patients, make appointments, attend to your correspondence, look after the linen, and take a general interest in the welfare of the office.

Although 100 years old, this description of dental assisting is remarkably appropriate today. Modern *dental assistants* assist in the direct care of dental patients under the supervision of a dentist and perform other auxiliary responsibilities in the dentist's office. The scope of the assistant's responsibilities is influenced by the employer, educational preparation, and the regulations of the dental practice act of the state in which the dental assistant is employed.

Dental assistants may provide support to the dentist on several levels. They provide chairside support: taking and exposing radiographs, recording vital signs, making preliminary impressions for study casts, and participating in "four-hand procedures," where they serve as the dentist's other set of hands. When assisting chairside, the dental assistant must anticipate the dentist's and the patient's needs, quickly and deftly handing the dentist the necessary instrument, preparing filling materials and cements, taking impressions, keeping the patient's mouth comfortable and the area being worked on free of debris. The dental assistant and the dentist work as a team to treat the patient's dental needs efficiently and comfortably. Dental assistants may provide clinical support: preparing and dismissing patients, sterilizing and disinfecting instruments and equipment, explaining postoperative and oral hygiene instructions to patients, preparing tray setups for dental procedures, assisting in the prevention and management of medical and dental emergencies, and maintaining accurate patient treatment records. They may offer laboratory support: pouring, trimming, and polishing study casts; fabricating custom impression trays from preliminary impressions; cleaning, repairing, and polishing removable appliances; and fabricating temporary restorations. And depending on the size and arrangement of the dentist's practice, dental assistants may also provide business office support: answering telephones, coordinating appointment schedules, organizing supply controls, setting up payment plans, and processing insurance payment claims (almost half of all dentists also employ full-time personnel who handle only business and insurance related matters and are referred to as dental business assistants or practice managers).

The specifics of a dental assistant's work are a function of the size of the dental practice, the state in which she or he works, and the number of other auxiliary dental personnel working with her or him. Usually, the more dental auxiliaries (hygienists and other assistants) there are in an office, the more closely defined a particular dental assistant's responsibilities will be.

A dental assistant may work for a general dentist or for a dentist who concentrates on one specific type of dentistry, such as endodontics (the treatment of the dental pulp—usually with root canal therapy), orthodontics (bite correction), oral surgery, pediatric dentistry (children's dentistry), periodontics (the treatment of gums). The nature of the specialty will determine the specific functions that a dental assistant must perform.

Each state has its own laws governing the expanded functions of dental assistants (in some states, dental assistants may independently take impressions, apply medications, and remove oral sutures).

Dr. Kell's 1893 description of his ideal dental assistant missed the mark in one big area, however. He wrote, "She should realize that her duties do not include entertaining the patients, and should understand that the less she has to say the better satisfaction she will give." Today's dental assistant also plays an important role in personalizing the dental experience for patients. The best dental assistants offer understanding, comfort, and information that can allay a patient's apprehension about the pending dental treatment. Many patients feel more comfortable talking to their dental assistant than to their dentist.

SETTINGS, SALARIES, STATISTICS

Most dental assistants work in the private offices of dentists who are in solo or group practice. Dental assistants also work in hospital dental departments, state and local departments of public health, mobile dental units, nursing homes, the Public Health Service, the Department of Veterans Affairs, the military, in clinics, and in dental schools. Many teach dental assisting or are representatives for dental practice products. Although dental assistants typically work forty hours per week, Saturday office hours and evening hours are often required. At least 12 percent of all dental assistants work part-time.

There are approximately 200,000 dental assistants in the United States at this time. The vast majority of them are female.

Salaries depend largely on the type of practice, the specific responsibilities assigned, and geographic location. Starting salaries tend to be low. Students with on-the-job training start at about $10,500 annually, and students with formal training begin at approximately $11,500 per year. Experienced dental assistants who work for private dentists earn between $13,000 and $16,000 annually, and approximately 20 percent of all dental assistants earn $25,000 a year or more.

Advancement as a dental assistant in a private practice is limited, but many dental assistants who want additional challenges go on to acquire the education necessary to become a dental hygienist, or they enter other allied health professions (such as radiography). Some dental assistants become sales representatives for companies that manufacture dental equipment and dental products.

HOW TO BECOME A DENTAL ASSISTANT

While most dental assistants are still trained on the job by the dentists who hire them, in the past twenty years there has been a steady trend toward formal dental assistant educational programs that are offered by community and junior colleges, trade schools, and vocational/technical schools. Approximately 270 of the hundreds of programs offered nationwide are accredited by the Commission on Dental Accreditation of the American Dental Association. There are basically two formal accredited educational routes to the training necessary for employment as a dental assistant: one-year study and training programs offered by vocational and technical institutes that award a certificate or diploma (these make up one-half of all the formal educational programs) and two-year associate's degree programs offered by community and junior colleges. Either educational route usually requires a high school diploma or its equivalent, above-average grades in science and English, and a high school grade point average of C or better. Some programs also require applicants to take a college entrance examination, such as the School and College Ability Test (SCAT) or the American College Test (ACT), and re- quire a certain standard of performance on these tests as a prerequisite for admission.

There are also nonaccredited four- to six-month dental assistant courses offered by private vocational schools. Some dental assistants learn their skills in the armed forces.

The curriculum of an approved dental assistant program typically consists of classroom, laboratory, and preclinical instruction. Subjects taught include chairside assisting, dental anatomy and pathology, dental terminology, steril- ization and bacteriology, laboratory techniques, local and general anesthesia for oral surgery, preventative dentistry, pharmacology, dental radiology, first aid, ethics, care of dental equipment, and office management practices. Prac- tical experience is acquired during work assignments in dentists' offices, hospital dental departments, dental laboratories, and other dental settings. In 1993, approximately 4,100 men and women successfully completed accred- ited educational programs for dental assistants.

In high school, students who are interested in dental assisting should take courses in biology, chemistry, mathematics, health, English, typing, book- keeping, and other business subjects.

Personal qualities that are important to effective performance and enjoy- ment as a dental assistant include manual dexterity, a friendly personality, a neat appearance, common sense, the ability to think quickly, and willingness to follow instructions.

Graduates of accredited dental assisting programs who pass a competency examination administered by the Dental Assisting National Board, Inc. and satisfy other requirements become certified dental assistants and may use the letters CDA after their names. Individuals who have two years of dental as- sisting experience but have not completed an accredited dental assistant program may also become eligible for certification by then passing an exam- ination.

Although not required for employment, certification is generally accepted as evidence of a high level of preparation. The Dental Assisting National Board also offers examinations in Dental Radiology and Infection Control.

THE FUTURE

According to the Bureau of Labor Statistics, employment opportunities for dental assistants should be excellent for the next several years. As many as 60,000 new positions should be added in the next twelve years, bringing the number of dental assistants in the U.S. to 225,000. The largest contributor to this growth is the increased use of dental assistants by dentists. Most dentists today find that hiring one or more assistants is essential to providing the dental services patients expect and to enlarging their practices. In addition, the number of Americans is increasing, the percentage of Americans over sixty-five years old is increasing and will continue to increase (senior citizens tend to require more dental care), more people today are able to pay for dental care because of dental insurance plans, and there is an increased awareness of the importance of regular dental care. These factors should create a greater demand for dental services and, therefore, for more dental assistants. In addition, there may be a shortage of dentists by the turn of the century which could lead to more expanded functions being performed by assistants and, therefore, more demand.

For more information about dental assistants, write to the:

> American Dental Assistants Association
> 203 LaSalle Street, Suite 1320
> Chicago, Illinois 60601

DENTAL HYGIENIST

Dental hygienists perform prophylactic dental treatments and provide other direct patient care. Although their functions vary by law from state to state, they typically include cleaning and polishing teeth; removing calculus and plaque (hard and soft deposits) from above and below the gum line (using various handheld instruments called curettes and often a machine called a cavitron that removes calculus with ultrasonic vibrations); and examining teeth and gums; taking medical and dental histories; charting the condition of decay and disease for the dentist's analysis; exposing, processing, and interpreting dental X rays; screening patients for oral cancer; taking blood pressure readings. (Although this function may seem incongruous in a dental setting, dental hygienists often record blood pressure readings because high blood pressure—the silent killer—can easily be detected by taking a patient's blood pressure with a sphygmomanometer, and many dentists and dental hygienists seize the opportunity to take the patient's reading while he or she is in for routine dental care or cleaning). Other duties of the dental hygienist include making impressions of teeth for study models; instructing patients in home oral health care procedures (proper brushing, selecting the proper toothbrush, flossing); putting temporary fillings in teeth; analyzing patients' diets and counseling them on diet as it pertains to good dental and gum health; applying topical, cavity-preventative agents such as fluoride and sealants; and designing and implementing community and school dental health programs. Another responsibility of the dental hygienist is to ensure that appropriate protocols and procedures are followed so that both patient and hygienist are protected from infectious disease and other hazards. In some states, dental hygienists may perform certain pain control and restorative procedures as well.

Until recent years, dental hygienists worked under supervision. Today, supervision levels vary from state to state. Also, in some settings (nursing homes and other institutions), they do not require supervision.

SETTING, SALARIES, STATISTICS

Most dental hygienists work in the private offices of dentists who are in solo or group practice. Dental hygienists are also employed in the dental department of hospitals, health maintenance organizations, private and state institutions, dental and dental hygiene schools, community agencies, primary and secondary schools, private industry, and the military. The Peace Corps and the World Health Organization offer dental hygienists opportunities abroad. Some dental hygienists who have the appropriate experience and educational background work as researchers, educators, consultants, and administrators of dental programs or as representatives of companies that manufacture dental products. Dental hygienists who work in private offices usually work 30 to 35 hours per week, including Saturday and evening office hours. Many dental hygienists work part-time, and hours are often flexible. Some dental hygienists work for more than one dentist.

Dental hygienists who work full-time in private offices earn an average of between $25,500 and $29,500 annually. Most dental hygienists who work in private offices are salaried or hourly employees, but in some cases dental hygienists are paid a commission for the work they perform or they receive a combination of salary and commission.

There are approximately 100,000 dental hygienists in the United States, and most of them are women.

HOW TO BECOME A DENTAL HYGIENIST

Dental hygiene is a licensed profession, and to be eligible for licensure a candidate must complete a minimum educational requirement of at least two academic years of college in a dental hygiene program that is accredited by the Commission on Dental Accreditation of the American Dental Association. At this time, there are 210 such programs offered by community colleges, dental schools, colleges, universities, and technical schools. Most of these programs award an associate's degree, and this credential is usually sufficient for employment in a private practice. Other programs lead to a bachelor's degree in dental hygiene. To work in a public or school health program, a minimum of a bachelor's degree is necessary. A master's degree in dental hygiene is also offered by five universities, and such graduate work is usually necessary for research, administrative, and teaching positions in dental hygiene.

Dental hygiene educational programs offer laboratory, clinical, and classroom instruction. The curriculum typically incudes course work in anatomy, physiology, chemistry, microbiology, oral pathology, oral anatomy and histology, nutrition, periodontology (the study of gums), pharmacology, dental materials, first aid, psychology, sociology, and public health. In high school, students considering a career as a dental hygienist should take courses in biology, mathematics, chemistry, health, and, if offered, speech.

Upon graduation from an accredited educational program, a dental hygienist is eligible to sit for the six-hour-long written National Board Dental Hygiene Examination, which is administered by the American Dental Association Joint Commission on National Dental Examinations, and a state or regional practical/clinical examination. The candidate must pass both the written and the practical/clinical examinations and be licensed by the state board of dental examiners in the state or states in which he or she intends to practice (there is little interstate reciprocity). For the clinical part of the examination, the candidate is required to perform specific dental hygiene procedures. In all states, candidates may satisfy the written part of the licensing examination by passing the National Board Dental Hygiene Examination. The states that do not recognize this examination provide their own, or a regional, written test of competency.

Personal qualities that can contribute to success and satisfaction as a dental hygienist include manual dexterity (important for handling the various dental instruments in the mouth where every minute fraction of an inch matters), appreciation for detail, personal neatness and cleanliness, good health, and good communication skills. A good hygienist is able to understand a patient's apprehensions and preferences to that he or she can institute an effective dental-care regimen that the patient will follow. A dental hygienist also interfaces with the other dental-care providers in his or her workplace, so the ability to work as part of a team is crucial. Dental hygiene is a very people-oriented profession. A dental hygienist must enjoy people.

THE FUTURE

Although the demand for dental hygienists varies according to geographic area, for the coming ten years, at least, the nationwide demand for dental hygienists should significantly outpace supply. Spurring this growth are several factors: increased awareness of the importance of preventative dental care (98 percent of all American adults have some degree of periodontal—gum—disease); the proliferation of dental insurance plans; and population increases (there will be more Americans and more older Americans). Another factor is the greater number of medically complex patients (individuals with long-term illnesses, persons with multiple disabilities, and others) who today are living longer and may be able to benefit from dental hygiene procedures or who, because of their treatment, require them. Finally, as a growing number of dentists accept the dental hygienist's role and benefit (increased productivity), the demand for dental hygienists will increase.

For more information about dental hygienists, write to the:

American Dental Hygienists' Association
Professional Development Division
444 North Michigan Avenue, Suite 3400
Chicago, Illinois 60611

DENTAL-LABORATORY TECHNICIAN

also known as
Dental Technician

Dental-laboratory technicians make and repair single and whole sets of prosthetic teeth, crowns, inlays, fixed bridges, partial removable bridges, and corrective orthodontic appliances following the specifications and instructions provided by dentists. Working from models made from impressions of the patient's teeth or mouth and the dentist's prescription, they fabricate these various dental prostheses out of the appropriate materials (choosing from, and sometimes combining, gold, silver, platinum, stainless steel, various plastics, porcelain, and other ceramics). They use small hand-tools (wax carvers, heated spatulas, scrapers, knives), precision measuring instruments (micrometers, articulators), bench-fabricating machines (fine electric drills, electric lathes, buffing wheels), metal-melting torches, high-heat furnaces, and other specialized laboratory equipment and electrical devices. The end product is a dental prosthesis that fits perfectly, is strong enough to do its job, and, as closely as possible, satisfies the patient's aesthetic expectations.

Along the fabrication route, there are five dental-laboratory technician specialists who carry out certain specific functions in the dental laboratory. *Orthodontic technicians* construct (out of metal and plastics) and repair appliances for straightening teeth (retainers, tooth bands, positioners) according to an orthodontist's prescription. *Dental ceramists* apply layers of carefully color-matched porcelain paste or acrylic resin over a metal framework to form crowns, bridges, and tooth facings (the prosthesis is placed in an oven to harden, more layers of ceramic material are added and baked on until the denture exactly conforms to specifications). *Complete denture specialists* set teeth in a denture base for complete upper and/or lower restoration. *Partial denture technicians* fabricate removable partial dentures from acrylic or a combination of metal framework and acrylic teeth for patients who have lost one or more of their natural teeth, and *crown and bridge technicians* design fixed restorations for one or more adjacent teeth from metal and porcelain, which are cemented into the patient's mouth.

Although dental-laboratory technicians rarely work directly with patients, their contributions to the patient's well-being—in terms of comfort, appearance, and health—are significant.

SETTINGS, SALARIES, STATISTICS

Most dental-laboratory technicians are employed in commercial dental laboratories. These laboratories are usually small, privately owned businesses, although there are a few dental laboratories employing a hundred or more technicians. Some dental-laboratory technicians own their own laboratories. Seventeen percent of all dental-laboratory technicians work directly in dentists' offices (usually in group practices). Dental-laboratory technicians are also employed in the dental departments of hospitals and by various governmental agencies, including veterans' hospitals and clinics and the armed forces. Opportunities also exist in sales, research, and education. Salaried dental technicians usually work a standard forty-hour week.

There are approximately 58,000 dental-laboratory technicians in the United States. Over half of them are male.

The average annual starting salary for a dental-laboratory technician working in a commercial laboratory is approximately $11,000. Depending on skill, education, and specialty (dental ceramists earn the highest salaries), an experienced dental-laboratory technician in a commercial laboratory may earn between $24,500 and $36,500 per year. Supervisors and managers in private laboratories earn even higher salaries, and self-employed dental technicians who work alone or who own their own laboratories and employ other dental technicians can earn significantly more.

HOW TO BECOME A DENTAL-LABORATORY TECHNICIAN

In Florida, Kentucky, South Carolina, and Texas, the basic educational requirement for a dental-laboratory technician is a high school diploma or its equivalent; in the other 46 states, a high school diploma or its equivalent is necessary only if the dental-laboratory technician intends to become certified. In high school, prospective dental-laboratory technicians should take courses in art, various sciences, metal shop, and metallurgy. After high school, a student interested in dental technology may receive his or her training on the job or in one of the many two-year diploma, certificate, or associate's degree formal training programs in this field offered by community colleges, technical institutes, vocational schools, and dental schools around the country.

Formal training programs are designed to provide instruction in both the technology and the principles of the five dental technology specialties: complete dentures, partial dentures, crowns and bridges, ceramics, and orthodontics. Formal programs are usually broken into two segments. The curriculum for the first year typically includes course work in anatomy, chemistry, metallurgy, dental law and ethics, and laboratory techniques; in the second year, students are given supervised practical experience. Following the completion of a formal two-year classroom program, prosthetic students perfect their skills by working under the direction of an experienced dental-laboratory technician. Approximately 60 of these formal programs, all of which award an associate's degree, are accredited by the Commission on Dental Accreditation in conjunction with the American Dental Association.

On-the-job training in a commercial dental laboratory is also a valid route to the education necessary to become a dental-laboratory technician. Apprenticeships usually last five years, during which time the technician is paid for his or her work.

Certification for dental-laboratory technicians is available through the National Board for Certification, which is a trust established by the National Association of Dental Laboratories. Dental-laboratory technicians who have completed formal accredited training programs and have two years of employment experience can obtain certification status by successfully passing the board's examination testing applicants' skills and knowledge. Upon satisfying these requirements, a dental-laboratory technician becomes a Certified Dental Technician and may use the CDT after his or her name.

Technicians who are trained in apprenticeship programs are not eligible to take the certification examination until they have completed five years of employment experience and successfully passed a comprehensive examination covering all five dental technology specialty areas.

Although not usually required for employment, certification is a respected credential that is growing in importance.

Personal qualifications for a career in dental-laboratory technology include a high degree of manual dexterity, a well-developed sense of color perception, the ability to follow instructions, and an appreciation for accuracy. In this field, precision is extremely important.

THE FUTURE

Employment opportunities for dental-laboratory technicians—especially for graduates of formal, accredited training programs—are expected to be very favorable. The expansion of dental insurance plans, the growing population, and especially the increasing number of older Americans (who may require dentures) together should contribute to the creation of thousands of new job openings for dental-laboratory technicians before 2000.

For more information about dental-laboratory technicians, accredited training programs, and certification, contact the:

National Association of Dental Laboratories
National Board for Certification in Dental Laboratory
   Technology
555 East Braddock Road
Alexandria, Virginia 23314

DIAGNOSTIC MEDICAL SONOGRAPHER

also known as
Ultrasound Technologist

Ultrasound (also called sonography or ultrasonography) is the use of sound waves to obtain visual information about various health conditions within the human body. Sound wave frequencies that are hundreds of times higher than the human ear can detect are directed into the body from a transducer, which is a medical device capable of converting electrical energy into sound waves. The transducer is moved back and forth over the patient's skin surface (gel is applied to the skin first so that the transducer will be in direct contact with the skin surface without air and interference coming between the two), and the sound waves (or echoes) it produces are directed into the patient's body. As they come in contact with structures deep within the body, they are reflected back to the body surface where they are received by the transducer and electronically converted into a picture revealing the contours and composition of the body tissue. These images are then displayed on a TV-like screen, giving health care professionals a clear, immediate, easily obtainable, and often otherwise unavailable view of various situations (among them, tumors, cysts, blockages, and even the developing fetus) deep within the patient's body.

Ultrasound is generally considered safe, and in many cases its use spares the patient more complicated, uncomfortable, invasive procedures. Ultrasound is a noninvasive procedure—that is, it does not involve surgery, injection, or even radiation. It is a new and very important diagnostic tool. With it, doctors can study the contour and inner structures of the brain (this specialty is called neurosonology), the structure and action of the heart (echocardiography), various organs, the eyes, blood vessels, lymph nodes, and other parts and systems of the body to determine if there is disease or malfunction. The use of sonography in obstetrics is rapidly becoming commonplace. Using ultrasound, an obstetrician can see an outline of the unborn child and predict multiple births, detect many abnormalities *in utero*, determine more accurately the specific state of prenatal development, and exactly locate the position of the fetus before amniocentesis or a Caesarean-section delivery is performed.

Diagnostic medical sonographers are the specially educated and trained health care professionals who, working under the supervision of a doctor of medicine or osteopathy, perform diagnostic medical sonographic examinations. They select the appropriate equipment for the tests ordered, explain the procedure to the patient, position the patient to facilitate optimum image making, position and operate the transducer and other equipment, and then, while moving the scanner, they view the oscilloscope screen and record the images produced. Prior to the testing, the sonographer will review the results of any other diagnostic procedures already performed on the patient and take any additional medical history needed to supplement the images produced during the ultrasound scanning. Because the sonographer's job is to obtain the information needed for the diagnosis, he or she must be able to recognize obstructions, abnormalities of function and shape, and the subtle differences between healthy and pathological areas. A sonographer must exercise discretion and judgment and have a high degree of technical skill and knowledge of anatomy and physiology.

SETTINGS, SALARIES, STATISTICS

Diagnostic medical sonographers work in hospitals, clinics, doctors' offices, and research facilities. Nationwide, diagnostic medical sonographers earn annual salaries ranging between $23,500 and $47,000, although these figures vary with responsibility, experience, and type of employer. Advancement to positions of administrative and supervisory authority and teaching positions can bring higher pay levels.

Sonographers typically work forty-hour weeks, but night hours and emergency calls are common. Much of this time is spent standing or sitting, producing and reading the ultrasound printouts.

HOW TO BECOME A DIAGNOSTIC MEDICAL SONOGRAPHER

A student may receive the education and experience necessary to carry out the responsibilities of a diagnostic medical sonographer either in a formal educational program or, sometimes, through on-the-job training. Most diagnostic medical sonographers are already registered nurses, radiologic technologists, respiratory therapists, medical technologists, or other allied health professionals who have received special on-the-job instruction in sonography.

There are 56 diagnostic medical sonography educational programs that are approved by the Commission for the Accreditation of Allied Health Education Programs (CAAHEP), which on July 1, 1994, succeeded the American Medical Association's Committee on Allied Health Education and

Accreditation (CAHEA) in accrediting educational programs for this, and twenty-one other, allied health professions. CAAHEP is an independent body in which the AMA participates as one sponsor among many. These accredited programs are between one and four years in length and award one-year certificates, two-year associate degrees, or baccalaureate degrees, depending on the candidate's preparation and the length of the program. Programs are offered by hospitals, medical centers, community colleges, and universities. None of these programs accepts a large number of students each year. For the academic year 1993–1994, enrollment in accredited programs was approximately 1,200.

Formal sonography programs consist of classroom education plus supervised clinical education in an actual clinical environment. All of these programs require a high school diploma or its equivalent and previous training in a clinically related health field or its equivalent. Some programs specifically accept only RNs and radiologic technologists.

The curriculum typically contains course work in acoustical physics and the physical principles of ultrasound, imaging and display techniques, equipment standards (calibration, operational standards, quality control), the biological effects of ultrasound, human anatomy and physiology, histology, organ and system relationships, certain clinical diseases, the effects of pathological conditions on anatomy, ultrasound characteristics of abnormal tissues, clinical medicine, medical ethics, patient psychology, emergency care, the applications and limitations of ultrasound, image evaluation, and administration (record keeping, coding, indexing, and laboratory management).

Approved programs that teach echocardiography also include courses in circulatory anatomy and physiology, cardiac anatomy, symptomatic impairment in congenital and acquired cardiac diseases, alterations in hemodynamics, the fundamentals of cardiac physical examinations and history taking, nuclear cardiology, pulse recording, and such diagnostic techniques as phonocardiography, apex cardiography, exercise stress testing, Doppler echocardiography, cardiac cineangiography, and catheterization.

Personal qualities important to successful and satisfying performance in this career include patience; attention to detail; and the ability to work well and communicate well with patients, their families, physicians, and other health care personnel. Good vision is needed for observing and studying ultrasound images. A sonographer must also be strong enough to lift and position patients.

Certification in this profession is offered through the American Registry of Diagnostic Medical Sonographers (ARDMS), which annually administers two-day, comprehensive, qualifying examinations in various sonographic specialties—abdomen, adult echocardiography, neurosonology, obstetrics and gynecology, ophthalmology, pediatric echocardiography, and peripheral vascular Doppler. The examinations cover the specialties plus general ultrasound physics and instrumentation concepts. Certification is voluntary, but, increasingly, it is enhancing employment opportunities. Since it began this examination in October of 1975, the ARDMS has certified approximately 20,000 sonographers worldwide.

To sit for the ARDMS registry exams, a candidate must (1) have completed training in a two-year, AMA-recognized, allied health occupation (RN, radiologic technologist, respiratory therapist, physical therapist, occupational therapist, medical technologist) plus have a minimum of 12 months of full-time clinical ultrasound experience; or (2) complete an accredited ultrasound educational program; or (3) be enrolled in a bachelor's degree program in ultrasound or radiology with a minor in ultrasound and have at least 12 months of full-time clinical ultrasound experience; or (4) have two years of formal education past high school plus a minimum of 24 months of full-time clinical ultrasound experience; or (5) have 24 months of on-the-job training in any recognized allied health occupation plus 24 months of full-time clinical ultrasound experience.

Upon successful completion of the certifying examination, a candidate may use the title *registered diagnostic medical sonographer* and put RDMS after his or her name. To maintain certification, a registered diagnostic medical sonographer must obtain 30 hours of continuing education every three years. Most registered sonographers are certified in more than one specialty. At this time, no states require diagnostic medical sonographers to be licensed.

THE FUTURE

At present, the demand for sonographers exceeds the supply, and the long-range job outlook for this field appears to be excellent. Educators, researchers, and administrators in this field are also very much in demand. New technologies and new applications of sonography plus the constant expansion in hospital health services and the expanding and aging American population should, over the coming ten years, together contribute to as much as a tenfold increase in the number of sonographers needed. Developments in this profession are unfolding rapidly. Obstetric sonograms and echocardiograms were rarely performed 15 years ago; today they are commonplace. "Real-time" devices, which use multiple transducers, record pictures in a way that resembles a motion picture, thereby enabling the ultrasonographer to observe motion within the body as well as the internal functioning of organs and structures. They are called real-time devices because they observe and record functions as they occur. Such important advances in the use and application of sonography should make the coming decade an exciting and challenging time to work as a sonographer. With the benefits of sonography clearly established, more small and rural hospitals as well as private offices are instituting sonography services, and this trend should make the coming ten years a very good time for sonographers to find well-paying positions.

For more information about diagnostic medical sonographers, write to the:

> Society of Diagnostic Medical Sonographers
> 12770 Coit Road, Suite 508
> Dallas, Texas 75251

For a list of accredited educational programs, write to the:

> Joint Review Committee on Education in
>   Diagnostic Medical Sonography
> 20 North Wacker Drive, Suite 900
> Chicago, Illinois 60606-2901

And for information about certification, contact the:

> American Registry of Diagnostic Medical Sonographers
> 2368 Victory Parkway, Suite 510
> Cincinnati, Ohio 45206

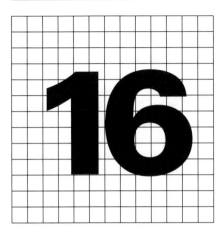

DIETETICS PROFESSIONS

including
Dietitian
Dietetic Technician
Dietary Manager (formerly known as Dietetic Assistant)
Dietetic Worker
Dietary Clerical Worker

DIETITIAN

Dietitians are nutrition experts who counsel individual patients and groups in health care institutions, the community, and the food industry on the principles of sound nutrition; design and supervise foodservice systems in hospitals, nursing homes, schools, and other facilities; and carry out educational and research programs that promote good health through proper diet. Dietitians know what foods are essential for the maintenance of good health and the prevention of disease at each stage of life, what foods or deficiencies are suspected of contributing to illness, and what modifications in diet can correct or alleviate certain health conditions.

There are five major areas of practice in dietetics: clinical, management, consultation, community, and education/research. *Clinical* (or *therapeutic*) *dietitians* specialize in the nutritional care of patients in hospitals, clinics, nursing homes, and other health care institutions. Their job is to assess the patient's nutritional needs (determine what foods must be eliminated, added, or restricted to improve the patient's health or maximize the effects of therapy); plan and implement an appropriate nutrition plan; follow up on the patient's progress; and instruct the patient and his or her family on the importance of the diet and on ways of maintaining it after discharge from the hospital or clinic. They work along with hospital pharmacists, physicians, and nurses in nutritional support units or teams to build up seriously undernourished patients and tackle other complicated nutritional conditions that may threaten the life or affect the treatment of a patient.

Management dietitians are experts in applying the principles of nutrition and food management to the large-scale food requirements of hospitals, long-term health care facilities, schools, universities, restaurants, hotels, company cafeterias, prisons, and other institutions. Their job is to run all aspects of what are often multimillion-dollar-a-year foodservice systems—from menu development and evaluation, preparation of food, and enforcement of safety and sanitary standards to the hiring and training of food personnel, food and equipment procurement, and budgeting.

Consultant dietitians offer a variety of services to health care facilities and consult patients on an inpatient or outpatient basis, or in private practice.

Community dietitians (also called nutritionists, although this term is often used generically to refer to anyone trained in nutrition) engage in nutrition counseling and research at the community level. Most work for public and private health and social service agencies (prenatal and child government nutrition programs, meals on wheels), teaching individuals and groups how to maintain general good health, prevent or alleviate the effects of certain diseases, rehabilitate by eating the right foods in the right quantities, plan and prepare meals, shop prudently, and budget.

Research dietitians usually have advanced degrees and work in medical centers, educational facilities, government agencies, or community health programs directing experiments to explore new nutritional approaches to preventing, curing, and alleviating certain diseases; improving health at every stage of life; and meeting the nutritional needs of the expanding populations of the future. *Dietetic educators* teach the principles of dietetics and new developments in the field of nutrition to members of the health care team in hospitals and in educational settings.

There is an additional category—the *business dietitian*. But as this occupation exists in industry (the business dietitian advises the food development, purchasing, marketing, advertising, sales, and public relations fields), it is not considered a health care career.

SETTINGS, SALARIES, STATISTICS

Dietitians work at a wide variety of functions in a wide variety of settings. Over 7,000 dietitians are currently in part-time or full-time private practice providing individual client counseling or in consultation to health care facilities or industry. Some dietitians engage in practice with physicians whose patients need careful guidance. Dietitians also work in local, state, and federal health agencies; the military; school systems; daycare centers; hotels; at colleges and universities; for industrial food services and restaurants; and in research institutions. However, the vast majority of dietitians (64 percent) work in hospitals, clinics, and related health facilities. There are approximately 100,000 dietitians in the United States at this time. Surveys show that 97 percent of them are female.

Because of the wide variety of settings in which dietitians work, there is significant variety in the salaries they earn. Education, experience, and region are also factors here. In its most recent survey, the American Dietetic Association (ADA), which is the nationwide professional organization for dietitians, nutritionists, and dietetic technicians, found salaries ranging from a low of $11,000 to a high of over $75,000 per year. Nationwide, entry-level salaries for dietitians average approximately $28,500 annually. Median annual incomes for community dietitians are approximately $30,200; for management dieticians, $38,700; for dietetic researchers and educators, $37,600; and for dietetic consultants, $35,200.

Advancement is possible in all fields of dietetics. With experience, a dietitian may be promoted to a supervisory capacity as assistant director or director of an institution's dietetics department. A graduate degree opens the door to teaching, business, management, and research. In all facets of dietetics, graduate study enhances the prospects for promotion, and approximately 40 percent of all dietitians have advanced degrees in related areas.

HOW TO BECOME A DIETITIAN

The basic educational requirement for a career in dietetics is a bachelor's degree in dietetics, nutrition, home economics, food science, or food service management. Approximately 290 colleges and universities around the country offer ADA-approved programs in these fields. Areas of studies covered in ADA-approved or accredited educational programs include biology, organic and inorganic chemistry, biochemistry, anatomy, physiology, microbiology, diet therapy, advanced nutrition, community nutrition, foodservice basic management, food service systems management, quantity food production, accounting, statistics, and data processing.

In high school, a student who is interested in becoming a dietitian should study chemistry, biology, health, mathematics, business administration, and home economics.

Most jobs in dietetics are very people oriented; therefore, in addition to an aptitude for and interest in food science and nutrition, the personal qualities that are important to effective and satisfying performance in this career include the ability to relate well with people and to communicate with them in effective ways. In some settings, dietitians instruct patients, other health professionals, and clients on nutrition and diet modification. Therefore, they should like and be comfortable in the role of teacher.

Most dietitians are registered dietitians, or RDs (in May of 1993, the number of RDs in the U.S. was approximately 54,400), which means that they have satisfied the classroom, clinical, and examination requirements established by the Commission on Dietetic Registration. Being credentialed is important because it provides evidence that certain high standards of education and training have been met, and it is required for employment in most positions in dietetics.

To become registered one of two educational routes must be completed. Each route calls for a combination of classroom education and experience. The first route requires a student to supplement his or her bachelor's degree and ADA-approved course work with an ADA-accredited dietetic internship or ADA-approved preprofessional practice program. There are approximately 94 internships and 136 preprofessional practice programs sponsored by universities and health care facilities across the country. These programs provide a minimum of 900 hours of supervised practice, are usually eight months to one year in length, and many offer graduate credit.

The second education/experience route to becoming an RD is to enroll in an ADA-accredited coordinated program. These four- to five-year programs combine academic work with experience, so that upon successful completion of the curriculum, a student is awarded a bachelor's or master's degree and has already fulfilled the ADA's experience requirements. At this time, there are 52 coordinated programs in dietetics being offered by universities in the United States.

Upon successful completion of either of these two educational plans, a candidate is eligible to take the registration examination for dietitians which is offered by the Commission on Dietetic Registration. This half-day-long test is given nationwide in April and October, and it covers six major areas of study: normal nutrition, clinical nutrition, community nutrition, management, foodservice systems, and food science. Upon passing this examination, a person becomes a registered dietitian and is eligible to use the letters RD after his or her name. To maintain registration, every five years an RD must accumulate a minimum of 75 hours of approved continuing education. If this continuing education requirement is not satisfied or if for any other reason the credential lapses, the ADA examination must again be passed for one to be reinstated.

Legislation requiring licensure or certification to practice as a dietitian has been enacted or is pending in thirty states.

THE FUTURE

Employment opportunities for dietitians (and especially for RDs) are expected to grow faster than the average for other occupations through the year 2000. Openings for additional dietitians are anticipated to meet the demands of hospitals, long-term health care institutions, and industry serving an expanding, aging, and more health-conscious American population. Public and private health care insurance plans should do much to make better health care available to many more individuals, thereby enhancing the job picture for dietitians. However, it remains, at this time, unclear specifically what kinds of nutritional services will be covered under future health care reform. It is possible that reimbursement will only be for nutritional counseling during covered preventative-care visits to doctors and as part of treatment for chronic conditions.

Still, as awareness of good nutrition and its preventative potential continue to increase, many more opportunities at the community, public, and health clinic level should open up. Careers in research should also expand.

For more information about dietitians and ADA-approved/accredited educational programs, write to:

The American Dietetic Association
Membership Department
216 West Jackson Boulevard, Suite 800
Chicago, Illinois 60606-6995

There are two other levels of employment in the field of dietetics. In addition to dietitians, there are *dietetic technicians* and *dietetic assistants*. The nature of the work, the variety of work settings, the personal qualifications, and the job outlook are basically the same for all three types of dietetics professionals. However, there are differences in the scope of responsibility, the education required, and salaries.

DIETETIC TECHNICIAN

There are many junior and community colleges across the country offering basic educational programs for the training of *dietetic technicians*. Approximately 71 of these programs are approved by the American Dietetic Association. A high school diploma or its equivalent is the minimum educational prerequisite for acceptance.

Upon graduation from an ADA-approved dietetic technician program, students are eligible to take the National Registration Examination for Dietetic Technicians, which is offered by the Commission on Dietetic Registration. Dietetic technicians who pass this exam are then eligible to use the credential DTR to signify professional competence. DTRs must accumulate 50 hours of approved continuing education every five years in order to maintain registration.

The specific functions that a dietetic technician may perform depend on the nature and size of the employer. In smaller institutions, dietetic technicians tend to assume supervisory positions and, working under the supervision of a consultant dietitian, they are responsible for the foodservice operation; whereas in medical centers and large hospitals, dietetic technicians usually work directly under the supervision of a registered dietitian. Dietetic technicians manage cafeterias, train and manage personnel, handle budget responsibilities, develop and standardize recipes, and enforce sanitation and safety standards. Upon satisfactory completion of an ADA-approved dietetic technician program, a student is awarded an associate's degree.

Advancement in this career comes in the form of promotion to supervisory positions. There is little "career laddering" in dietetics—that is, not much, if any, of the classroom work and practical training necessary to become a dietetic technician is applicable toward the educational requirements for becoming a dietitian. If there is any integration between the two educational programs, it is where they are both offered by the same educational institution. When a dietetic technician is trained in one institution and then applies to enter a dietitian educational program offered by a different school, usually little credit is given for the technician's training. (For this reason, it is prudent to inquire in advance about a school's policy on credit transfer and acceptance.)

Approximately 100,000 men and women work as dietetic technicians, and annual salaries range from $10,000 to $40,000.

For more information about dietetic technicians, write to:

> The American Dietetic Association
> Membership Department
> 216 West Jackson Boulevard, Suite 800
> Chicago, Illinois 60606-6995

DIETARY MANAGER

A *dietary manager* (also known as a dietetic service supervisor or food service supervisor) carries out various activities in the food service operation of a hospital, long-term care facility, school, correctional facility, or other institutional setting. Specific job responsibilities vary depending on the size, locale, and nature of the institution, but dietary managers are trained in understanding the basic nutritional needs of their clientele. Dietary managers work in partnership with registered dietitians. The dietary manager is responsible for purchasing, storing, preparing, and delivering balanced meals, in most cases three times a day, 365 days a year. They are charged with providing menu variety and appetizing entrées while maintaining nutritional requirements within cost/profit objectives. Many postsecondary vocational/technical schools and community colleges around the country offer dietary manager training programs. They are typically one-year programs, and graduates of these programs are eligible for certification from the Dietary Managers Association (DMA) upon passing an exam. Those who pass the exam are known as CDMs (certified dietary managers). Approximately 14,000 dietary managers across the country are members of DMA. Of that number, nearly 10,000 are certified.

To learn more about this career, contact:

> Dietary Managers Association
> One Pierce Place, Suite 1220W
> Itasca, IL 60143

DIETETIC WORKER AND DIETARY CLERICAL WORKER

Two other types of dietetic personnel usually found working in the foodservice operation of larger institutions are *dietetic workers* (also called dietary aides or hospital food service workers) and *dietary clerical workers*.

It is the dietetic worker who actually prepares the food and serves it to patients and employees in hospitals, nursing homes, long-term health care facilities, and other institutions. Among their specific functions are the storage, preparation, and cooking of the food; serving in the institution's cafeteria or dining room; and dishwashing and kitchen maintenance. Dietetic workers are trained either on the job or in vocational high schools. Their workweek is usually 40 hours long, and the average annual salary earned is approximately $14,000. Dietetic clerical workers type menus, purchase orders, and recipes; prepare worksheets; calculate costs; and otherwise handle the paperwork associated with the running of an institutional food service. Basic high school stenographic and clerical training are required.

For more information about dietetic workers and dietary clerical workers, write to:

> The American Dietetic Association
> Membership Department
> 216 West Jackson Boulevard, Suite 800
> Chicago, Illinois 60606-6995

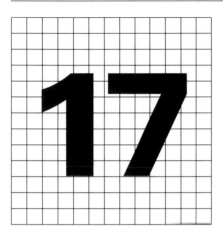

ELECTROENCEPHALOGRAPHIC TECHNOLOGIST AND ELECTROENCEPHALOGRAPHIC TECHNICIAN

also known as
EEG Technologist
EEG Technician
Electroneurodiagnostic Technologist
Electroneurodiagnostic Technician

Electroencephalography (EEG) is a scientific field devoted to the recording and study of the brain's electrical activity. ("Encephalo" is from the Greek work *enkephalos*, meaning "of the brain.") This electrical activity reflects the functional state of the brain at any given waking or sleeping moment. The instrument used to collect, record, and amplify these millionth-of-a-volt electrical impulses is an electroencephalograph, and the written tracing this machine produces is called an electroencephalogram, or brain wave record. Neurologists and other physicians use electroencephalograms in diagnosing and evaluating head trauma, stroke, infectious diseases, brain tumors, epilepsy, and other medical conditions. In cases where a patient experiences severe adjustment or learning difficulties, EEG is used to determine if the source of the problem is organic. Electroencephalograms are also used to determine when a person is medically dead, this being an issue of increasing significance in light of advances in the field of organ transplants.

An *electroencephalographic technologist* (EEG technologist) is the trained health care worker who is responsible for recording a patient's EEG activity. After briefing the patient and taking a medical history, the EEG technologist applies to the patient's scalp small electrodes that are connected to the electroencephalograph. The EEG technologist is trained to understand the optimal use of the electroencephalograph and how to apply EEG procedures to a specific patient's problem. EEG technologists must know what normal and abnormal brain activity look like on an electroencephalogram, what combinations of electrodes and instrument controls are necessary to obtain the required information, and how to record that information in a meaningful way. A fundamental understanding of EEG equipment and of diseases and conditions commonly encountered is essential.

Throughout the recording period, the EEG technologist monitors the patient's neurological, cardiac, and respiratory data, and keeps a careful record of the patient's behavior. EEG technologists are also trained to respond appropriately to medical emergencies that may arise during the session.

When the testing is completed, the EEG technologist debriefs the patient and then writes a descriptive report of the tracing for the electroencephalographer or other physician. The responsibilities of an EEG technologist may also include management of the EEG laboratory, and more senior technologists supervise and train EEG technicians.

SETTINGS, SALARIES, STATISTICS

EEG technologists work primarily in the neurology department of hospitals, and the work is usually a full-time, forty-hour week with little overtime. Some hospitals require the EEG staff to rotate and be on call. If sleep studies are being conducted, night hours may be necessary. Some EEG technologists work in clinics, and there are also openings in the private offices of neurologists and neurosurgeons. EEG technologists employed by the federal government are called medical machine technicians.

There are approximately 8,000 EEG technologists presently working in the United States. Eighty-five percent of them are women.

Salaries vary from area to area in the United States and also depend on the technologist's training, experience, and initiative. According to a survey conducted by the American Society of Electroneurodiagnostic Technologists, in 1993 the most common salary range was $23,500 to $26,500. Entry-level salaries were in the $14,000 to $17,500 range. Experienced technologists often have salaries exceeding $33,000.

Advancement in this career may come in the form of promotion to a supervisory position (chief EEG technologist), or an experienced EEG technologist may work with a highly specialized neurosurgery team or teach in an EEG training program at a university. At medical teaching centers there are also often positions for experienced technologists who are interested in doing medical research.

HOW TO BECOME AN ELECTROENCEPHALOGRAPHIC TECHNOLOGIST

There are two educational routes to a career as an electroencephalographic technologist. One entails on-the-job training at a hospital. The other route entails graduation from a formal EEG training program. Both types of preparation require that a student have a high school diploma or its equivalent and a good academic record. Successful EEG technologists usually are in the upper one-third of their high school graduating classes. High school courses in health, biology, human anatomy, and mathematics are recommended. Further education at the college level tends to strengthen a candidate's application. On-the-job training to become an EEG technologist usually consists of six months of instruction followed by six months of supervised practice. Most on-the-job trainees are paid during this learning period.

Formal educational programs are one to two years in length and are offered by hospitals, medical schools, community colleges, senior colleges, universities, and vocational/technical institutes. There are approximately 30 formal training programs in the United States, 14 of which are approved by the Commission for the Accreditation of Allied Health Education Programs (CAAHEP), which, on July 1, 1994, succeeded the American Medical Association's Committee on Allied Health Education and Accreditation (CAHEA) in accrediting educational programs for this and twenty-one other allied health professions. (CAAHEP is an independent body in which the AMA participates as one sponsor among many.) These formal programs usually include laboratory experience plus classroom instruction in neurology, anatomy, neuroanatomy, physiology, neurophysiology, electronics, and instrumentation. Upon successful completion of a formal EEG technologist educational program, depending on the institution, a graduate will receive either an associate's degree or a certificate. Last year, approximately 115 men and women graduated from approved EEG technologist educational programs.

An EEG technologist must be tactful, patient, compassionate, dedicated, and able to handle the very ill. In addition, he or she must possess good communication skills, manual dexterity, good vision, an aptitude for working with electronic equipment, the ability to deal with visual concepts, and the ability to take the initiative.

There are no state licensing requirements in this field at this time. EEG personnel who have one year of training and laboratory experience and who successfully complete an examination administered by the American Board of Registration for Electroencephalographic and Evoked Potential Technologists, Inc. (which uses the acronym ABRET) are designated registered electroencephalographic technologists (or R. EEG T.) ABRET also offers an examination in evoked potentials. (The American Board of Certified Registered EEG Technicians-Technologists, which for many years was a registry for this field, was dissolved in 1991.)

ELECTROENCEPHALOGRAPHIC TECHNICIAN

Electroencephalographic technicians (EEG technicians) perform duties similar to those carried out by electroencephalographic technologists; however, their training is shorter and less in depth, they are supervised by both a physician and an EEG technologist, and they tend to be paid less for their services. Like EEG technologists, EEG technicians are trained to prepare patients for EEG recording, take patient histories, apply electrodes and monitor their function, check the electroencephalograph for proper function, and handle certain medical emergencies in the laboratory. However, the typical six-month, on-the-job training required is not as broad as the technologist's training, and, because it tends not to go into the theory behind the diagnostic test, it does not prepare the technician for the professional judgments that EEG technologists make. Many students begin as EEG technicians and add to their education and training to proceed to technologist status.

SETTINGS, SALARIES, STATISTICS

Like EEG technologists, most EEG technicians work in the neurology departments of hospitals. Private labs, clinics, and the private offices of neurologists and neurosurgeons provide other job opportunities. The workweek is usually 40 hours long, with rotating emergency, evening, weekend, and holiday hours. Salaries tend to be lower than those for technologists. Starting salaries average approximately $14,000 per year, and experienced EEG technicians may earn approximately $24,000 annually.

It should be noted here that the title *EEG technician* is being phased out by the American Society of Electroneurodiagnostic Technologists and that the title *electroencephalographic technologist* will be used to refer to both electroencephalographic technicians and electroencephalographic technologists. *Technician* will probably continue to be used by some institutions for some time. Be aware of this change in semantics so as to avoid confusion when inquiring about educational requirements and certification.

HOW TO BECOME AN ELECTROENCEPHALOGRAPHIC TECHNICIAN

Most EEG technicians are trained on-the-job in hospitals. This training typically covers basic science, neurological disease, instrumentation, electrical safety, and basic technique in clinical electroencephalogy. A high school diploma or its equivalent is usually prerequisite.

There is much patient contact in this profession. Compassion, a pleasant personality, and good communication skills are important to satisfactory performance and satisfaction in this occupation, as are manual dexterity, attention to detail, good vision, and electronic aptitude.

At this time, no licensing requirements exist in this field. Information regarding registration for electroencephalographic technicians is available from the American Board of Registration for Electroencephalographic and Evoked Potential Technologists, Inc.

THE FUTURE

In the coming decade, employment opportunities for EEG technologists and technicians should grow significantly—perhaps by as much as 40 percent for technologists and 35 percent for technicians. This favorable job outlook is based on several factors. Most significant is the increased use of EEG in surgery and in diagnosing and monitoring patients suffering from brain diseases. EEG is playing an ever-greater role in research of the brain. Recent advances in clinical neurophysiology have created more kinds of electro-physiological examinations for EEG personnel to perform.

In addition, the expanding American health industry, the increasing size and age of the American population, and the greater access to health care made possible by public and private insurance programs should together contribute to a favorable job outlook for EEG technologists and technicians. At this time, this field is very understaffed, and there is a need for several hundred technologists as well as more technicians.

For more information about EEG technologists and technicians, write to the:

American Society for Electroneurodiagnostic
    Technologists (ASET)
204 West 7th
Carroll, Iowa 51401

American Board of Registration for
    Electroencephalographic and Evoked Potential
    Technologists, Inc. (ABRET)
P.O. Box 11434
Norfolk, Virginia 23517

And for information about accredited educational programs for EEG tech-nologists, write to the:

Joint Review Committee for the Accreditation of EEG
    Technology Training Programs
P.O. Box 11434
Norfolk, Virginia 23517

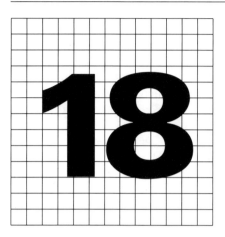

EMERGENCY MEDICAL TECHNICIAN

including
Emergency Medical Technician-Basic
Emergency Medical Technician-Intermediate
Emergency Medical Technician-Paramedic

Emergency medical technicians (EMTs) provide often lifesaving prehospital care to individuals in emergency situations (i.e. heart attacks, unscheduled childbirths, psychiatric crises, drownings, poisonings, fires, explosions, athletic injuries, environmental injuries, industrial accidents, radiation accidents, child abuse cases, rapes, gunshot wounds, automobile accidents).

Emergency medical technicians are alerted to emergencies by a police, fire department, hospital, or emergency medical service dispatcher who provides the exact location of the victim and any preliminary information available regarding the nature of the emergency. The emergency medical technicians, working in ambulance corps or advanced life support units, then rush to the emergency and immediately set to work assessing the victim's injuries, taking vital sign readings (pulse, respiration, blood pressure), and initiating the appropriate lifesaving measures. Depending on the situation, they may open and maintain airways, restore breathing, control bleeding, treat for shock, immobilize the victim's neck and spine, splint fractures, and dress wounds. They are also trained to manage mentally disturbed patients, institute emergency burn treatments, assist in childbirth, apply an automatic defibrillator to "shock" the heart and restore the pulse, and provide whatever other prehospital medical care and comfort are indicated.

As assessment of the condition is being conducted, the emergency medical technicians will look for any identification indicating preexisting medical conditions (allergies, diseases, medications taken) in the victim that might affect treatment. As assessment proceeds, the emergency medical technicians will radio or phone the emergency department physician in the hospital to which the patient will be transported; it is under the direction of this physician that the emergency medical technicians will institute treatment. Intravenous therapy may be initiated, medications administered, electrocardiograms may be taken, oxygen administered, cardiopulmonary resuscitation initiated, or, to restart a stopped heart, defibrillation may be required. Working within the limits of his or her training, the laws of the jurisdiction in which the emergency is taking place, and the directions of the hospital physician, the emergency medical technician may provide a wide spectrum of prehospital medical procedures to save the patient and prevent further damage.

The emergency medical technicians then move the patient to the ambulance and transport him or her to the hospital. During the ride, the emergency medical technicians constantly monitor the patient and provide additional treatment as needed. If necessary, radio or telephone communication with the emergency room physician is maintained. At the hospital, the emergency medical technicians transfer the patient from the ambulance to the emergency department and report their observations and care of the patient to the emergency department staff. Often, the emergency medical technicians will help the emergency room physicians and nurses as they treat the patient.

After a run, the emergency medical technicians clean the vehicle (including decontaminating the interior if the patient was contagious), restock it with linens and supplies, check all of the medical equipment aboard, and refuel and check the vehicle itself so that it is prepared for the next call. Some EMTs reach their patients by airplane and/or helicopter.

With over 14 million calls for emergency medical services coming in every year in this country, the role of the emergency medical technician is vital.

SETTINGS, SALARIES, STATISTICS

As emergency medical services evolved in towns and cities across the country, they responded to different geographic, social, and economic demands. As a result, many different levels of prehospital, emergency medical care personnel and many types of emergency medical services exist in the United States today. From state to state and community to community, emergency medical services are organized differently and are operated and managed by different agencies. In some towns, emergency medical personnel work for the fire department; in others, they work for the police department. Some emergency medical services are county operated. In urban areas, ambulance service is often provided by private companies. Some geographic areas are served by hospital-dispatched ambulances. Emergency medical personnel may be full-time paid professionals, or they may be part-time community volunteers. Emergency medical technicians come from many backgrounds. They are emergency ambulance, rescue, military field service, and military independent duty personnel; patient/health care personnel such as RNs, LPNs, surgical technicians, lab technicians, X-ray technicians, and orderlies; as well as law enforcement officers and industrial safety workers.

The National Registry of Emergency Medical Technicians recognizes three separate levels of emergency medical technician: Emergency Medical Technician-Basic, Emergency Medical Technician-Intermediate, and Emergency Medical Technician-Paramedic.

An *Emergency Medical Technician-Basic* (EMT-B) carries out basic life-support skills such as cardiovascular resuscitation, bleeding control techniques, fracture care, treatment of shock, and assistance in childbirth.

An *Emergency Medical Technician-Intermediate* (EMT-I) performs all of the functions of an EMT-B but may also establish intravenous life-lines, perform trauma patient assessment, use antishock garments, and carry out other, more advanced prehospital procedures.

An *Emergency Medical Technician-Paramedic* (EMT-P) is trained to perform the most advanced emergency medical service care, including defibrillation, interpreting electrocardiograms, administering medications, and carrying out advanced airway maintenance techniques.

There are approximately 600,000 emergency medical technicians in the United States, 55,000 of whom are EMT-Ps. Approximately 250,000 of the men and women in this field are paid employees, and 350,000 are full- or part-time rescue squad volunteers.

Paid EMTs earn approximately $25,700 annually. Salaries vary depending on level, employment setting, and geographic location. On average, in 1993 EMT-Bs earned $23,200, EMT-Is earned $24,700, and EMT-Ps earned $29,200 (and some very experienced EMT-Ps in cities, where salaries tend to be highest, earned as much as $40,000). Fire departments tend to pay the highest salaries, hospitals the least, and private ambulance services somewhere in between.

Unpaid emergency medical technicians earn (and deserve) the heartfelt appreciation and admiration of the communities they serve so well without financial reward.

HOW TO BECOME AN EMERGENCY MEDICAL TECHNICIAN

Only in the last two decades has formal education for EMTs been mandatory. The basic educational requirement is a 110-hour program of instruction and practice in dealing with such emergencies as bleeding, shock, fractures, soft tissue injuries, airway obstruction, chest and abdominal injuries, environmental injuries, extrication of trapped victims, cardiac arrest, and emergency birth, as well as in the legal aspects of prehospital care, the use of common emergency equipment (backboards, suction machines, splints, oxygen apparatus), vehicle operation and maintenance, communications, and documentation. Basic emergency medical technician programs are available in all fifty states and the District of Columbia and are offered by police, fire, and health departments; hospitals; colleges; universities; and medical schools. The 110-hour standard training course designed by the U.S. Department of Transportation is commonly followed. This basic training prepares the student to quality as an EMT-B. An applicant for entry into a basic program must be a minimum of eighteen years old, hold a high school diploma or its equivalent and a valid driver's license, read at the high school level, and meet certain criteria of emotional and physical ability.

If a technician wishes to advance from the basic EMT level, he or she may acquire the additional training and experience necessary to progress to the EMT-I level, or he or she may skip this level and proceed directly to an EMT-P program of training. EMT-Is usually supplement the basic program with courses and experience in patient assessment, shock management, utilization of intravenous lifelines, fluid administration, use of antishock garments, and more advanced methods of airway maintenance.

EMT-P training entails 700 to 1,000 hours of intensive didactic instruction, in-house hospital clinical practice, and supervised field internship, during which time the student gains a more in-depth knowledge of physiology, and of psychological and clinical symptoms, and perfects such skills as patient assessment, cardiac monitoring, intravenous fluid administration, defibrillation, medication administration, and endotracheal intubation. There are approximately 450 EMT-P training programs in the United States, 92 of which are accredited by the Commission for the Accreditation of Allied Health Education Programs (CAAHEP), which on July 1, 1994, succeeded the American Medical Association's Committee on Allied Health Education and Accreditation (CAHEA) in accrediting education programs for this and twenty-one other allied health professions. (CAAHEP is an independent body in which the AMA participates as one sponsor among many.) Last year, almost 2,500 men and women graduated from accredited programs in this field. To qualify for EMT-P training, a candidate must be 18 years old, a high school graduate, and a nationally registered EMT-B or EMT-I. Some paramedic programs combine EMT-I and EMT-P training.

Registration for EMT-Bs, EMT-Is, and EMT-Ps is available from the National Registry of Emergency Medical Technicians, which has established specific training, field experience, and examination criteria at each level. Technicians who satisfy these requirements earn the title Registered EMT-Basic, Registered EMT-Intermediate, and Registered EMT-Paramedic, respectively. Twenty-nine states require registration. Also, in all fifty states and the District of Columbia, some form of certification procedure for emergency medical technicians exists. In many states, registration with the National Registry is necessary, and in several other states, the candidate is offered the choice of taking a state certification examination or the National Registry exam. Most states accept National Registry as the basis for reciprocity. In several states, specific licensing of EMT-Ps exists.

Personal qualifications necessary to carry out this important work include good health, the ability to lift and carry up to a hundred pounds, good vision or good corrected vision, accurate color discrimination (important in examining patients—blue lips might indicate oxygen deprivation), manual dexterity and motor coordination, the ability to give and receive accurate verbal directions, emotional stability, compassion, and the all-important ability to react correctly, efficiently, and calmly in extremely stressful situations. Indeed, stress is a major cause of turnover in this field.

THE FUTURE

Growth in this profession should be average through 2005. Opportunities will be most plentiful in hospital and private ambulance services. Because of the job security, benefits, and good pay, employment with fire, police, and rescue squads should remain attractive. As the American population ages, demand for EMT services will increase, and this demand should be translated into larger appropriations for emergency services.

For more information about emergency medical technicians, contact the:

National Association of Emergency Medical Technicians
102 West Leake Street
Clinton, Mississippi 39056

National Registry of Emergency Medical Technicians
P.O. Box 29233
Columbus, Ohio 43229

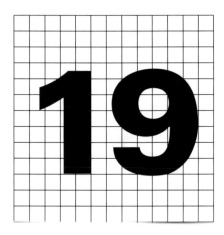

FOOD TECHNOLOGIST

also known as
Food Engineer
Food Scientist
including
Food Technician

Food technologists are scientists who apply the principles of the biological and physical sciences and engineering to the selection, preservation, processing, packaging, distribution, and use of safe, nutritious and wholesome food. Working in the laboratory, the test kitchen, and on the production line, food technologists seek ways of improving the nutritional value, purity, taste, appearance, shelf life, convenience, safety, and cost of foods; they also develop new food products. Frozen concentrated orange juice, freeze-dried coffee, dehydrated soups and eggs, precooked sausages, granola bars, low-fat or fat-free products, and juices in "juice boxes" are among the thousands of improved and new foods that food technologists have helped to develop.

Some food technologists apply their scientific and engineering talents to the challenge of increasing the nutritional level of diets in underdeveloped nations. They seek methods that will improve and preserve the quality of harvests and convert low-cost food sources, such as soybeans, grains, and nutrients reclaimed from wastes, into foods that will be both nutritious and palatable.

The majority of all food technologists are employed by industry and work in food processing plants, food ingredient plants, and food manufacturing plants. Food processing plants convert raw foods into beverages, cereals, dairy products, meats, poultry, game, fish and seafood products, fruit and vegetable products, snack and convenience foods, and animal foods. Food manufacturers differ from food processors in that they build entirely new kinds of foods from new, previously unthought of, or unusual sources (for example, powdered artificial cream made from soy protein). Food ingredient plants process and manufacture salt, pepper, spices, flavors, preservatives, antioxidants, vitamins, minerals, and stabilizers.

In all these industrial settings, there are numerous points at which the expertise of the food technologist is needed—in the research, development, and pilot testing of a new food, process, piece of equipment, or packaging system; in the chemical analysis of food composition and ingredients; and in the supervision of quality control, plant safety, sanitary standards, and waste management. Often food technologists are among the top executives of food companies, and some food technologists own their own food companies.

Many food technologists work at the federal and state levels of government in education or research. In government, food technologists work for the Food and Drug Administration, the Environmental Protection Agency, and other regulatory agencies and in the Departments of State, Defense, Commerce, and Agriculture, carrying out much the same work in chemistry, microbiology, food safety and quality, inspection, and research as food technologists in industry conduct. Some food technologists work for NASA in Houston, developing foods for space travel. The United Nations employs food technologists in its Food and Agriculture Organization and in the World Health Organization. Food technologists who work in basic research study the structure and composition of food and the changes that occur during processing and storage. Food technologists who are in education and/or research usually work for major colleges, universities, or education and health foundations. Still other food technologists work in private testing labs or in the business end of the field—in sales, marketing, technical service, advertising, private consulting, technical writing, and patent law.

SETTINGS, SALARIES, STATISTICS

There are approximately 70,000 food technologists in the U.S. alone. Of them, 27,000 are members of the Institute of Food Technologists (IFT), which is the international professional organization of food technologists. Although in 1970, only 11 percent of them were women, that percentage had risen to 32 percent by 1993.

Food technologists can be found working in every state of the Union and throughout the world. The foods and products with which the food technologist works are often defined by region—potatoes in Idaho and Maine, cereals and meat products in the Midwest, and citrus and vegetables in California and Florida. Two-thirds of all food technologists work in private industry, and the remaining third work in government, education, and research.

Salaries for food technologists vary because there is a great variety of work situations in this field. Food technologists with bachelor's degrees start at approximately $28,500, and those with 20 or more years of experience average approximately $47,000 annually. Food technologists who hold master's degrees begin at salaries of approximately $37,000 annually, and those with 20-plus years of experience earn an average of $51,500 per year. Food technologists holding doctorate degrees may start out earning an average of $44,000 and, with experience, earn an average of $65,000 annually. Salaries tend to be highest in the Pacific and South Atlantic states.

Food technologists usually work regular 35 to 40-hour weeks, although much of the food processing industry is seasonal, and overtime hours may be necessary during peak periods.

HOW TO BECOME A FOOD TECHNOLOGIST

Students should plan on a minimum of four years of college study. A bachelor's degree in food technology, food service, or a related science such as chemistry, biochemistry, agriculture, microbiology, nutrition, or food engineering is the minimum educational requirement for entrance into the food technology profession. Approximately 60 colleges and universities around the country offer programs that provide the necessary course work, and 45 of these have been approved by the Institute of Food Technologists. Most of the schools with undergraduate food technology programs also offer advanced degrees in the field, and almost half of all food technologists do have master's or doctorate degrees. Food technologists holding master's and doctorate degrees have more job opportunities available to them (a Ph.D. is generally required for teaching, for example), tend to be in greater demand, and earn higher salaries.

In general, the course work in a food technology program will include courses in food science (including processing, microbiology, chemistry, food analysis, engineering), humanities and social sciences, physics, mathematics/statistics, biosciences, communications, and electives (with economics and business administration strongly recommended for students planning to work in the management aspects of the business). Courses that develop computer skills and critical thinking may also be required.

Personal qualities important to the successful execution of jobs in this field include a love of science; an orderly, inquisitive mind; honesty; perseverance; and good communications skills. The ability to work in a team is also essential.

For men and women who are interested in entering this field at the technical level, there are two-year programs offered by numerous junior colleges, technical training schools, and community vocational schools that prepare students to become *food technicians*. Associate certificates are awarded upon satisfactory completion of these programs. Food industries on the West Coast employ food technicians extensively.

At this time there are no certification or licensure requirements for food technologists or food technicians. The Institute of Food Technologists offers member status to all individuals in the field or related fields. Members with a bachelor of science degree or an advanced degree in food technology, plus five years of professional experience, may apply for professional member status.

THE FUTURE

Employment for food technologists and food technicians should remain steady or show small growth in the next ten years. The ever-pressing need to feed the poor and underdeveloped nations and the ever-present consumer demand for new, healthier, and more convenient foods may generate an approximately 14 percent increase in job openings by 2001.

For more information about food technologists and food science and technology, write to:

Institute of Food Technologists
221 North LaSalle Street
Chicago, Illinois 60601

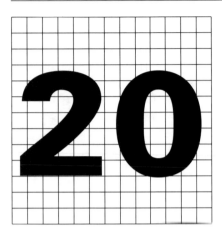

GENETIC COUNSELOR

Genetics is the study of the passing of traits from parents to offspring. In the 41 years since James D. Watson and Francis H. C. Crick gave the world its first glimpse of DNA's double helix structure and explained how DNA stores and passes on hereditary information (these discoveries earned them the Nobel Prize), genetics research has progressed so fast that today, through the use of a variety of diagnostic procedures, parents can get a genetic "glimpse" of their offspring before they are born.

The medical community has developed technologies and techniques that are capable of detecting hundreds of genetically transmitted diseases and conditions in the unborn. In amniocentesis, for example, samples of the amniotic fluid which surrounds the developing unborn child are withdrawn with a fine needle. Amniotic fluid contains cells that have been lost by the fetus. These cells are cultured so that the chromosomes in them can be studied microscopically for abnormalities. Chromosomal abnormalities suggest genetic disease and/or genetic anomaly. Amniotic fluid also has waste materials containing proteins that come from the fetus. Analysis of these proteins can reveal other genetic disorders. Another technique, chorionic villus sampling (CVS), similarly samples fetal chromosomes. For the common alpha-fetoprotein (AFP) test, a small sample of the mother's blood is tested for abnormally high or low levels of a protein that the fetus produces. In ultrasound testing, sound waves are sent through the amniotic fluid, producing on a screen an image of the developing fetus that parents and physician can see.

Together, the results from these prenatal diagnostic tests create a "genetic picture" of the unborn child. Among the hundreds of genetic conditions that can be tested for (and there are many more for which there are no tests) are Down's Syndrome, hemophilia, Tay-Sachs, certain forms of mental retardation, muscular dystrophy, cystic fibrosis, and sickle cell disease. Ultrasound scans can reveal malformations of the spine and various organs (heart, kidneys, lungs) and the size of the baby. One baby in fifty is born with a congenital condition. Happily, most of these conditions are not devastating or life-threatening. New ground is being broken in the surgical correction or alleviation of certain conditions while the baby is still *in utero*. Human genetics is one of the fastest changing fields in medical science, and with such rapid and drastic change has come a myriad of medical, ethical, and emotional considerations. In an increasing number of hospitals, genetic counselors are helping parents and prospective parents understand their genetic situation and options.

A *genetic counselor* is a health care professional who, by virtue of extensive education and training, is specially equipped to communicate technical genetic information to individuals and families who want to know more about a suspected or actual genetic disorder. The genetic counselor is a member of the medical genetics team. While it is the physician who orders the prenatal screening tests and presents their results to the patient, the genetic counselor's job is to explain the results and then to devote as much time as necessary to one-to-one patient counseling.The counselor uses specially developed communications skills to explain test results, short- and long-range consequences of a genetic disease or anomaly, and options to parents. Some counselors specialize in a particular genetic disease.

Genetic counselors also work with prospective parents who are concerned about possible genetic conditions in their offspring because they suspect that they are in a high-risk group (persons with a family history of childhood deaths or pattern of genetic anomaly, members of certain nationalities in which there is a high incidence of certain defects, individuals who have been exposed to certain potentially harmful materials).

Genetic counselors not only provide crucial information, they provide important emotional support and critically needed coping skills to parents and prospective parents going through what is a very personal and often bewildering and highly emotional experience.

Genetic counselors also participate in clinical research projects as well as teach other members of the health care community (general practitioners, nurses, social workers) and consumers about genetic disorders.

SETTINGS, SALARIES, STATISTICS

Genetic counselors work in major medical centers where genetic screening and prenatal diagnosis are offered, most commonly in departments of obstetrics and pediatrics, and in specialty clinics where children and adults with genetic disorders are treated. They also work in federal and state government departments of health and private diagnostic laboratories. In addition, a growing number of genetic counselors are in private practice.

There are about a 1,000 certified genetic counselors in the United States at this time. The majority of them are females.

Genetic counseling is still a relatively new profession, and programs and salaries vary greatly.

HOW TO BECOME A GENETIC COUNSELOR

To practice as a professional genetic counselor, a master's degree in human genetics is necessary. The first master's-level program in this specialty was established in 1969 at Sarah Lawrence College in Bronxville, New York. Today, there are 17 master's degree genetic counseling training programs in the nation, with an additional program slated to open in early 1995 (at Beaver College in Glenside, Pennsylvania.) Most of the programs require applicants to have taken the following courses as undergraduates: general biology, developmental biology (vertebrate embryology), Mendelian and molecular genetics, basic chemistry, psychology, and probability and statistics. Recommended prerequisites may include organic chemistry, the psychology of personality, and fluency in a foreign language (preferably Spanish).

The master's program of study typically entails two years of full-time enrollment. Some schools offer part-time programs. Courses include biochemistry, human anatomy and physiology, clinical medicine, human genetics laboratory, issues in clinical genetics, client-centered counseling, medical genetics, and delivery of genetic services. There may be group sensitivity workshops. At Sarah Lawrence, 600 hours of field training experience are required. Students are placed in clinical settings and in a cytogenetics laboratory for this fieldwork.

A certificate program in genetic counseling is offered at Mt. Sinai Hospital in New York City for individuals with a minimum of a master's degree or Ph.D. in a related field (i.e., psychology, medical genetics, cytogenetics). The length of this certificate program depends on what supplemental education and training are necessary.

Personal qualities important for satisfaction and effectiveness as a genetic counselor include extremely strong communication and counseling skills. A counselor deals with individuals and families coping with very personal, often very emotional issues. One might expect a high rate of burn-out among women and men doing this work, but, in fact, no higher level is reported for genetic counselors than for persons in other helping professions. Ideally, a genetic counselor has that special blend of objectivity and sensitivity so crucial to the successful practice of so many health care professions.

Graduates of the master's degree programs in genetic counseling are eligible to sit for the certification examination given by the American Board of Genetic Counseling. This board was formed in 1993 and certifies only genetic counselors. (Until 1991, certification was awarded by the American Board of Medical Genetics, but this organization now only certifies individuals working in the field of genetics who hold MDs or Ph.D.s.)

THE FUTURE

Genetic counseling is still a relatively new field. That 100 percent of the available graduates of genetic counseling programs are employed in the field of human genetics demonstrates both acceptance of this health profession and strong demand for the services of these health professionals.

For more information on genetic counselors, write to the:

National Society of Genetic Counselors, Inc.
233 Canterbury Drive
Wallingford, Pennsylvania 19086

American Board of Genetic Counseling
9650 Rockville Pike
Bethesda, Maryland 20814-3998

Human Genetics Program
Sarah Lawrence College
Bronxville, New York 10708

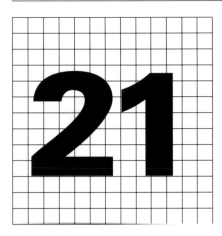

HEALTH INFORMATION MANAGEMENT PERSONNEL

including
Medical Record Administrator
Medical Record Technician
Coding Specialist

In the course of diagnosing and treating a patient's illness or injury, a lot of information is generated, and all of it is potentially significant. To make a diagnosis, for example, a doctor will examine and observe the patient, interview the patient about symptoms and about his or her medical history, and, often, order one or more laboratory, radiologic, and/or other diagnostic tests and evaluate the results. Diagnosing is putting all of the pieces of information gathered together to identify and assess the patient's health condition. It is, therefore, important that none of this information be lost.

Over the course of the subsequent treatment, more important information comes in. What medications is the patient taking? How much? When is it taken? With what results? What is the patient's fluid intake? Output? Blood pressure? Temperature? Blood count? How many stitches were used to close the incision? What anesthesia was used? How was it tolerated? What treatments are being administered? For how long? With what results? What dietary restrictions are being imposed? What did the X rays show? The amount of information grows with the nature, complexity, and duration of the patient's condition, and any part of it can have important bearing on the patient's subsequent treatment, the assessment of his or her progress, and the handling of any future medical problems. Sometimes, this information can have bearing on the health of the patient's family members or coworkers. It is, therefore, vitally important that all of this information be collected, recorded, organized, and preserved so that all of the details of the patient's situation can be communicated clearly and quickly to other medical personnel handling the case, thereby maximizing the value of what has already been learned about the patient and reducing the chance of error. A patient's health (or medical) record is that important communicator. A health record is a permanent document of the history and progress of a patient's illness or injury. It is made by the patient's physician(s) and any other health professionals who come in contact with the patient, and it contains information about when and how the condition first came to medical attention; how the diagnosis was arrived at; the patient's medical history (which includes his or her age, sex, height, weight, occupation, habits, family illnesses, allergies, information about chronic health conditions and previous injuries, treatments, and medications, plus observations made by the physician taking the history); the findings of the patient's physical examination; the doctors' orders and progress reports; the nurses' notes; diet orders; medications and doses prescribed; treatments administered; the results of any laboratory tests administered; X rays; electrocardiogram tracings; and a report of any surgery performed. Ideally, it is a complete, clear, objective, and readily available profile of the patient's medical history.

In addition to helping the medical team in diagnosing and treating the patient expeditiously, accurate and complete health records are important for several other reasons. Public health officials depend on health records to provide data that indicate disease patterns and trends; researchers use them to uncover, correlate, and compare data that may lead to new methods of diagnosis and treatment; and hospitals and health care facilities often use the information in health records to facilitate planning and to substantiate performance for accreditation purposes. Health records are also used for the evaluation of treatments and medications, as case studies for the training of medical personnel, and for legal actions.

Most recently, health records are the primary source documents for insurance claims. Hospitals and other health care facilities depend on health information coding for reimbursement purposes.

The amount of information that accumulates in the course of one patent's illness or injury can be substantial. Multiply by the number of patients treated in a health care facility over a many-year period, and the volume of information that must be processed and maintained can be astronomical. Microfiche and computers have revolutionized the handling and storage of all this information. Still, fundamental to the recording, organization, and retrieval of this data are health care personnel who are experts on medical information. Medical record administrators and medical record technicians are the specially trained and educated members of the medical team who are responsible for the processing, organization, and maintenance of these important health records.

MEDICAL RECORD ADMINISTRATOR

Medical record administrators plan, develop, and supervise systems for the acquisition, analysis, retention, and retrieval of health records that are consistent with the medical, administrative, ethical, and legal requirements of the particular health care delivery system. More specifically, they develop, analyze, and technically evaluate health records and indexes; supervise personnel who are engaged in coding the health records; collect and analyze patient and institutional data for health care and health care-related programs and research; develop in-service educational materials for the health care personnel; assist the medical staff in evaluating the quality of patient care; develop and implement policies and procedures for processing medical legal documents and insurance and correspondence requests that are in accordance with professional ethics and in conformity with federal, state, and local statutes; safeguard the confidentiality of the health records; and, when necessary, testify in court about records and record procedures. The specific scope of the medical record administrator's responsibilities depends on the size and type of the institution.

SETTINGS, SALARIES, STATISTICS

Medical record administrators work in general, specialized, and teaching hospitals (together, these make up the largest employer of medical record administrators); ambulatory care centers; outpatient clinics; nursing homes; rehabilitation centers; health maintenance organizations; group practices; insurance companies (where they determine liability for payment of clients' medical fees); professional services review organizations; local, state, and federal government research centers; private industry; and on the teaching staffs of colleges and universities.

Most large hospitals have chief medical record administrators who supervise other medical record administrators, medical record technicians, and clerks. A smaller hospital may need only two or three personnel to run its health information management department. In the case of certain small health care facilities, sometimes only one (or one part-time) medical record administrator is employed.

Working conditions are generally pleasant, and a typical workweek is forty hours long. There are also part-time opportunities available.

Approximately 17,000 medical record administrators are employed at this time. The majority of them are female.

Annual salaries range from approximately $20,000 to $80,000, depending upon position, education level attained, years of experience, type of employer, and region. The average starting salary for medical record administrators working in hospitals is approximately $23,000 per year; and for those employed by the federal government, it is approximately $20,000 annually. Salaries on the east and west coasts tend to be highest.

HOW TO BECOME A MEDICAL RECORD ADMINISTRATOR

Preparation for this career entails a minimum of four years of study after high school which leads to a bachelor's degree in medical record administration or health information management. There are currently 52 colleges, universities, and medical schools offering educational programs in medical record administration that are approved by the Commission for the Accreditation of Allied Health Education Programs (CAAHEP), in collaboration with the American Health Information Management Association (AHIMA). (CAAHEP, which on July 1, 1994, succeeded the American Medical Association's Committee on Allied Health Care Education and Accreditation, or CAHEA, in accrediting education programs for most allied health professions, is an independent body in which the AMA participates as one sponsor among many.) These accredited programs offer several educational options. More than half of them require applicants to have successfully completed at least two years of college. These programs are typically two years in length and award a bachelor of science in medical record administration or health information management (HIM). Almost one-quarter of the programs require a minimum of only a high school diploma or its equivalent and are four years in length. They, too, award a bachelor's degree. Several programs are approximately one year in length and are for undergraduates who have completed three years of college. This alternative also leads to a bachelor of science in medical record administration or HIM. For individuals who are already college graduates and have taken required courses in the liberal arts, biology, and statistics, a small number of accredited postgraduate certificate programs in medical record administration are available.

The curriculum will vary slightly from program to program, but basically, in addition to liberal arts and sciences, a student medical record administrator will study fundamentals of medical science, anatomy, physiology, medical terminology, disease classification, medical record administration, statistics, research methods, medical law, and computer science and will have an opportunity for carefully supervised practice in accredited health care institutions. Last year approximately 630 women and men graduated from accredited medical record administrator or HIM educational programs.

In high school, students considering a career in medical record administration should elect the general college preparatory course, including classes in biology, chemistry, mathematics, English, health, computer science, business administration, anatomy, and physiology.

Personal qualities that are important to success and satisfaction in this career include the ability to plan and to organize well, facility with numbers and details, strong communication skills, integrity, the ability to teach others, sensitivity, flexibility, alertness, competence, and good vision.

Upon graduation from an approved medical record administrator educational program, a student is eligible to take the national registration examination, a one-day test given yearly in October by AHIMA. Passing this examination entitles the candidate to use the letters RRA (which stand for registered record administrator) after his or her name. Registration is voluntary, but it is a widely accepted standard of proficiency in this field, and it can significantly enhance job opportunities and salary. Many employers demand this credential. To maintain registration, an RRA must fulfill certain continuing education requirements and must be a member of AHIMA.

THE FUTURE

Our growing population, our aging population, the ever-increasing out-pouring of data from an ever-broadening spectrum of tests and procedures, and the growing demand for medical information from third-party payers (insurance companies, U.S. government agencies), researchers, and various accrediting and monitoring agencies should, together, result in increasing employment opportunities for medical record administrators and especially for those who are certified. It is expected that opportunities will grow much faster than average through the year 2000, and most job openings will be in hospitals. The American Hospital Association projects that by 2000, the number of unfilled jobs for registered medical record administrators will have increased by 54 percent.

For more information about medical record administrators and a list of accredited programs, write to the:

> American Health Information Management Association
> 919 North Michigan Avenue, Suite 1400
> Chicago, Illinois 60611-1683

MEDICAL RECORD TECHNICIAN

Medical record technicians serve as technical assistants to medical record administrators. In large hospitals and health care facilities, they are usually responsible for supervising many of the health information management (or HIM) department's day-to-day functions and for carrying out many of the more demanding technical functions. Medical record technicians code diseases, operations, and therapies according to recognized classification systems (these codes are used to abbreviate the medical facts of the case to facilitate review). They enter these codes in patients' medical records; maintain registries; analyze records; cross-index medical information; abstract records; review records for accuracy and consistency and from them, gather statistics that may be needed by insurance companies, law firms, government agencies, and researchers, and for studies of bed utilization, operating room use, disease, and other aspects of health care delivery. Like medical record administrators, they may be called upon to take records to court. Medical record technicians also supervise medical record clerks, medical record transcriptionists, and coding specialists. Medical record clerks, transcriptionists, and coding specialists provide support for technicians and administrators. The term *health information personnel* is used to describe all five of these levels of employment in this field.

SETTINGS, SALARIES, STATISTICS

Medical record technicians work in the same settings as medical record administrators. Most work in hospitals, but an increasing number are finding opportunities in ambulatory health care facilities, industrial clinics, state and federal health agencies, group practices, medical research organizations, health maintenance organizations, and insurance companies. Some are self-employed consultants. In addition, medical record technicians are often employed as directors of health information management departments in small hospitals and some nursing homes. A forty-hour workweek is typical, and work conditions are usually pleasant.

There are approximately 50,000 medical record technicians. Most of them are female. Salaries will vary greatly depending on the type of institution, scope of responsibility, and region. Recently graduated medical record technicians working in hospitals average approximately $18,500 annually, and experienced technicians in the same setting average about $25,000 annually. Earnings for medical record technicians who work for the federal government are somewhat lower.

Advancement in this field is available in the form of promotion to positions of greater authority within the medical record department. Also, medical record technicians may become medical record administrators by supplementing their educations and passing the American Health Information Management Association (AHIMA) competency examination.

In a recent AHIMA survey, almost 300 respondents stated that they are both certified medical record administrators and accredited medical record technicians. An increasing number of medical record technician and medical record administrator educational programs are being coordinated to allow ease of progression with a minimum of credit loss and subject matter duplication.

HOW TO BECOME A MEDICAL RECORD TECHNICIAN

Increasingly, medical record technology students are receiving their educations and training in the two-year associate degree programs accredited by the Commission for the Accreditation of Allied Health Education Programs (CAAHEP), in collaboration with AHIMA. (CAAHEP, which on July 1, 1994, succeeded the American Medical Association's Committee on Allied Health Care Education and Accreditation, or CAHEA, in accrediting education programs for most allied health professions, is an independent body in which the AMA participates as one sponsor among many.) Because these programs must maintain certain high standards in preparing students, most employers prefer their graduates. There are 130 accredited medical record technician or health information technology/technician programs offered by community and junior colleges, universities, and vocational/technical institutes across the country. All of these programs require students to have a high school diploma or its equivalent.

Educational programs for medical record technicians include theoretical instruction plus practical hospital experience. Required courses include medical terminology, medical law, anatomy, physiology, processing of health data, medical transcription, and hospital procedures.

Upon successful completion of an approved medical record technician educational program, a candidate is eligible to take the national accredited medical record technician examination, which is administered once a year, in the fall. Those who pass this examination are entitled to use the letters ART after their names. A second route to certification is to enroll in AHIMA's Independent Study Program in Medical Record Technology (ISP/MRT). Upon successful completion of the course of study and the accumulation of a minimum of 30 semester hours of college credit in designated areas, these candidates may also take the accreditation examination to become ARTs. While having this credential is not required for employment, it often results in greater career opportunities, positions of greater responsibility, and higher starting salaries.

The American Health Information Association also offers certification for a third classification of health information management personnel—the coding specialist. *Coding specialists* are trained (through a combination of on-the-job experience and coding education workshops, seminars, and coding tracks within medical record technology programs offered by AHIMA) to analyze medical records and then to assign and sequence numerical classification codes to diagnoses and procedures. A high school diploma or its equivalent is prerequisite. Upon completing this training, a candidate may sit for the AHIMA certification examination, and upon passing it may use the designation CCS (for Certified Coding Specialist) after his or her name. On average, CCSs earn $10.50 per hour.

Personal qualities important to the satisfactory execution of this job include mental acuity; good vision; manual dexterity for data entry, transcribing, and filing; an analytical mind; maturity; and respect for the important and sensitive nature of the material being handled.

THE FUTURE

As is the case with medical record administrators, the job outlook is favorable, especially for those medical record technicians who are accredited. The American population is growing larger and living longer, and generating more and more health information. In addition, with the creation of each new diagnosis, treatment, and therapy, more types of information are being created. Add to these factors the dramatic increase in demand (from researchers and insurers) for this information, and a positive job picture emerges. Employment of medical record technicians is expected to grow faster than average for all occupations, with a projected increase of about 40 percent by 2000.

For more information about medical record technicians and accredited schools and also about other health information management personnel, write to the :

American Health Information Management Association
919 North Michigan Avenue, Suite 1440
Chicago, Illinois 60611-1683

HEALTH SCIENCES LIBRARIAN

also known as
Medical Librarian
Hospital Librarian
Health Information Professional

An information explosion is taking place in the health sciences. New medical tests, treatments, pharmaceuticals, equipment, procedures, research results, data, and theories emerge almost daily, affecting the way illness and injury are handled and adding to the already huge body of knowledge for which health care professionals must be responsible. The volume of new medical information is so great and mounting so rapidly that it has been estimated that more medical and health literature has been published in the last ten years than in all the years before that put together. Last year alone, over 3,000 new books and 1,050 new audiovisual programs on medical and health subjects were made available to the American medical community, and there are presently over 8,000 different journals serving these fields, each generating numerous issues per year. According to a 1992 survey by the Association of Academic Health Science Library Directors (AAHSLD), there are approximately 200,000 bound volumes in the average health science library in the U.S. Major teaching hospitals may have health science libraries that contain 500,000 bound volumes, subscribe to 4,000 journals, maintain thousands of audiovisual programs, and provide access to thousands of indexes via on-line searching. This is a tremendous amount of incoming information that must be cataloged, organized, and maintained in a manner that will allow effective and efficient dissemination to the health sciences practitioners, students, educators, researchers, and administrators who depend on them.

Health sciences librarians are specially trained information specialists who are responsible for the collection, compilation, and dissemination of this essential biomedical information. Using knowledge of both library science and the health sciences, they select and purchase books, journals, and other materials on the health sciences; classify and catalog acquisitions for easy access; instruct health care students and professionals in the use of information resources; prepare guides to reference materials; compile bibliographies; answer mail and telephone requests for information; help health care personnel track down elusive information; translate or find a translator for biomedical pieces written in foreign languages; and manage the operation of the library (including budget and long-range planning and the supervising of health sciences library technicians and other library personnel).

Using computerized data bases, health sciences librarians can quickly produce complete and current bibliographies on almost any medical or health-related subject, and, through participation in national networks of information resources, they can locate specific books and journals in libraries around the country. Computerization and interlibrary cooperation have revolutionized the health science library. For example, with the push of the right buttons, MEDLINE, a world-wide on-line bibliographic retrieval system (initiated in 1971 by the National Library of Medicine, the largest health sciences library in the United States), can lead the health sciences librarian to over seven million citations within seconds. Other data bases on specific aspects of medicine and health care also exist: CANCERPROJ provides access to bibliographies on cancer research projects; BIOETHICSLINE contains information about ethics and related public policy issues in health care and biomedical research; DENTALPROJ covers ongoing dental research projects; GENE-TOX is a chemical mutagenicity data base; POPLINE houses population information; HISTLINE is a bibliography retrieval system for information on the history of medicine; TDB is a toxicology data bank; and AIDSLINE contains information on Acquired Immune Deficiency Syndrome. There are hundreds of biomedical data bases, and new ones are constantly being developed.

Some health sciences librarians who work in hospitals are also responsible for providing book-cart services and programs for patients who are ambulatory as well as for those who are confined to bed.

SETTINGS, SALARIES, STATISTICS

Health sciences librarians work in schools of medicine, nursing, pharmacy, veterinary medicine, and allied health; hospitals; pharmaceutical companies; professional associations; federal and state agencies; research centers; health maintenance organizations; and health planning organizations. Two-thirds of all health sciences libraries are located in hospitals. Approximately 12 percent (the second largest percentage) are in medical, professional, and vocational schools. There are approximately 3,700 health sciences librarians in the United States. Ninety-five percent of them are female.

Starting salaries for health sciences librarians range between $18,000 and $25,000 per year. Nationwide, the average annual salary for all health sciences librarians is approximately $35,000, but a few very experienced health sciences librarians in positions of high authority earn as much as $60,000. Institutions in the mid-Atlantic region of the United States tend to pay the most.

HOW TO BECOME A HEALTH SCIENCES LIBRARIAN

A master's degree in library science, preferably from a college or university accredited by the American Library Association (ALA), is the usual and preferable preparation for professional librarians. There are, at this time, approximately 60 ALA-accredited, one- or two-year graduate librarian education programs in the United States and 7 in Canada. Of these, a total of 44 offer one or more specific courses in health sciences librarianship (science literature; biomedical communications; the evaluation, selection, and use of bibliographic and informational resources in medicine and the allied sciences; introduction to the organization and administration of the medical library; standard informational systems; budgeting; personnel; book selection). Many of these schools also offer postgraduate programs leading to a doctor of philosophy or doctor of library science; however, the ALA does not review and accredit these programs.

As an undergraduate working toward a bachelor of arts or bachelor of science degree, a prospective health sciences librarian should consider courses in the physical and biological sciences (chemistry, physics, mathematics, biology, zoology, anatomy), the life sciences (psychology, sociology, anthropology), computer science, and management. Health sciences librarians with undergraduate majors in these fields tend to be in greater demand. Applicants to master's programs must have a good reading knowledge of at least one foreign language.

Personal qualities essential to success as a health sciences librarian include intelligence, patience, imagination, intellectual curiosity, strong communications and organizational skills, friendliness, the ability to handle details, and a genuine interest in the subject matter.

Advancement in this career can come in the form of promotions up the administrative ladder or in the form of specialization in a single area of responsibility.

While not compulsory, certification by the Medical Library Association (MLA) is a useful credential that can enhance job opportunities and salaries. The MLA offers four levels of certification. Entry-level certification requires a postbaccalaureate degree from an ALA-accredited program or a postbaccalaureate degree in a related field (i.e., informatics, information science, computer programming) from a program accredited by the appropriate agency and demonstration of competency in seven areas of health librarianship that have been designed by the MLA (library schools, library associations, and other institutions offer courses in these areas of knowledge). Membership in the Medical Library Association, which was once required, is now optional. Combinations of additional course work, research, published papers, and service to the MLA qualify candidates for higher certification status. The formal designation that MLA-certified librarians use after their names is AHIP, which stands for Academy of Health Information Professionals.

THE FUTURE

Employment prospects for health sciences librarians in the coming decade are expected to be average. Competition for positions is now, and should continue to be, strong, but very qualified health sciences librarians will continue to be in demand to manage the biomedical information explosion.

For more information about health sciences librarians and for a list of accredited educational programs in this field, write to the:

> Medical Library Association
> Professional Development Department
> Six North Michigan Avenue, Suite 300
> Chicago, Illinois 60602-4805

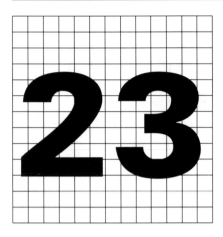

HEALTH SOCIOLOGIST

also known as
Medical Sociologist

Health sociologists identify and explain the influence of social factors on health and health care. They conduct research on how social factors affect the incidence and course of disease (this is called social epidemiology), on patients' and the general population's responses to various health conditions and health care settings, and on the acceptance or rejection of specific treatments. They gather data and then look for common social values and behavioral and attitudinal orientations in an attempt to discover trends in what prompts patients to seek medical attention, how patients cope with terminal illness, how patients and practioners behave, how members of the health profession interact, and how a community will react to a new medical technology. Health sociologists then share this information with medical personnel to help them identify and deal with health trends and deliver health care more ideally suited to the varied needs of the community.

A good way to understand the work of health sociologists is to look at the research that the men and women in this field have done on the medical and social crisis, Acquired Immune Deficiency Syndrome, or AIDS. Health sociologists were part of the research team at the Centers for Disease Control (of the U.S. Public Health Service) that discovered the first cluster of sexually transmitted cases of AIDS. They documented the spread of AIDS and presently are studying changing behavior patterns in the homosexual community, focusing on mental health and sexual conduct. Intravenous drug users and others considered to be high-risk also are being studied. How do persons with AIDS and those close to them cope with the anger, isolation, despair, loss of self-esteem, and legal and economic consequences that may accompany this disease? Who gets AIDS, and who does not? Why do some individuals expose themselves to AIDS while others do not? What motivates some AIDS patients to endanger other people

while others cannot? How does society respond to AIDS and persons with
AIDS? How can a community and its resources cope with AIDS and all
that it means? These are some of the questions health sociologists are try-
ing to answer. They also are studying and analyzing the effectiveness and
acceptability of various methods of avoiding AIDS exposure, as well as
the effectiveness and acceptability of various methods of educating not
only the public, but the health care management community as well about
AIDS. Because of their special and thorough work on AIDS, the National
Academy of Sciences recently asked health sociologists to design strate-
gies for improving health care and social services for those afflicted with
the illness and for allaying the public's fear of AIDS. A number of sociologists have organized the Sociologists' AIDS Network, which acts as a
clearinghouse for sociological research and activity on AIDS.

SETTINGS, SALARIES, STATISTICS

Health sociologists work in universities, for federal health agencies, in state
and local health departments, in major hospital and research institutes, and
for medical, nursing, and other professional schools.

The exact number of health sociologists is difficult to determine. The
medical sociology section of the American Sociological Association (ASA)
in Washington, D.C., lists 1,100 members. A total figure slightly in excess of
1,100 men and women is probably close.

Salaries range greatly depending on the type of employer, position, and
region. In general, however, health sociologists who are employed by the
government earn the highest salaries, research tends to pay the second
highest salaries, and teaching positions at universities pay the least but
also often entail the fewest workweeks per year. Nationwide, the average
starting salary for health sociologists holding doctorate degrees is approximately $31,500 annually. Health sociologists with Ph.D.s who work for
the federal government earn an average of approximately $49,000 per
year.

HOW TO BECOME A HEALTH SOCIOLOGIST

Most health sociologists are Ph.D.s, which means that after four years of
college with a major in sociology or an allied field, they have successfully
completed the course work, thesis, and examination requirements for the
master's degree in sociology and then gone on to satisfy the requirements
for a doctorate in sociology, including the writing of a doctoral thesis based
on advanced research. While the master's degree is sufficient for employment in this field, the Ph.D. greatly enhances the range of employment and
advancement opportunities. About 50 universities in the United States offer
specific health or medical sociology educational programs. Another 50 or
so universities offer a significant number of courses in health or medical

sociology. In this competitive field, acquiring the best credentials—that is, the best grades from the best schools and learning from the best minds in health sociology—is extremely important.

In high school, interested students should take as much English and mathematics as possible, and as an undergraduate majoring in sociology or an allied field, students should take courses in biology, health, and environmental science. Good computer skills are also necessary.

Personal qualifications for success and satisfaction in this field include inquisitiveness; strong speaking, writing, and analytic skills; objectivity; and perseverance.

There is no licensing for health sociologists, but there is certification which, although not required for all work in health sociology, is necessary for employment in most federal hospitals for veterans and in many research situations. Certification is offered by the American Sociological Association, which has as its requirements a Ph.D. in sociology, a minimum of two years of practice, letters of recommendation from colleagues, course work in medical sociology, and membership in ASA. Certification is also offered by the Sociological Practice Association, which confers the designation CCS, for certified clinical sociologist, on health sociologists in nonacademic, clinical settings who satisfy their requirements.

THE FUTURE

Although employment for sociologists in general is expected to increase more slowly than average for all occupations through 2000, the demand for health sociologists will increase. There should also be a significant increase in the demand for social gerontologists, and in this prediction may be a large part of the reason why health sociology is expected to grow. Social gerontologists are sociologists who study the special problems faced by aged persons in our rapidly changing society. The American population is not only growing larger, it is growing older. It is predicted that by the year 2030, one in five Americans (or 20 percent of the population) will be 65 years of age or older. This trend has been called "the graying of America." More of us are living longer, and as the "boom" babies born after World War II and through the 1950s become senior citizens, there should be a "boom" of elderly Americans requiring health care. With this large aging population should come new health sociology issues regarding the distribution of illness and patterns of response to health problems and to the delivery of health care. In addition, health care is rapidly changing and becoming more complex. Each change, new discovery, new technique, illness uncovered, illinois treated, and illness cured has sociological ramifications and raises sociological questions. It is clearly a very interesting time to be a health sociologist.

For more information about a career as a health sociologist, contact the:

American Sociological Association
1722 N Street, N.W.
Washington, DC 20036

Sociological Practice Association
c/o Mary C. Sengstuck, Ph.D.
Department of Sociology, 2247 FAB
Wayne State University
Detroit, Michigan 48202

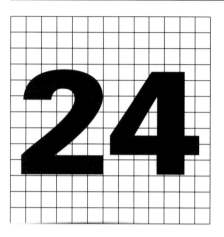

HISTOLOGIC TECHNICIAN AND HISTOTECHNOLOGIST

Histology is the branch of biology concerned with the microscopic study of the structure of tissues. Histotechnology is the preparation of human or animal tissue samples for microscopic and other types of examination for diagnostic, research, or instructional purposes. The health care personnel who are primarily responsible for preparing such specimens are *histologic technicians*. *Histotechnologists* usually function as supervisors and instructors and perform the more complex laboratory procedures.

Tissue sections prepared by histologic technicians and histotechnologists are used to detect and diagnose body dysfunction and malignancies. The methods by which histologic technicians process sections of body tissue include fixation, dehydration, embedding, sectioning, microincineration, mounting, and the use of various contrast stains, all of which are performed so as to make visible discrete changes in the tissue that could indicate disease or other abnormality—or, on the other end of the spectrum, that could indicate normality or improvement.

Advances in slide preparation and sophisticated new methods of examining tissue samples today allow for important early detection of many types of cancer. Tissue samples are often taken from patients during surgery, and, while the surgical team waits, they are immediately prepared by a histologic technician or histotechnologist and promptly examined by a pathologist and/or the attending physician. Depending on what is revealed, the surgery may proceed and abnormal tissue removed, or it may be determined that additional surgery is not warranted or appropriate. Clearly, the work carried out by histologic technicians and histotechnologists is extremely important and requires intelligence and precision.

SETTINGS, SALARIES, STATISTICS

Most histologic technicians and histotechnologists work in clinics, hospitals, and universities. In the hospital setting, they play an extremely important role as health care team members in the care of patients. Duties range from performing frozen section stat procedures while the patient is on an operating table, to performing special, painstaking staining procedures for infectious disease diagnosis in the lab. Current technology includes immunohistochemistry, flow cytometry, DNA hybridization, and image analysis.

Many histologic technicians and histotechnologists work in industry in the laboratories of chemical, pharmaceutical, petrochemical, personal care products, and household products manufacturers. Opportunities also exist in the government.

Histologic technicians and histotechnologists usually average 40 hours of work per week, with weekend and night shifts sometimes required. There are approximately 30,000 histologic technicians and histotechnologists in the United States, and 85 percent of them are female.

Annual salaries range from $13,500 to as high as $45,500 for a highly experienced histotechnologist who has supervisory responsibilities. Salaries in large cities and on the West Coast tend to be higher.

HOW TO BECOME A HISTOLOGIC TECHNICIAN OR A HISTOTECHNOLOGIST

In the past, histologic technicians were trained on the job, and while examples of such informal training persist, the strong trend today is toward formal histotechnological training. It is hoped that formalized educational programs in this field will upgrade and unify competency standards, and students planning careers in histotechnology should anticipate committing the necessary time to a formal educational program. There are 35 histologic technician/technologist educational programs that are accredited by the National Accrediting Agency for Clinical Laboratory Sciences (NAACLS). The majority of programs are offered by hospital and medical centers, and several community and junior colleges also have programs that are approved. In 1993, approximately 120 individuals graduated from NAACLS-accredited histologic technician/technologist programs. Of these 35 programs, 7 award associate's degrees upon successful completion and the rest award certificates (or diplomas, as they are called by a few institutions). The associate's degree programs are all approximately 24 months long, and all but one require only a high school diploma or its equivalent. Approximately two-thirds of the certificate programs require only a high school diploma, and the rest require associate's degrees or anywhere from one to four years of college preparation.

The curriculum of an accredited program consists of classroom instruction, practical demonstration, and actual, extensive, hands-on laboratory experience. The curriculum covers medical ethics, medical terminology, chemistry, laboratory mathematics, anatomy, histology, histochemistry, quality control, instrumentation, microscopy, processing techniques, preparation of museum specimens, and records and administration procedures.

In high school, students who are interested in becoming histologic technicians or histotechnologists should take science and mathematics courses.

In addition to an aptitude for and interest in the biological sciences, other personal aptitudes and qualities that are important to success in this career include manual dexterity, good vision and particularly good color differentiation, attention to detail, a strong sense of responsibility, and maturity. Handling tissue specimens is important medical work requiring care, concentration, and precision. Histologic technicians and histotechnologists must be temperamentally suited to doing such exacting, often repetitive work and also to handling specimens of diseased tissues. Although modern laboratory safety procedures minimize the risks, exposure to environmental toxicity is a potential hazard.

Certification in this field is available through the Board of Registry of the American Society of Clinical Pathologists (ASCP).

To be eligible for ASCP certification at the histologic technician level, a candidate must successfully complete a NAACLS-accredited histotechnology program; or have an associate's degree or at least 60 semester hours (including a combination of 12 in biology and chemistry) of academic credit from an accredited college or university plus at least one year of full-time, acceptable, supervised clinical laboratory experience in histopathology; or a high school diploma or its equivalent plus two years of full-time, acceptable, supervised clinical laboratory experience in histopathology. Upon passing the ASCP's examination, a candidate is then entitled to use the initials HT (ASCP)—which stand for histologic technician certified by the American Society of Clinical Pathologists—after his or her name.

Histotechnologists seeking ASCP certification must hold a bachelor's degree with a combination of 30 semester hours of biology and chemistry plus one year of full-time, acceptable, supervised clinical laboratory experience in a histopathology laboratory. Or, a candidate may hold a bachelor's degree as described above and successfully complete one of the NAACLS-accredited histologic technician educational programs. Upon passing a competency examination, a candidate may use the designation HTL (ASCP)—which stands for histotechnologist who is certified by the American Society of Clinical Pathologists—after his or her name.

At present, several states require histologic technicians and histotechnologists to be licensed.

THE FUTURE

Job opportunities should remain stable over the next ten years. Factors that will contribute to growth in this field include the increased frequency with which doctors are turning to laboratory tests when diagnosing and treating patients; the ever-expanding array of tests available; the growing American population; the aging American population; the new health consciousness;

and methods of third-party payment that allow more people to afford more medical care, including any tests that are ordered.

For more information about a career in histotechnology, write to the:

National Society for Histotechnology
4201 Northview Drive, Suite 502
Bowie, Maryland 20716

Board of Registry
American Society of Clinical Pathologists
P.O. Box 12277
Chicago, Illinois 60612

National Accrediting Agency for
 Clinical Laboratory Sciences
8410 West Bryn Mawr, Suite 670
Chicago, Illinois 60631

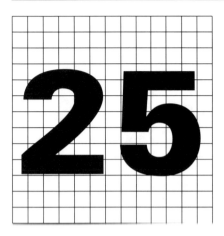

HOME CARE AIDE

also known as
Homemaker-Home Health Aide
Homemaker
Home Health Aide
Personal Care Aide
Home Attendant
Home Helper
Home Nursing Assistant
In-Home Support Worker

Home care aides (this term has replaced the lengthy "Homemaker-Home Health Aide" title) are health care paraprofessionals who visit the homes of the ill, disabled, elderly, socially disadvantaged, and others who are unable to perform basic tasks themselves to provide a wide spectrum of personal and homemaking assistance. The specific functions carried out by the home care aide depend on the nature and extent of the physical, emotional, or social problems affecting the patient and the patient's family.

The personal assistance may include bathing and otherwise aiding the patient in carrying out personal hygiene; helping the patient with walking and any prescribed exercises (and especially in the case of the bedridden patient, helping to rotate the patient to prevent bed sores and other complications of inactivity); checking respiration, heartbeat, and blood pressure; administering medications; changing surgical dressings; helping the patient with orthoses (braces) and prostheses (artificial limbs); and offering important human contact, comfort, emotional support, and instruction on how to manage and carry out fundamental tasks and, if necessary, how to adapt to the limitations caused by the disability.

Homemaking functions carried out by the home care aide may include changing bed linens and doing the patient's laundry; cleaning the patient's home; planning, shopping for, and preparing meals that often must conform to special dietary restrictions; and caring for, dressing, and feeding any young children in the family.

A home care aide usually works with a particular patient and his or her family over an extended period of time, thereby allowing the aide to observe the progress made. On a regular basis, this progress is reported back to the home care aide's supervisor (usually a registered nurse or social worker) who uses this information to determine if services should be changed.

Home care aides are very important deliverers of direct health care. Because of their efforts, many patients who would otherwise require hospitalization are able to remain in their own homes. Home care aides improve the quality of the lives of many patients struggling at home.

SETTINGS, SALARIES, STATISTICS

Home care aides work for local health and welfare departments, hospitals, community voluntary agencies, and private health care agencies. Some opportunities also exist in nursing homes. In all, there are approximately 15,000 agencies across the country that employ home care aides. Aides usually work alone in the patient's home, traveling from assignment to assignment. Many aides work part-time, and weekend hours are common.

Best estimates place the number of home care aides at about 370,000. The vast majority of them are female.

Salaries tend to be low. Most home care aides earn between $10,000 and $16,000 per year. In 1993, home care aides who worked on an hourly basis earned an average of between $4.75 and $7.50 per hour, although in large cities, where wages are highest, some home care aides earn as much as $11.00 an hour. Some home care aides work for agencies that provide them with insurance benefits, sick leave pay, and paid vacations. Others do not receive these benefits at this time.

The title used for workers in this field will vary geographically. In some parts of the country, the title *homemaker* is used; in others, the title *aide*; and in others, the title *homemaker–home health aide*. In some parts of the country, the titles *homemaker* and *aide* are used to designate two different levels of experience.

HOW TO BECOME A HOME CARE AIDE

Educational requirements in this field are in flux. Previously, preparation typically consisted of a several-week-long training course plus on-the-job training, which were provided by the employer agency. The trend today is toward more, and more formal, education. Twenty states currently require formal training, and many other states recommend it. A significant number of these states use as their educational standard the national standards suggested by the National Home Caring Council (NHCC), which call for 60 hours of training coupled with a 15-hour practicum. The National Home Caring Council is a division of the Foundation for Hospice and Homecare.

Training programs for home care aides are offered by community colleges, adult basic education programs, state programs for the aging, and private agencies. Typically, a student is taught how to bathe, lift, and turn the patient; plan and prepare nutritious meals; monitor vital signs; administer medications; and manage the patient's household. The home care aide also learns about the emotional problems common to illness, dealing with the elderly, and how to offer support at what is often a very stressful time.

In Spring of 1994, the Home Care Aide Association of America (HCAAA) presented a detailed position paper entitled "National Uniformity for Paraprofessional Title, Qualifications and Supervision," in which a three-level career ladder for home care aides is proposed.

A Home Care Aide I (or HCA I) would assist with housekeeping and homemaking (performing such duties as cleaning, shopping, doing laundry, performing essential errands, planning and preparing basic meals, etc.), maintain a safe environment, observe and monitor the client's condition, and teach the client those tasks that increase the client's independence. The HCA I would not, however, provide any personal care.

A Home Care Aide II (or HCA II) would assist the client and client's family with home management activities and with nonmedically directed personal care. Specifically, an HCA II would perform all of the duties of a Home Care Aide I, plus assist with ambulation, bathing, hair care/grooming, dressing, toileting, transfer activities, and special diets. An HCA II would not, however, perform duties under a medically directed plan of care and would not be assigned duties related to assistance with medications or wound care.

A Home Care Aide III (or HCA III) would work under a medically supervised plan of care to assist the client and client's family with both household management and personal care. Specifically, an HCA III would carry out all of the functions of an HCA I and an HCA II, plus perform nonsterile wound care, assist with self-administered medications, assist with prescribed exercises and rehabilitation activities, and help with assistive devices.

Specific training, supervision, and yearly in-service education requirements for each of these categories are also detailed in the Home Care Aide Association of America's position paper. It is highly likely that these titles and standards will be approved and formally accepted.

Personal qualifications for work as a home care aide include maturity, genuine willingness to help people, compassion, patience, common sense, a sense of humor, and enough strength to life and support patients.

THE FUTURE

The demand for home care aides should grow dramatically in the future as a result of the rapidly increasing elderly and chronically ill populations and because of the cost effectivness of home care. In fact, of the ten occupations requiring a high school diploma or less that are predicted to grow the fastest by the year 2005, home care aide is listed first. Job opportunities in this field should increase by an incredible 92 percent. An additional 250,000 jobs are expected in this field. It is hoped that salaries will increase significantly as well. Home care is an essential component of health care reform. Shortened hospital stays will mean ever greater importance for the home care aide's services. The Home Care Aide Association of America's newly proposed HCA I, II, and III classifications and standards reflect an anticipated increase in the importance of the home care aide's role. Indeed, the creation of home care aide specialties (i.e., pediatric, mental health, Alzheimers, developmental disabilities, and HIV home care aides) is under discussion. As hospital and other institutional costs skyrocket, and as hospitals and third-party payers have moved to establish limitations on the lengths of hospital stays, the emphasis on home care is increasing and should continue to grow.

For more information about home care aides, contact the:

Home Care Aide Association of America
519 C Street N.E., Stanton Park
Washington, D.C. 20002-5809

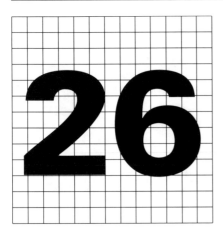

HORTICULTURAL THERAPIST

In ancient Egypt, physicians often prescribed walks in the garden for their disturbed patients. Today, many physicians prescribe *working* in the garden, greenhouse, crop field, or orchard for certain patients who have mental, physical and/or social disabilities.

Horticulture is the growing of flowers, fruits, vegetables, and shrubs for ornament and pleasure. Horticultural therapy is the use of gardening activities to evaluate, rehabilitate, train, and otherwise improve the life skills and lives of individuals who are physically and/or mentally impaired.

Horticultural therapy is based on several basic human tendencies and needs. Fundamental to its theory is the universal, almost innate, human delight in perceiving natural beauty. Horticultural therapy brings to its patients natural beauty in the form of flowers, shrubs, and other plant life. Flowers and organic motifs appear in the art of almost every culture in every age. Plants and flowers are part of our rituals and celebrations. We plant them in our yards and bring them into our homes and even our workplaces because they are among the most beautiful things in nature, and that beauty has a positive effect on us. Seeing a garden in bloom can be calming, renewing, and inspiring for any person but perhaps especially for a patient who has been shut off from the mainstream of life by physical and mental limitations. Perceiving the color, fragrance, and form of a beautiful flower can, in very elemental ways, make a person feel better.

Horticultural therapy is also founded on the concept that work experiences can be therapeutic. Tending a garden is a lesson in patience, responsibility, and faith. Watching day by day as seed turns into blossom is fascinating and fun. Harvesting the fruits—and flowers—of one's labors can provide a sense of personal accomplishment. In addition, society not only values the beauty of plants and well-landscaped grounds, it values those individuals with a knack for tending them. On many levels, making things grow can be a personal growth experience.

Horticulture therapists are specially educated and trained members of re-habilitation and therapy teams (along with doctors, psychiatrists, psychologists, occupational therapists, behavioral specialists, vocational skills instructors, and others) who involve the patient in all phases of gardening (and, sometimes, even in the activity of selling the produce and plants grown) as a means of improving those patients' lives. Horticultural therapists are experts on the medical and psychological benefits of gardening. Horticultural therapy can enhance self-esteem; alleviate depression; improve motor skills; provide opportunities in problem solving; encourage work adjustment, social interaction, and communication; as well as teach certain marketable horticultural and business skills—all toward the goal of integrating the individual into the everyday community life stream.

For many patients whose conditions (and treatments) have rendered them feeling passive and dependent, having living plants to nurture creates a role reversal. Horticultural therapy places the patient in the care-giving role, and this often engenders confidence and a renewed sense of purpose. Because the education required to become a horticultural therapist stresses not only horticulture and agriculture but also psychology and the social and behavioral sciences, the therapist is able to help analyze the patient's problems, assess his or her limitations and cognitive abilities, tailor activities to fit the disabilities and goals set, and gauge progress.

Patients include individuals who are mentally retarded, mentally ill, visually impaired, elderly, socially maladjusted, alcohol and/or drug abusive, disadvantaged, recuperating from surgery, as well as individuals who have sustained spinal cord injuries or stroke, or who have cerebral palsy or other conditions resulting in physical impairment.

The Wheelchair Orchard at Kansas State University's Horticultural Research Farm is an example of how an understanding of horticulture and disabilities, creative thinking, and sensitivity can happily come together in a horticultural therapy program to provide mental and physical therapy and pleasure to patients who use wheelchairs. In the Wheelchair Orchard, apple and pear trees have been wired and trained to grow onto low overhead trellises so that the branches are accessible to the wheelchair-bound gardener, and pruning, pinching, and otherwise tending these trees—and picking their fruit—are possible.

SETTINGS, SALARIES, STATISTICS

Horticultural therapists work in general hospitals; psychiatric hospitals; convalescent homes; juvenile centers; nursing homes; schools, work co-ops, and training centers for individuals who have mental disabilities; public school special education programs; alcohol rehabilitation centers; and correctional facilities. Horticultural therapists work indoors and outdoors, usually with groups but also on a one-to-one basis with patients. In 1879, the Pennsylvania Friends Asylum for the Insane built the first greenhouse in the United States for use with the mentally ill. Today, there are over a thousand horticultural therapy programs across the country providing this therapy to an estimated 23,000 individuals.

Recent surveys of part-time and full-time horticultural therapists revealed an average annual salary of $28,000. Since part-time therapists' salaries are factored in, it can be assumed that full-time, certified horticultural therapists can earn significantly more.

HOW TO BECOME A HORTICULTURAL THERAPIST

A minimum of a bachelor's degree in horticulture is required. Fourteen colleges of agriculture and departments of horticulture and forestry in universities and colleges offer course work in horticultural therapy, (one, at Kansas State University, offers correspondence course work). Of these 14, only Kansas State awards a bachelor of science degree specifically in horticultural therapy. It also is the only institution awarding a master's degree in horticultural therapy. Three other institutions award B.S. degrees in horticulture with a horticultural therapy option. The curriculum typically includes courses in agriculture, horticulture, sociology, psychology, the behavioral sciences, horticultural therapy, and an internship.

The American Horticultural Therapy Association (AHTA), which was formerly the National Council for Therapy and Rehabilitation through Horticulture, or NCTRH, has established two professional classifications for horticultural therapists that are based on educational level and employment experience. They are: registered horticultural therapist (HTR), which is for horticultural therapists holding advanced degrees in horticultural therapy who have also interned for a minimum of one year (2,000 hours) of paid employment; and master horticultural therapist (HTM), which is for horticultural therapists who have attained higher levels of education in this field, worked extensively in horticultural therapy, and have extensive educational and/or professional achievements (a minimum of a master's degree in horticultural therapy and four years of full-time paid employment). The horticultural therapy technician (HTT) classification once offered to students in the process of obtaining their bachelor's degree and/or practical experience is no longer offered.

At this time, registration with the AHTA is voluntary, and there are no state licensing laws.

The AHTA advises high school students to obtain well-rounded, solid horticultural backgrounds by spending their summer vacations working in greenhouses, nurseries, or for landscaping companies and volunteering at facilities where it is possible to learn about various disabilities.

Of the personal requirements for success in this career, most important are the subtle, special qualities that make an individual a good "relater"—

sensitivity, empathy, compassion, patience, the ability to listen, and a genuine willingness to help. While plant care can call for physical strength and dexterity, there are horticultural therapists who are physically disabled and who, because of their physical limitations, may have the added effectiveness of serving as positive role models for their patients.

THE FUTURE

Several recent studies of emerging fields and occupations have identified horticultural therapy as an area that should experience rapid growth in the coming decade. The number of facilities and, therefore, job opportunities should increase as the American population grows older and larger. There are 65 million households in the United States where gardening is regularly carried out. Many people do not have to be told by professionals about the therapeutic effects of gardening; they know about them from experiences in their own backyards. Gardening is pleasurable and inexpensive, and it is expected that as our population ages, more people will naturally continue to garden or easily turn to gardening as a form of therapy. Gardening is an excellent life-long activity, and as more programs offering formal horticultural therapy are created or expanded, opportunities for therapists will grow.

For additional information about a career in horticultural therapy and a list of educational programs, contact the:

American Horticultural Therapy Association
362A Christopher Avenue
Gaithersburg, Maryland 20879

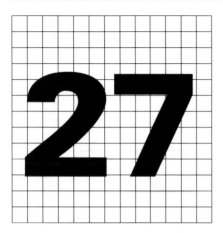

MEDICAL ASSISTANT

A *medical assistant* is a multiskilled allied health care professional who has been trained to perform administrative and/or clinical duties in an ambulatory or immediate care setting under the supervision of a licensed health care practitioner. Most medical assistants have both clinical and clerical responsibilities. Clinical functions vary depending on the scope of duties permitted by the laws of each state. They may include helping the physician by obtaining the patient's medical history; taking and recording the patient's height and weight; obtaining and recording vital signs (pulse, temperature, respiration, blood pressure); preparing the patient for examination and/or treatment; drawing blood; assisting in the examination and/or treatment; performing routine laboratory tests and EKGs; applying dressings; instructing the patient in preparation for X rays and laboratory examinations; preparing and administering medications as directed by a physician; instructing the patient on medication and home care; preparing the examining room; cleaning and sterilizing instruments; disposing of contaminated supplies; stocking laboratory supplies; and maintaining the examining, consultation, and waiting rooms in a clean and orderly condition.

The clerical, or administrative, responsibilities that a medical assistant may be expected to perform include scheduling and receiving patients; maintaining medical records; procedural and diagnostic coding; typing and taking dictation; medical transcription; arranging for hospital admissions and laboratory procedures for patients; and handling telephone calls, correspondence, reports, insurance matters, office accounts, fees, and collections.

The size of the office in which the medical assistant works usually determines the ratio of clinical to clerical work expected. In larger offices with several staff members, medical assistants usually specialize in either patient care or office functions, whereas in a small practice, a medical assistant may have to handle both facets of the work. (Although they may carry out clerical responsibilities, by virtue of their education and training, medical assistants are different from medical secretaries, who rarely perform clinical duties.)

Medical assistants work in all medical specialties. For example, *medical assistants in pediatrics* are medical assistants who have specialized in pediatrics (the branch of medicine dealing with the development and care of infants and children). Working as members of the pediatric health care team under the supervision of a pediatrician, they perform many of the same clinical and clerical functions carried out by medical assistant-generalists. They prepare examining rooms and patients for examination, take temperatures, measure height and weight, sterilize instruments, and assist the pediatrician as he or she examines and treats the infant or child. A medical assistant in pediatrics may also administer and interpret specific screening and diagnostic tests, recognize acute medical conditions, and administer specific medications—all under the supervision of the pediatrician. Any clerical responsibilities they may assume are also the same as the medical assistant's and may include secretarial, receptionist, bookkeeping, and medical record-keeping functions. There are also *geriatric medical assistants, podiatric medical assistants, ophthalmic medical assistants* (see Chapter 39), *orthopedic medical assistants, family practice medical assistants,* and many more.

A medical assistant must adhere to the ethical and legal standards of medical practice, demonstrate professional characteristics, and know how to respond to medical emergencies. Medical assistants serve another important purpose. Ideally they act as liaison between patient and physician (and in the case of a medical assistant in pediatrics, between family and physician as well). A medical assistant can offer important guidance, support, comfort, and warmth to the patient while freeing the physician for more technical functions. The medical assistant's role in understanding, evaluating, and accurately relaying patients' telephone calls for assistance is extremely important. A medical assistant who is efficient and personable can do much to enhance both the delivery of health care to the patient and the atmosphere in which that health care is delivered.

SETTINGS, SALARIES, STATISTICS

Sixty-five percent of all medical assistants work in the offices of physicians (single practitioners and group practices) who are in private practice. (More medical assistants are employed by practicing physicians than any other type of allied health personnel.) Medical assistants work for primary care physicians and for specialists; in clinics, health maintenance organizations, hospitals, and nursing homes. Although they usually work forty-hour weeks, evening and weekend office hours may be required.

Of the medical assistants who have specialized in pediatrics, the vast majority are employed by pediatricians who are in solo or group practice. Child care centers, community and neighborhood health centers, well-baby clinics, and other ambulatory child health care facilities that are supervised by a physician also employ medical assistants in pediatrics.

There are approximately 200,000 medical assistants currently employed in the United States. Most medical assistants are female; however, more and more males are entering the field.

Salaries for medical assistants vary widely. The medical assistant's training, years of experience, scope of responsibility, the volume of the physician's practice and the geographic location can all affect income. Annual salaries in the $12,500 to $20,000 range are average for experienced medical assistants. Starting salaries for medical assistants who are graduates of accredited formal educational programs range between $10,500 and $18,500 per year.

Opportunities for direct advancement in the office setting may be limited. In larger offices, promotions to supervisor or office manager may be possible. Most medical assistants who seek greater challenges and salaries undertake additional formal training so that they may enter other allied health professions. Opportunities also exist in teaching and consulting. Many medical assistants work in specialty areas of other types of facilities, such as medical records departments, emergency rooms, outpatient treatment centers, and insurance companies.

HOW TO BECOME A MEDICAL ASSISTANT

While some medical assistants are still trained on-the-job by the physician for whom they work, most medical assistants are graduates of formal education programs offered by postsecondary institutions. Hundreds of public and private vocational schools, community colleges, and junior colleges now offer medical assistant programs providing courses in medical terminology, biology, anatomy and physiology, typing, transcription, accounting and record keeping, as well as instruction in laboratory techniques, clinical procedures, and the use of medical equipment.

Medical assistant programs offered by community colleges usually entail two years of class work and supervised clinical experience leading to an associate's degree. Other programs available are approximately one year in length and award diplomas or certificates. Last year, approximately 23,000 students graduated from formal medical assistant educational programs.

The Commission for the Accreditation of Allied Health Education Programs (CAAHEP), which on July 1, 1994 succeeded the American Medical Association's Committee on Allied Health Education and Accreditation (CAHEA) currently accredits approximately 211 educational programs for medical assistants. (CAAHEP, which accredits educational programs for this and twenty-one other allied health professions, is an independent body in which the AMA participates as one sponsor among many.) An accredited medical assistant curriculum includes courses in anatomy and physiology, medical terminology, medical law and ethics, psychology, written and oral communication, medical assisting administrative procedures (including office procedures, business correspondence, typing, transcription of medical dictation, medical office management, bookkeeping, and insurance), and medical assistant clinical procedures (including examination room techniques, aseptic practices and techniques, care of supplies and equipment, first aid and cardiopulmonary resuscitation, laboratory orientation, and principles of pharmacology). These programs also require students to extern in qualified physicians' offices, accredited hospitals, and other health care facilities. Last year, approximately 5,700 men and women graduated from CAAHEP-accredited medical assistant programs.

The Accrediting Bureau of Health Education Schools (ABHES) also accredits medical assistant educational programs. Last year, almost 7,400 students graduated from the approximately 160 programs that are ABHES-accredited.

A high school diploma is almost always required for formal education as well as for on-the-job training in medical assisting. In high school, students should take mathematics, health, biology, typing, and business courses.

Personal qualities that are important to success and satisfaction as a medical assistant include intelligence, common sense, strong oral and written communication skills, friendliness, compassion, conscientiousness, manual dexterity, maturity, respect for the confidential nature of medical information, and a genuine interest in and willingness to help individuals who are ill. Medical assistants in pediatrics should, of course, enjoy children.

Certification in this field is offered by the American Medical Technologists (AMT) and the American Association of Medical Assistants (AAMA). To be eligible for certification by the AMT, a medical assistant must complete an ABHES-accredited course in medical assisting, or complete a medical assistant course accredited by a regional accrediting commission (the accrediting body for two-year public colleges), or complete an armed forces training course. Graduates of certain other private vocational training programs in this field who also have a minimum of one year of experience may also apply for certification, as may high school graduates who have a minimum of five years of employment experience in the medical assisting profession. Upon passing the AMT's certification examination, a candidate becomes a Registered Medical Assistant and may use the designation RMA after his or her name.

To be eligible for AAMA certification, a medical assistant must complete an accredited medical assistant educational program or show evidence of 12 months of full-time or 24 months of part-time experience as a health professional working under the supervision of a physician or other licensed health care practitioner (osteopath, clinical psychologist, podiatrist, dentist, veterinarian). Upon passing the AAMA's written competency examination, a candidate is entitled to use the designation Certified Medical Assistant (CMA) after his or her name.

While voluntary, both AAMA certification and AMT certification are widely accepted as evidence of a high level of preparation, and both tend to improve job opportunities and starting salaries. Although there is no licensing for medical assistants, some states require a short course or test before medical assistants may draw blood, give injections, take X rays, and so on.

THE FUTURE

The job outlook for medical assistants—and especially for medical assistants who have graduated from formal, accredited training programs—is excellent. Government and private economists report that medical assisting is the nation's second-fastest growing occupation for the second decade in a row. Several factors should contribute to this favorable picture. First, there are more than 400,000 practicing physicians in the United States, and this number is growing rapidly. As more doctors hang out their shingles, more opportunities for medical assistants should be created. Second, the expanding American population, the increasing percentage of older Americans in that population, the new health consciousness, and the improved ability to pay for medical care that third-party payment now affords many Americans should, together, create a situation where the demand for health services increases significantly. And if demand for medical care grows, so, too, should the demand for the clinical and clerical services provided by medical assistants. The U.S. Department of Labor projects that there will be approximately 290,000 openings for medical assistants by 2005.

For more information about medical assistants, write to the:

American Association of Medical Assistants
20 North Wacker Drive, Suite 1575
Chicago, Illinois 60606-2903

Registered Medical Assistants of American Medical
   Technologists
710 Higgins Road
Park Ridge, Illinois 60068-5765

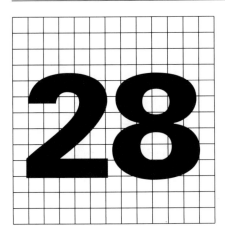

MEDICAL ILLUSTRATOR

also known as
Graphic Communicator in Medicine
Medical Artist

A *medical illustrator* is a highly trained, specialized artist who creates graphic representations of medical or biological subjects for the various bioscience communications media—medical textbooks, professional journals, pamphlets, instructional films and exhibits, general magazines, and television. Medical illustrators are communicators and educators who use their artistic talents and creative insights to record facts and progress in many health fields. They sometimes work directly with health care and research teams using their drafting skills to provide illustrations that assist with research problems or their modeling skills to prepare artificial body parts (noses, eyes, ears) to be used when cosmetic or functional improvement is required. For one assignment, a medical illustrator may be called upon to draw an extremely accurate, representational rendering of an anatomical part or microorganism or even an entire surgical procedure in an operating room; for the next project, the assignment may be to reduce a complex idea to an abstract, easy-to-understand diagram or schematic concept. But a medical illustrator is not just a talented artist—he or she is a talented artist who has a solid educational foundation in anatomy and general medicine. Students preparing at schools of medical illustration learn neuroanatomy and physiology right along with three-dimensional modeling techniques and illustration. This medical foundation is essential because the artist must understand the demands of an assignment, and the work executed must be authentic and correctly interpreted.

Because of the variety of assignments a medical illustrator must be able to fulfill, he or she must be accomplished in a variety of artistic techniques and media—drawing, painting, modeling, diagraming, and creating graphic and audiovisual aids. He or she must possess a basic knowledge of typography, layout and design, and know how to prepare artwork for publication.

While the majority of medical illustrators handle an ever-changing variety of assignments, some medical illustrators specialize in a single art medium or concentrate on a particular medical specialty (such as pathology, embryology, ophthalmology), working with physicians, research scientists, educators, and authors in that particular specialty only.

SETTINGS, SALARIES, STATISTICS

Most medical illustrators are employed by medical schools and large medical centers having teaching and research programs. They also work in private, state, and federal hospitals; clinics; dental and veterinary schools; medical publishing companies; pharmaceutical manufacturers; and advertising agencies. Many of these artists also take on freelance assignments, and some medical illustrators work exclusively on a freelance basis. Some medical illustrators are in solo practice; others are members of large multimedia production units working with other medical illustrators, graphic designers, chart artists, art assistants, biological photographers, television personnel, and educational specialists.

The number of men and women in this field is small. The Association of Medical Illustrators (AMI), which is the international professional association for medical illustrators, reports a membership of approximately 910 men and women and estimates that this figure represents 80 percent of the total number of individuals in this field.

The average starting salary for graduates of schools of medical illustration is approximately $25,000 per year, and the average experienced staff medical illustrator may earn anywhere from $35,000 to $60,000. A few medical illustrators command six-figure incomes. Many staff illustrators significantly supplement their incomes by freelancing at hourly rates that vary according to the region of the country and the artist's expertise.

Advancement in this field usually comes in the form of promotion to director/producer of an audiovisual service department.

HOW TO BECOME A MEDICAL ILLUSTRATOR

Medical illustrating requires talent and training in art as well as interest and education in the biological sciences. To become a medical illustrator today, specialized training in both disciplines is necessary. There are very few schools of medical illustration in the United States, and only five of them (the Medical College of Georgia, University of Illinois, Johns Hopkins University School of Medicine, University of Michigan, and University of Texas) are accredited by the Association of Medical Illustrators, which has established standards for the professional training of medical illustrators. Each of these programs accepts only between three and twelve students per year. Membership in the AMI is useful because many employers rely on it as an indication of proficiency.

In 1987, the American Medical Association's Committee on Allied Health Education and Accreditation (CAHEA) recognized the medical illustration occupation, and, until July 1, 1994, it accredited medical illustration educational programs. The newly created Commission for the Accreditation of Allied Health Education Programs (CAAHEP), which is CAHEA's successor, now accredits programs. CAAHEP is an independent body in which the AMA participates as one sponsor among many. At this time, the five programs recognized by AMI are also accredited by CAAHEP.

All five accredited educational programs for medical illustrators are master's degree programs, and they range in length from two to three years. Requirements for admission to these programs vary to some degree, but, basically, the following preparation is recommended. In high school, an aspiring medical illustrator should follow the general college preparatory program with strong emphasis on art. Biology and other science courses should be included. At the college level, a student should concentrate on art, premed biology, and humanities courses. The art courses should include drawing, life drawing, painting, color theory, design, illustration techniques, layout, photography, and typography. The science courses usually required include zoology, comparative vertebrate anatomy, embryology, physiology, chemistry, biology, and histology. Most of the students admitted to schools of medical illustration major in art. Some students, however, choose zoology as their undergraduate major or have double or interdisciplinary majors in art/biology. Because these schools accept very few students annually competition is stiff. A strong academic record is essential, and a portfolio of the candidate's artwork is also reviewed.

Although there is some variety from school to school, most educational programs for medical illustrators include courses in gross human anatomy (including dissection), histology (the microscopic study of cells and tissues), human physiology, embryology, neuroanatomy (the nervous system), pathology, illustration techniques for publication (wash, carbon dust, pen and ink, watercolor, gouache, acrylics, ink, and air brush), illustration techniques for nonprint media (slide-tape, motion picture, filmstrip, television), surgical illustration (including surgical observation), anatomical illustration (including autopsy observation), three-dimensional modeling techniques, chart design, graph design, table design, exhibit design and construction, prosthesis design and construction, cinematography, and animation.

To succeed in this profession, artistic ability, creativity, the ability to interpret information clearly, plus a strong interest in the subject matter are needed.

At this time, certification is optional. There are no state licensing requirements for medical illustrators.

THE FUTURE

Employment opportunities for medical illustrators are favorable. As medical research, new technologies, and new techniques evolve ever faster, the need for artists who can record and communicate these advancements will grow, and medical illustrators holding master's degrees from accredited educational programs will be in greatest demand.

For more information about medical illustrators and a list of accredited schools of medical illustration, write to the:

Association of Medical Illustrators
1819 Peachtree Road N.E., Suite 712
Atlanta, Georgia 30309

MEDICAL SOCIAL WORKER AND PSYCHIATRIC SOCIAL WORKER

It is widely agreed that health is more than just the absence of disease or illness; it is the complete physical, mental, and social well-being of the individual. *Social work* is defined as a system of organized activities carried out by a person with particular knowledge, competence, and values, that is designed to help individuals, groups, or communities toward a mutual adjustment between themselves and their social environment. A professional social worker is an expert who helps people cope with complex interpersonal and social problems and obtains for them the resources they need to live with dignity. A *medical social worker* is a social worker who specializes in helping patients and their families cope with personal problems—be they social, emotional, or financial—resulting from severe or long-term illness or disability, recovery, and rehabilitation and who obtains the resources they will need to get through their health situation with a minimum of stress. A *psychiatric social worker* is a social worker who specializes in helping psychiatric patients and others overcome emotionally stressful situations. Once patients overcome their acute problems, the psychiatric social worker helps them reenter the community and serves as an important communications link between the patient and his or her family and between the family and the professionals treating their loved one.

If personal problems and fears are severe enough and go unanswered, they can slow a patient's progress toward health and well-being. The job of the medical and psychiatric social workers is to understand the patient's concerns and to bring to him or her the hospital personnel and services and the community resources that can alleviate these fears and the conditions that cause them so that the best recovery can be achieved. Medical and psychiatric social workers are vital members of the health care team along with doctors, nurses, psychiatrists, therapists, and other health care professionals.

There are more social workers employed in the nation's mental health facilities than any other single profession (40 percent of the staff of all mental health facilities are social workers, compared to 32 percent psychiatrists, 23 percent psychologists, and 5 percent psychiatric nurses). Half of all the mental health treatment in the United States is given by professional social workers. Often, it is the social worker's sensitivity, knowledge, skills, and insights that make the big difference in a patient's recovery or adjustment.

A complete list of the specific duties carried out by a medical social worker is almost impossible to compile—medical social workers have to respond to the many problems caused by illness and injury. They assist individuals and their families in coping with a wide range of problems related to physical illness, disability, recovery, and death: directing the parents of a newborn with a congenital disability to the resources in the community that they will need; organizing rehabilitation services and support groups within the community; finding shelter for young children left untended because of parental hospitalization; arranging for the regular delivery of special dietetic meals to an elderly patient after he or she is discharged from the hospital and convalescing at home, or smoothing that patient's transition into a nursing home, should that become necessary. Medical social workers help patients handle their fears about their medical condition and their worries about how their health may affect future family relationships, work, and finances. They conduct individual and family assessments, educate people about personal health care, refer patients to the appropriate health services, and follow up on these referrals. Medical social workers advocate on behalf of patients and groups of patients, work with groups of people who have similar health problems, help communities secure access to needed health resources and services, direct social service programs in institutional and noninstitutional settings, design programs, teach, and conduct research. The AIDS epidemic has presented new challenges to the work of medical social workers.

The specific functions and responsibilities carried out by psychiatric social workers are as numerous and varied as the problems that can be generated or aggravated by mental illness. Fundamentally, the psychiatric social worker's responsibilities include obtaining and preparing a history of each new patient admitted to a mental hospital or other mental health facility; serving as a constant and friendly liaison between patient and family throughout what is often a long period of treatment; and serving, too, as liaison between the family and the psychiatrist and other professionals treating the patient, explaining to them the patient's illness and progress and communicating to the professional staff any family concerns or information that may bear on the treatment. The psychiatric social worker helps smooth the patient's return to normal life in the community by using a carefully cultivated repertoire of community resources and producing remedies for the concrete, day-to-day problems that may face patients as they adjust to the outside world and, too, by remaining in touch with patients and providing continuing support and help as they work to overcome their problems and

fears. For psychiatric social work, too, AIDS has presented new issues, problems, and interventions. Some psychiatric social workers conduct research,
and others teach psychiatric social work.

SETTINGS, SALARIES STATISTICS

Medical social workers practice in a wide variety of settings: free clinics;
union health centers; specialty outpatient clinics; health maintenance organizations; solo and group medical practices; home health agencies; industry;
the emergency, intake, discharge, maternity, pediatric, intensive care, psychiatric, burn, surgical, and medical areas of general, specialized, government,
and military hospitals (over half of the country's hospitals have social services departments or offer social services); nursing homes; long-term health
care facilities; public health departments; alcohol and drug abuse programs;
sex education programs; crisis clinics; rape prevention and child abuse services; national and international voluntary agencies; rural health planning
agencies; native American reservations; the Department of Health and
Human Services; vocational rehabilitation offices; mental health/retardation
boards; health and disaster relief programs; private practice; and schools of
social work, medical, nursing, public health, pharmacy, and dentistry schools
and allied health paraprofessional training programs where they teach medical social work. This long and diverse list of work settings should suggest
what is special about the nature of medical social work—medical social
workers are wherever people are faced with health and medical situations,
dilemmas, and problems. Social workers began their involvement with
health issues in the United States at the turn of the century. Their first concerns were with making health services available to the poor and improving
social conditions that bred tuberculosis and other infectious diseases. Today,
medical social workers are found in every aspect of our health care system.

Psychiatric social workers work in mental hospitals, the psychiatric departments of general hospitals, mental health clinics, hospitals for individuals who are mentally disabled or who have epilepsy, federal and state mental
hospitals, rehabilitation organizations, community mental health centers, in
the courts, in research, and in educational institutions.

There are, at this time, approximately 55,000 social workers employed in
health and mental health settings. This number represents approximately
one-third of all social workers practicing in this country.

Average salaries range from $25,000 for a social worker who holds a
bachelor's degree to $42,000 for an experienced social worker who has a
graduate degree and is certified. Starting salaries range from approximately
$18,500 for medical social workers holding bachelor's degrees to $25,500
for those with master's degrees. Salary levels will, of course, vary in different regions and institutions. Institutions in the West (Arizona, Idaho, Utah,
Nevada, Oregon, Washington, California, Hawaii, Alaska, Montana, and
Wyoming) tend to offer the highest salaries. Social workers who are em-

ployed by the federal government are among the highest paid members of this profession.

HOW TO BECOME A MEDICAL SOCIAL WORKER OR A PSYCHIATRIC SOCIAL WORKER

There are three levels of professional social work education: the bachelor's degree (B.S.W.), the master's degree (M.S.W.), and the doctorate (D.S.W. or Ph.D.). Preparation for professional social work requires a minimum of a bachelor's degree, and there are approximately 400 bachelor of social work degree programs that are accredited by the Council on Social Work Education (CSWE). An accredited undergraduate curriculum will include course work in human behavior and the social environment, social welfare policy and services, methods of social work (which is the process of intervening in the flow of events to help solve a problem or develop a resource), research, and field practice.

An M.S.W. is usually required for more advanced medical social work positions. There are approximately 115 universities that offer two-year master's programs. To apply for a graduate degree in social work, a person need not have a bachelor's degree in this field. A number of graduate schools offer health concentrations in their curricula, and a few offer interdisciplinary degrees with public health schools.

A doctorate (Ph.D. in Social Work or D.S.W., for Doctor of Social Work) is usually required for faculty positions in colleges and universities and for most research positions. The CSWE accredits 45 doctorate programs, presently.

Personal qualities that are essential for success and career-long satisfaction in the field of medical social work include a genuine love for people and concern for their needs, warmth, the important ability to work as a member of a team, freedom from prejudices, sound judgment, and a special balance of empathy and professionalism, faith and objectivity.

Voluntary certification in this field is available through the Academy of Certified Social Workers (A.C.S.W.). To become certified, a candidate must complete a master's degree program in social work, have a minimum of two years of post-master's work experience, be a member of the National Association of Social Workers, and pass a written examination. Upon successful completion of the certifying process, a social worker may use the title certified social worker (ACSW). Certification tends to enhance salary and advancement. At this time, all fifty states and the District of Columbia require social workers to be registered, licensed, or certified.

THE FUTURE

The U.S. Department of Labor's Bureau of Labor Statistics predicts that between now and 2005, job opportunities for social workers will expand greatly, and social work will indeed be in the top 20 percent of all occupations in terms of growth. Ever-increasing awareness of the importance and application of this work, the expansion of the U.S. population, and, more specifically, of the older population, and the never-ending line of new medical problems and medical solutions, almost all of which present challenges to the patient and to society, should cause ever-greater demand for medical and psychiatric social workers.

For more information about what medical social workers and psychiatric social workers do and about education and certification requirements, write to the:

> National Association of Social Workers, Inc., Education
>   Office
> 700 First Street N.E., Suite 700
> Washington, D.C. 20002-4241

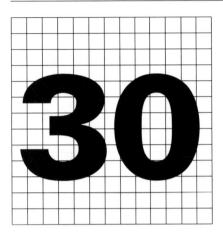

MEDICAL TECHNOLOGIST AND MEDICAL LABORATORY TECHNICIAN

also known as
Clinical Laboratory Scientist and Clinical Laboratory Technician
including
Clinical Laboratory Assistant

Medical technologists and *medical laboratory technicians* (increasingly known as clinical laboratory scientists and clinical laboratory technicians, respectively) perform diagnostic laboratory tests that play a crucial role in the detection of diseases and treatment of patients. Using microscopes, a variety of chemicals, complex precision instruments, and computers, they carry out serology, parasitology, toxicology, cytology, histology, bacteriology, urinalysis, environmental chemistry, hematology and blood typing, general chemistry, immunochemistry, nuclear medicine, and other tests that tell physicians and patients much about the nature and progress of health conditions. Last year, Americans spent about twenty billion dollars on the over one thousand different medical laboratory tests available today. A major hospital may process more than two million different laboratory tests in one year. Much of modern laboratory work is computerized. From one two-milliliter blood sample (about forty drops), more than twenty different tests can be run simultaneously, with the results being handled by laboratory information systems that can interface with patient care centers. Some laboratory tests are so sophisticated and specialized that they are performed by only one or a few laboratories nationwide. A hospital laboratory never completely shuts down. The need for vital laboratory information exists around the clock, and timely handling of important laboratory information leads to better patient care.

Medical technologists have a baccalaureate degree. They supervise laboratories and make critical judgments about laboratory results as well as carrying out complex testing procedures. Because of their comprehensive science background, medical technologists know how to solve problems and troubleshoot analytical systems. They understand the scientific theory behind a test, and they also are able to evaluate the effects that various pathological conditions may have on test results. They understand quality issues and monitor laboratory output for precision and accuracy as well as design and implement new test procedures. Some medical technologists are employed in facilities where they work in all the laboratory disciplines. They are known as generalists. Others specialize in clinical areas and become experts in that arena. Medical technologists are also employed in research, public health, and reference laboratories as well as performing private consulting for physician office laboratories.

Medical laboratory technicians usually have a two-year associate's degree. Working under the supervision of the medical technologist, a medical laboratory technician performs laboratory tests that are less complex and require less theoretical and technical knowledge. Medical laboratory technicians are expected to microscopically examine specimens, perform blood counts, operate automated testing equipment, and inoculate culture media to identify bacteria. With experience they may take on more responsibility and use more independent judgment.

Medical laboratory technicians who hold certificates from one-year educational programs are referred to as clinical laboratory assistants. They are trained to perform the most routine, least complicated laboratory procedures under direct supervision. These procedures involve the use of laboratory instruments in processes where discriminations are clear, errors few and easily corrected, and results can be confirmed with a reference test or source within the working area.

SETTINGS, SALARIES, STATISTICS

Most medical laboratory personnel work in a hospital laboratory. Other opportunities exist in independent laboratories; physicians' offices; clinics; HMOs; pharmaceutical companies; public and private research institutions dedicated to the study of specific diseases; the armed forces; city, state, and federal health agencies; and on the teaching staffs of programs that prepare medical laboratory personnel. A growing demand exists for private consultants to interface with physician office laboratories. The workweek is usually 40 hours long. Part-time opportunities exist in many work sites, and flexible hours are possible as hospitals are staffed for three shifts. Twenty percent of all medical laboratory personnel work part-time. Because the hospital laboratory never closes, hospital laboratory personnel can expect evening, weekend, and holiday duty. The work load can be extremely heavy.

There are approximately 220,000 medical technologists and 100,000 medical laboratory technicians in the United States. Approximately 6,100 medical laboratory personnel work in Department of Veterans Affairs hospitals and laboratories.

Salaries in this field depend on educational level, certification, region, and institution. Generally, medical laboratory personnel who work in large cities earn the highest salaries. Entry-level salaries range between $25,000 and $32,000 annually. Experienced medical technologists average between $32,000 and $40,000 per year. Entry-level salaries for medical laboratory technicians holding associate's degrees range between $15,000 and $21,500 annually. Nationwide, experienced medical laboratory technicians average approximately $23,000. Technicians who have certificates have a salary range from $12,000 to $19,500.

Medical laboratory technology is a field where "career laddering" definitely exists. The experience and training necessary to function at one level are applicable to the attainment of the higher levels. For example, without losing any credit or time, medical laboratory technicians can add course work and experience to their certificates or associate's degrees and qualify for medical technologist status. Similarly, medical laboratory technicians with certificates may apply their training toward the educational and experiential requirements for a medical laboratory technician associate's degree.

Technologists may advance to supervisory positions, and, with additional time and experience, a medical technologist may become the administrative medical technologist in a large hospital. Graduate education tends to enhance salaries and advancement.

HOW TO BECOME A MEDICAL TECHNOLOGIST OR MEDICAL LABORATORY TECHNICIAN

The educational requirement for an entry-level position as a medical technologist is a baccalaureate degree including or in addition to completion of a hospital internship. Generally as an undergraduate a student medical technologist will take course work in biological science, chemistry, and mathematics, which will provide a solid scientific foundation for the clinical internship in which he or she will participate.

Medical technologist educational programs are offered by many colleges, universities, and hospitals around the county. The curriculum offers courses in theory and extensive laboratory experience in hematology, microbiology, immunology, transfusion medicine, and clinical chemistry. Some programs are integrated and the student receives instruction in medical laboratory technology course work as a component of the baccalaureate degree. Other programs are referred to as three plus one. Students spend three academic years on a college or university campus studying the background foundational sciences and then relocate to a hospital setting for their final year of education.

Of the medical technologist education programs offered nationwide, approximately 400 are accredited by the National Accrediting Agency for Clinical Laboratory Sciences (NAACLS). (On July 1, 1994, the American Medical Association's Committee on Allied Health Education, or CAHEA, which for many years accredited programs for medical technologists and medical laboratory technicians, ceased its accrediting activities for these professions.) Students applying for admission to NAACLS-accredited, hospital-based programs must have a minimum of 90 semester hours from a college or university approved by a recognized accrediting agency, and this academic credit must include 16 semester hours of biological science, 16 hours of chemistry (including organic or biochemistry), and 3 semester hours of mathematics. Last year about 3,500 men and women graduated from NAACLS-accredited medical technologist educational programs.

Many institutions offer graduate work in medical laboratory technology. This graduate study prepares medical technologists for teaching, administrative, and research positions, and enables professionals to gain specialist certification in specialty areas of the laboratory.

Students embarking on the education necessary to become a medical laboratory technician have two formal educational options. After high school, they may enroll in a two-year, community or junior college associate's degree program that will prepare them to carry out the more complicated technical functions of laboratory work, or they may enroll in a one-year certificate program for medical laboratory technicians offered by a hospital, college, community college, or vocational/technical school. In addition, many practicing medical laboratory technicians learn their skills in the military, and some have been trained on the job. Several agencies accredit medical laboratory technician educational programs. The National Accrediting Agency for Clinical Laboratory Sciences accredits 213 associate's degree programs and 40 certificate programs at this time. Last year, approximately 1,800 men and women successfully completed these NAACLS-accredited associate's degree programs and 800 graduated from NAACLS-accredited certificate programs. The Accrediting Bureau of Health Education Schools (ABHES) and the Accrediting Commission of Independent Colleges and Schools (ACICS) also accredit medical laboratory technician educational programs.

Students in two-year medical laboratory training programs learn more theory than certificate students. The emphasis is on general knowledge, basic skills, and mastering laboratory testing procedures. The curriculum teaches procedures in hematology, serology, chemistry, microbiology, and immunohematology. Medical laboratory technician (certificate) students take introductory course work in medical ethics and conduct, medical terminology, laboratory solutions and media, quality control, blood collecting techniques, microbiology, hematology, serology, and immunohematology.

Abilities and personal qualities that can contribute to effective and enjoyable performance in this field include an aptitude for science, attention to detail, manual dexterity, good or good corrected vision, the ability to distinguish between fine color gradations, and the ability to work well under pressure.

At this time, 12 states and the city of New York require medical laboratory personnel to be licensed. New York and several of these states administer their own examinations, and several use a certification as the standard for licensure. Certification in medical laboratory work is offered by several national certifying agencies. The Board of Registry of the American Society of Clinical Pathologists is the oldest and largest of these certifying agencies. The Board of Registry has specific combinations of education and experience that entitle a candidate to sit for its examinations. Medical technologists who satisfy these requirements earn the designation MT (ASCP), which stands for medical technologist certified by the American Society of Clinical Pathologists. A medical laboratory technician who satisfies the requirements may use the designation MLT (ASCP)—for medical laboratory technician certified by the American Society of Clinical Pathologists—after his or her name.

The National Certification Agency for Medical Laboratory Personnel (NCA) also certifies medical technologists and medical laboratory technicians. A medical technologist who satisfies the NCA's educational, experience, and examination requirements is designated a CLS (NCA) (for clinical laboratory scientist), and a medical laboratory technician fulfilling the requirements is designated a CLT (NCA) (for clinical laboratory technician).

The American Medical Technologists (AMT) also certifies medical laboratory personnel, offering the designations MT (AMT) and MLT (AMT) to medical technologists and medical laboratory technicians, respectively, who meet its educational and experience requirements. Finally, certification is available from the International Society for Clinical Laboratory Technology (ISCLT). A medical laboratory technician who satisfies the ISCLT's preparation requirements and passes its competency examination is designated an RLT (which means that he or she is a registered laboratory technician). A medical technologist who satisfies the various requirements is designated an RMT, or registered medical technologist. ISCLT certification satisfies the licensing requirements in several states.

Certification is an important enhancement to employment, salaries, and advancement in this field, and, in many cases, it is a requirement for employment. Many medical laboratory workers are certified by more than one agency. The agencies' certification requirements are numerous and varied, and it is strongly recommended that students contact these organizations directly. In some parts of the country, certification by a particular agency is preferred by employers.

THE FUTURE

Several factors must enter any discussion of the employment out look for medical laboratory personnel. The American population is growing larger, and a larger percentage of it is older (a trend which is expected to continue at least for several decades); therefore, the number of people potentially requiring laboratory tests should increase. Simultaneously, that population is growing more and more health conscious and is willing to undergo medical tests. And, as third-party methods of payment have spread, that population is more able to pay for laboratory procedures. In addition, the number of tests available is growing, and their use by physicians to pinpoint diagnoses is growing. These factors should contribute to an increased demand for laboratory tests and, therefore, an increased demand for laboratory personnel. At the same time, however, the student population is smaller today.

A potentially complicating factor is the greater efficiency that accompanies the greater labor and cost effectiveness of computerized testing methods. Procedures that once were done one at a time, by hand, are now carried out with the push of a button by computers that are able to turn out large batches of results, quickly and inexpensively.

Adding these influences together, however, it is expected that demand for medical technologists and medical laboratory technicians should be strong well into the twenty-first century. Already many areas of the country are reporting acute shortages of laboratory personnel. Over 60 percent of the states and territories surveyed by the American Society for Medical Technology report a shortage of technologists. Forty-six percent report shortages of technicians. Some facilities have been forced to hire temporary technologists at extremely high fees from temporary agencies. Other facilities are offering substantial bonuses to employees who will commit to at least one year of employment in a rural hospital.

For more information about medical laboratory personnel, contact the:

American Society for Clinical Laboratory Science
7910 Woodmont Avenue, Suite 1301
Bethesda, Maryland 20814

Board of Registry
American Society of Clinical Pathologists (ASCP)
P.O. Box 12277
Chicago, Illinois 60612

American Medical Technologists
710 Higgins Road
Park Ridge, Illinois 60068

National Certification Agency for Medical
   Laboratory Personnel
7910 Woodmont Avenue, Suite 1301
Bethesda, Maryland 20814

International Society for Clinical Laboratory Technology
818 Olive, Suite 918
St. Louis, Missouri 63101

National Accrediting Agency for Clinical
   Laboratory Sciences
8410 West Bryn Mawr, Suite 670
Chicago, IL 60631

MENTAL HEALTH WORKER

also known as
Mental Health Associate
Mental Health Assistant
Human Service Worker
including
Psychiatric Technician
Psych Tech
Case Manager

Mental health workers are human service workers who perform a wide variety of therapeutic, supportive, and preventative functions for persons who are mentally ill and developmentally disabled. These patients include individuals who are mentally retarded; children, adolescents, and adults who are psychotic and emotionally disturbed; the acutely and chronically ill; the aged; and individuals who abuse alcohol and drugs. Mental health workers are usually generalists who must be able to assume a wide variety of specific functions. Working under the supervision of a psychiatrist, psychologist, social worker, or registered nurse, they interview and evaluate patients (called clients); provide behavior modification counseling; carry out therapeutic activities; keep client records; motivate clients and teach them new skills; advocate for clients; serve as community resources for clients and their families; help the transition to home for the client and the client's family; and follow up and report on the client's progress. Mental health workers must also be skilled in such nursing techniques as taking temperature and blood pressure, counting pulse and respiration, and assisting in the administration of medications and physical treatments. Basically, the mental health worker's function is to work closely with the client, providing (within the institution's and the state's definition of this occupation) instruction, care (feeding and dressing), and comfort that will help the person achieve his or her maximum level of functioning.

Although traditionally generalist in approach, in recent years (especially in California) there has been a trend toward specialization in mental health technology. Mental health workers may specialize in the problems of children who are mentally disturbed, the clinical training of individuals who are developmentally disabled, drug abuse counseling, psychiatric emergencies, and crisis intervention.

In Ohio, a new type of mental health worker, the case manager, has recently been recognized. A case manager finds and negotiates for the various services (housing, food stamps, vocational rehabilitation, transportation) that a patient who is about to be discharged from the hospital might need.

Another innovation in this field is the recruiting of mental health clients to be mental health workers, an arrangement that provides benefits all around.

Mental health workers provide important one-on-one, day-to-day contact for the people they serve. The personalized nature of their role and the continuity they afford to their clients make mental health workers important and very effective therapeutic and rehabilitative agents who are indispensable to the mental health delivery system in America.

SETTINGS, SALARIES, STATISTICS

Most mental health workers are employed in inpatient mental health settings: state and private mental health hospitals, schools for the mentally retarded, community health centers, and mental health clinics. Opportunities also exist in after-care programs, emergency and crisis centers, alcohol and drug programs, sheltered workshops, halfway houses, social rehabilitation centers, child guidance clinics, nursing homes, and the offices of private psychiatrists. A small number of mental health workers function as administrators and mental health educators.

There are approximately 160,000 paid mental health workers in the United States. Most mental health workers are female.

Salaries vary greatly depending on experience, type of agency and its funding, and the degree of responsibility assumed. Salary also depends on geographical location. In some parts of the country, mental health work is recognized as a career, with increased job performance matched by increased responsibility and pay. In other parts of the country, however, mental health work is considered a tightly defined job, and to advance, a mental health worker must acquire progressively higher academic credentials. Mental health workers who are employed in state mental health facilities are civil servants whose pay is based on the civil service scale. Entry-level salaries for workers holding an associate's degree usually range from $11,600 to $21,100 annually, but in some states, top mental health workers can earn $33,500 plus per year.

HOW TO BECOME A MENTAL HEALTH WORKER

How much education and training a person needs to function as a mental health worker depends on exactly where he or she wants to work. Some states and some settings do not require a high school diploma. In other situations, only a high school diploma and on-the-job training are needed. But in most employment situations, some post-high school classroom time is necessary, and this preparation usually entails the awarding of an associate's degree in mental health, human services, or mental health/human services. Many community colleges offer such educational programs. In California, where the more specialized mental health or psychiatric technician (or psych tech) level of mental health worker exists, course work in practical nursing is required.

The curriculum in a mental health technology program typically includes courses in basic and psychiatric nursing, general and abnormal psychology, mental health technology, sociology, personality and social development theory, group dynamics, and child development and growth. An opportunity for supervised experience working directly with clients in a mental health setting is also provided.

Personal qualities that are important for effectiveness and satisfaction as a mental health worker include emotional stability, patience, compassion, tact, a healthy sense of humor, good physical health, stamina, and a genuine desire to help individuals who are emotionally ill or mentally retarded. The ability to relate well to these patients and their families is essential.

At this time, licensure of mental health workers is required in only four states—Arkansas, California, Colorado, and Kansas. It is anticipated that, in time, more states will move toward licensure in this field.

THE FUTURE

Several trends should contribute to an increase in the number of job openings for mental health workers. First, the mental health establishment, third-party insurers, the states, and the public are becoming increasingly aware of the cost-effectiveness and safety of mental health worker practice. Secondly, the population of mental health clients in community based services and facilities is growing because of a trend toward earlier release of institutionalized patients and closure of large state facilities. This trend has created greater demand for mental health workers in transitional service agencies (sheltered workshops, halfway houses, crisis centers). Also, as more Americans in need of help reach out for help—or are reached out to—demands on our country's mental health services should increase.

For more information about mental health workers, contact the:

Center for Mental Health Services
Human Resource Planning and Development Branch
Room 15C 18
Rockville, Maryland 20857

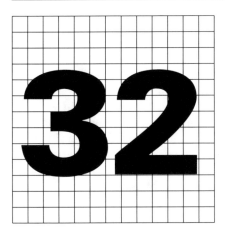

MUSIC THERAPIST

also known as
Adjunctive Therapist
Creative Arts Therapist
Music Specialist
Rehabilitation Therapist
Therapeutic Activities Worker
Expressive Arts Therapist

We learn early, perhaps from when we are babies rocked and lullabied to sleep (perhaps even before birth), that music can affect the way we feel. The lullaby, gentle and predictable in rhythm and tone, carries a message of security and calm—a soothing quality that, with luck, lulls baby to sleep.

Conversely, enter a room where hard rock is playing, and your body will tend to respond quite differently. Your visceral, or instinctive, reactions to the rock's fast, abrupt tempo; loud, pounding cadence; and the message or feeling of the song itself will generate in you a mood most likely quite different from the one in which you were put by that lullaby. Music therapy is based upon this human tendency to respond to certain musical sounds in certain ways.

The notion that music has healing value is as old as recorded history. Today, for many kinds of patients, music is part of the prescribed treatment plan. Modern music therapy is the systematic application of music in a therapeutic environment to bring about desirable changes in a patient's behavior. It is a useful, therapeutic tool in the rehabilitation of patients with a variety of behavioral, learning, and physical disorders, and has been demonstrated to be effective in improving self-control and self-esteem, relieving depression, enhancing attention span, and, in other ways, giving patients new insight into themselves and a better understanding of the world around them.

Music therapists are the trained health care professionals who plan and carry out the specific musical activities used in the rehabilitation of persons with disabilities. They work with socially and emotionally maladjusted adults and adolescents (the largest group of patients treated); the mentally retarded of all ages; geriatric patients; children with learning problems; individuals with hearing loss, visual and physical impairments; the homeless; AIDS patients; substance abuse patients; individuals with cerebral palsy; and persons with multiple disabilities, using a combination of music and psychology to achieve certain treatment goals involving the restoration, maintenance, and improvement of the patient's mental and physical health.

The programs devised by music therapists are designed to gain and maintain the patient's interest. Group and individual singing, musical instruments, and often dance and body movements are part of the therapy.

The music therapist is a member of the health care team, often working with other therapists, psychiatrists, psychologists, and social workers to analyze the patient's problems and establish treatment goals. How music therapy may help a particular patient is discussed, then specific group and individual activities designed to meet the patient's needs are planned and implemented by the music therapist. Patients are periodically evaluated to gauge the effectiveness of the music therapy.

SETTINGS, SALARIES, STATISTICS

Approximately 5,000 music therapists practice in the United States, working in psychiatric and general care hospitals, clinics, mental retardation centers, adult day-care facilities, government and community health agencies, nursing homes, hospices, halfway houses, correctional facilities, special education programs in public and private schools, and in the research departments of universities where work on projects in biofeedback, relaxation, and other areas where music therapy may play a role is conducted. Some music therapists have their own studios and work with children and adults who are referred by psychiatrists and other health professionals. Most music therapists have regular workweeks but may occasionally be called on to work evening or weekend hours. While 90 percent of music therapists are women, the number of men entering this field is growing steadily.

Starting salaries for music therapists are in the high teens, and experienced music therapists earn $28,000 or more per year on average. Prior education and experience and location will affect these figures. Some music therapy professors report earnings as high as $60,000 per annum. Music therapists who work in hospices or who specialize in gerontology tend to earn the least. Salaries are generally highest in the New England and western states and lowest in the south central states.

Advancement in the music therapy field is possible. There are positions, such as department supervisor, to which a music therapist may be elevated, but such promotions usually entail a reduction in therapy activities and increased administrative duties.

HOW TO BECOME A MUSIC THERAPIST

The people who are working as music therapists today bring to their careers a wide range of prior training and experience. Some have advanced degrees in music therapy from institutions offering special programs in this field; others have study and experience combinations that have led to employment in the music therapy field. As this form of therapy grows, however, more rigid educational standards are being established and adopted by more employers. Therefore, satisfying these standards is recommended to students starting in the field. The curriculum typically leading to a bachelor's degree in music therapy includes music and music therapy courses (60 percent of the program work), behavioral/health/natural science courses (20 percent), and general studies (20 percent).

At this time, approximately 67 colleges and universities offer bachelor's degree programs in music therapy. Of these, about a dozen institutions also offer master's and doctoral programs.

Personal qualities important to a successful and satisfying career in music therapy include good physical health, stamina, the emotional stability both to handle patients and to be a good role model for them, tact, patience, compassion, a healthy sense of humor, the ability to withstand frustration, and creativity. It is also important to work well as part of a team.

Registration of music therapists is available from the National Association for Music Therapy (NAMT) and from the American Association for Music Therapy (AAMT). Certification is available from the AAMT only, and there are two routes to this certification. The first is for students who have graduated from one of the music therapy educational programs that this organization accredits. The alternate route is for music therapists who have graduated from other educational programs or who have extensive experience in the field. These candidates must provide letters of recommendation and tapes of therapy sessions, be interviewed, and be observed on site. The NAMT accredits approximately 64 music therapy educational programs and requires that candidates for registration be graduated from one of these programs or have a bachelor's degree in a related major that is supplemented with required courses. A six-month internship at an accredited site is also required. The AAMT and NAMT have recently formed an independent testing body called the Certification Board for Music Therapists (CBMT). This board administers a standardized test once a year in November. Upon passing this test and maintaining certain continuing education requirements, a music therapist may use the designation *board certified*. Board certification is not a requirement for practice at this time, although this condition for employment may soon be instituted. However, presently two-thirds of the 3,000 registered music therapists in the United States are board certified. Either NAMT or AAMT registration or AAMT certification is usually required.

At this time, licensure is not required, except in the case of music therapists who work in public schools and who may, then, be licensed as special education instructors in the states in which they work.

THE FUTURE

The employment picture for this career looks very good. Music therapy is gaining in acceptance and popularity as the medical profession and the public recognize the benefits of alternative forms of medical care. Indeed, music therapy's significant benefits to the growing elderly population were the topic of recent governmental hearings, and on September 30, 1992, when amendments to the Older Americans Act became law, music therapy, as well as dance/movement therapy (see Chapter 11) and art therapy (see Chapter 2) were included and defined. This recognition makes certain federal grant money available for study and treatment. Research into music's part in biofeedback and relaxation as well as exciting new work on music's role in enhancing special education continue to increase interest in this therapy and create a demand for therapists. As with other auxiliary health care, however, the future of music therapy depends on the economy, coming health care trends, and governmental support and financing of health care.

Work as a music therapist can be challenging, creative, and personally satisfying. Music therapy is an important form of rehabilitation for many patients today. If the economy and health care delivery systems are favorable, jobs in this important field should open up.

For more information about music therapists, write to the:

National Association for Music Therapy, Inc.
8455 Colesville Road, Suite 930
Silver Spring, Maryland 20910

American Association for Music Therapy, Inc.
P.O. Box 80012
Valley Forge, Pennsylvania 19484

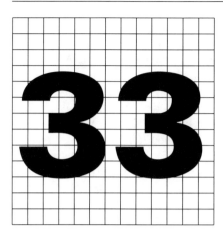

NUCLEAR MEDICINE TECHNOLOGIST

also known as
Radioisotope Technologist

Nuclear medicine is the science and clinical discipline of administering radioactive compounds (radionuclides and radiopharmaceuticals) to patients or to specimens of the patient's body in order to diagnose, treat, and investigate certain health problems. When these compounds are used directly on the patient, they are administered intravenously, intramuscularly, subcutaneously, or orally. In diagnostic procedures, tiny amounts of these isotopes are introduced into the patient's body to act as tracers. In the course of their journey through the body, these isotopes are altered, or they attach to certain tissues. A special camera is positioned over the region of interest (the brain, liver, lungs, thyroid gland, bones, whole systems), and when the radioactivity has concentrated in that region, it is detected and translated into spots of light that expose the camera's film. The developed film is called a scan or scintigram. The "picture" created by the radioactive tracer allows the physician to detect a variety of structural and functional abnormalities. By observing how and where the radioactive compounds go, a nuclear medicine physician is able to gain unique and valuable information about changes in the body's biological processes as well as alterations in anatomy.

When administered for therapeutic purposes, the radioactive compounds are used to selectively destroy diseased tissue.

A good example of how nuclear medicine is used to diagnose and evaluate health problems is the nuclear cardiology procedure known as the thallium scan, which is a test performed to detect blockage in the coronary arteries that supply the heart. In this procedure, the patient is connected to an electrocardiograph that will constantly monitor his or her heart activity. He or she then commences exercising on a treadmill. While the patient exercises, the radioisotope thallium 201 is injected into a vein in the patient's arm. Thallium 201 is a low-dose radioactive tracer. It enters the patient's bloodstream and circulates throughout his or her body. A gamma scintillation camera is positioned over the patient's chest, and it picks up the isotope as it progresses on to the coronary arteries leading to the heart muscle. A computer than translates the signals given off by the thallium and from them produces a computerized printout displaying the distribution of the thallium in the heart muscle. Where the blood flows unimpeded, the tracer also flows, giving off its radiation and creating spots of light on the scan. Where circulation is poor or a blockage exists, the flow of blood (and tracer) is impeded, and the computer picture will show a "cold spot." This test can reveal much about the patient's heart and is very accurate while being almost noninvasive (only an injection is required). The radiation dose used is only slightly greater than that in a conventional chest X ray.

A common example of nuclear medicine used in the treatment of diseases is the radioactive iodine capsule or liquid given to patients suffering from hyperthyroidism, which is overactivity of the thyroid gland. In this procedure, the patient swallows a carefully controlled amount of radioactive iodine. When it reaches the thyroid gland, the radioactive iodine destroys the overfunctioning tissue, thereby relieving the potentially serious symptoms. The advantage of using radioactive iodine is that it destroys this tissue nonsurgically, eliminating the hospital stay, greater expense, and potential trauma and risk that surgery entails.

Nuclear medicine technologists (NMTs) are the health care professionals who, working under the supervision of the nuclear medicine physician and other professionals in this field, position the patient; calculate, prepare, and administer the correct dosages of the radioactive drugs; run the gamma ray detecting equipment; examine the quality of the image made (either on film or on a computer screen); and then process the study, increasingly with the help of a computer. For most NMTs, diagnostic scanning is the primary function. They also perform certain *in vitro* diagnostic procedures (*in vitro* is Latin for in glass—that is, occurring not in the patient's body but in a laboratory situation). In these laboratory procedures, known as radioassay, radioactive materials are added to body specimens (such as urine and blood) to measure, for example, tiny amounts of hormones, vitamins, or vital drug levels. NMTs must, of course, be proficient in laboratory procedures. Nuclear medicine technologists apply their knowledge of radiation physics and radiation safety procedures so that radiation exposure to the patient, to the public, and to the radiation workers is kept within minimum levels. Nuclear medicine workers are also responsible for purchasing, handling, and proper disposal of the radioactive drugs; maintaining quality control; and maintaining patient records.

Nuclear medicine technologists must also understand and relate to the patient's concerns and fears about his or her illness and pending diagnostic procedures or therapies, and they must be able to recognize emergency situations and know how to initiate lifesaving first aid.

SETTINGS, SALARIES, STATISTICS

Eighty-five percent of all NMTs work in hospitals. NMTs also work in public health institutions, doctors' offices, and research institutions. Some NMTs teach nuclear medicine technology in colleges and universities.

There are approximately 16,000 nuclear medicine technologists in the United States. The majority of them are female. Salaries vary according to experience, responsibility, type of institution, and geographic area, but on average, starting salaries for nuclear medicine technologists range from $17,000 to $31,500 annually. Experienced technologists earn an average of $35,000. Salaries tend to be higher on the West Coast.

Advancement in the field of nuclear medicine technology may come in the form of promotion to supervisory and administrative positions. However, a bachelor's degree is important for such promotion and essential for teaching positions. Administrative personnel in this field can earn as much as $70,000 per year.

HOW TO BECOME A NUCLEAR MEDICINE TECHNOLOGIST

There are several ways to attain the education and clinical experience necessary to become a nuclear medicine technologist. Formal education programs of different lengths (usually twelve months to four years) accommodate the prior training and needs of candidates coming to this field from a variety of backgrounds—certified radiographers, certified radiation therapy technologists, RNs, medical technologists, and holders of associate's and bachelor's degrees in physics and the biological sciences. The length of the program and the credential awarded—certificate, associate's degree, or bachelor's degree—will depend on prior preparation, the educational needs of the student, and the specific institution. One-year certificate and two-year associate's degree programs are most common. Programs in this field are accredited by the Joint Review Committee on Nuclear Medicine Technology (JRCNMT). On-the-job experiences also can lead to the training necessary for employment as an NMT, but such training is becoming rarer and is considered, by an increasing number of employers, to be undesirable.

At this time, there are 119 accredited programs. Slightly more than half are offered by colleges and universities, and one-third are offered by hospitals and medical centers. Accredited programs also are offered by community colleges and the military. Last year, 500 men and women graduated from accredited NMT programs.

The curriculum in a formal program includes courses in patient care, nuclear physics, instrumentation, statistics, health physics, biochemistry, immunology, radionuclide chemistry, radiopharmacy, administration, radiation biology, clinical nuclear medicine, *in vivo* (in the patient's body) and *in vitro* (in the laboratory) studies, radionuclide therapy, and computer application and operation.

In many settings (hospitals, primarily), to work as a nuclear medicine technologist, a candidate must be certified and/or registered. Two organizations certify NMTs: the American Registry of Radiologic Technologists and the Nuclear Medicine Technology Certification Board. Many NMTs are certified by one or by both, depending on the employment requirements in their region and their long-range career goals. The American Registry of Radiologic Technologists (ARRT) offers its certification examination three times a year in approximately one hundred locations nationwide and in Puerto Rico. This three-hour-long test of competency is used not only by employers as a standard of preparation but also by those states that require licensing. To be eligible for this examination, a candidate must graduate from an accredited nuclear medicine educational program. In certain specific cases, candidates who have not attended one of these programs may file an appeal to sit for the examination. Upon passing the ARRT examination, a nuclear medicine technologist may use the title registered nuclear medical technologist and the letters R.T.(N)(ARRT) after his or her name. The letters stand for radiologic technologist in nuclear medicine certified by the American Registry of Radiologic Technologists. ARRT certification is recognized by Great Britain, Canada, Australia, and South Africa.

The Nuclear Medicine Technology Certification Board (NMTCB) also requires its candidates to graduate from accredited schools of nuclear medicine technology. Candidates with bachelor's or associate's degrees in one of the physical or biological sciences; individuals with certification in medical technology, radiologic technology, or clinical laboratory science; and RNs who began on-the-job training in this field prior to January 1, 1979, may satisfy the certification requirements by accumulating a minimum of three years of full-time experience in nuclear medicine technology under the supervision of a physician who is board certified in nuclear radiology, nuclear medicine, or isotope pathology or of an authorized physician-user of radioactive materials with special competency in nuclear medicine, or, if the clinical experience began on or after January 1, 1979, by accumulating four years of clinical experience under the same supervision. Certification options for nuclear medicine technologists who have been trained on-the-job exclusively have been phased out. As of January 1, 1996, to sit for the NMTCB examination, a candidate must either be a graduate of an accredited educational program in nuclear medicine technology or have taken the exam before within the past five years.

Upon successful completion of the NMTCB'S qualifying examination, a candidate may use the title certified nuclear medical technologist and its abbreviation CNMT after his or her name. Since 1980, the NMTCB has had reciprocity with the Canadian Association of Medical Radiation Technologists, which means that certification by the NMTCB is recognized in Canada, and vice versa.

At this time, almost half of the states and Puerto Rico require nuclear medicine technologists to be licensed. However, recent federal legislation encouraging state licensing should result in a trend toward more state regulation in the near future.

Individuals who are interested in nuclear medicine technology should have good verbal and numerical skills, manual dexterity, appreciation for the importance of accuracy, respect for the potentially dangerous materials being handled, the ability to work well and communicate well both with other health care professionals and with a wide variety of patients (many of whom are very anxious, very ill, or dying), compassion, patience, and the physical strength to lift and position patients.

THE FUTURE

The job outlook for nuclear medicine technologists will depend largely on what future technological advances dominate. Competing with nuclear medicine imaging methods are many new, less invasive methods such as magnetic resonance imaging and computerized tomography (CT) scanning. In turn, these innovations are likely to be replaced with the next generation of sophisticated, noninvasive diagnostic techniques. Simultaneously, new applications for nuclear medicine (in tumor treatment and in coronary output evaluation) that are more effective and/or safer than earlier procedures should increase the need for NMTs. Most NMTs work in hospitals, so hospital efforts at cost containment must also be factored into the job outlook. Taking these potentially conflicting factors into account, one may assume that employment opportunities in this field will grow at an average rate through 2005.

For more information about nuclear medicine technologists and the educational and other requirements for a career in this field, contact the following associations.

The Society of Nuclear Medicine,
   Technologists Section
1850 Samuel Morse Drive
Reston, Virginia 22090-5316

American Registry of Radiologic Technologists
1255 Northland Drive
St. Paul, Minnesota 55120

Nuclear Medicine Technology
   Certification Board
2970 Clairmont Road N.E., Suite 610
Atlanta, Georgia 30329-1634

And for information about accredited educational programs in nuclear medicine technology, contact the:

Joint Review Committee on Education Programs in
   Nuclear Medicine Technology
136 Madison Avenue
New York, New York 10016

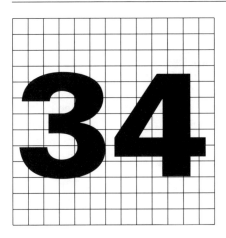

NURSE

including
Licensed Practical Nurse (LPN)
Registered Nurse (RN)
Advanced Practice Nurse
Clinical Specialties

In a recent survey, hospital chief executive officers who were polled pointed to the quality of an institution's nursing care as being the single most important factor contributing to overall hospital quality and patient satisfaction. Nurses are essential suppliers of health care in America. The goals of nursing are recovery and prevention. Working in a broad range of institutional and community settings, nurses care for and comfort the disabled and teach good health. Nursing is usually very people-oriented work that provides personal challenges and personal satisfactions.

There are four educational routes in nursing: (1) practical, or vocational, nursing programs; (2) associate's degree programs; (3) diploma programs; and (4) baccalaureate programs. All four options prepare the student to provide nursing services, but they differ in the depth and breadth of intellectual, interpersonal, and technical skills taught.

The first educational option entails one year of formal education plus supervised clinical instruction which prepare students to become *licensed practical nurses* (or *licensed vocational nurses*, LVNs, as they are called in Texas and California). Licensed practical nurses (or LPNs) provide bedside care to the ill, injured, convalescent, and physically disabled in hospitals, clinics, nursing homes, and similar institutions. Working under the supervision of registered nurses (RNs), they provide nursing care that requires technical knowledge and skill but not necessarily the in-depth professional education and training of a registered nurse. Their functions may include taking and recording the patient's temperature, blood pressure, pulse rate, and respiration rate; dressing wounds; giving alcohol rubs, massages, and injections; applying compresses, ice bags, and hot water bottles; administering certain medications; helping the patient with bathing and other personal hygiene routines; preparing the patient for medical examination; assisting the physician and registered nurse in examining the patient and carrying out nursing procedures; assisting in the delivery, care, and feeding of newborns; and observing the patient and reporting any significant symptoms, reactions, and changes in the patient's condition to the physician or nurse in charge.

Often, LPNs specialize in one of several related areas of medicine (pediatrics, obstetrics, coronary care, intensive care) or in one area of the hospital (the operating room, recovery room, emergency room), and such specialization may entail additional on-the-job training or continuing education courses. Some licensed practical nurses who work in hospitals supervise hospital attendants and nursing aides.

Licensed practical nurses who work in clinics and doctors' offices may prepare the patients for examination, apply dressings, instruct patients on home health care, and handle such administrative responsibilities as record taking and managing the appointment calendar.

The other three educational options all prepare students to become *registered nurses* (or RNs).

Nursing is a huge profession that encompasses many health care functions applied in a wide variety of settings. Where a registered nurse works and which area of nursing or specialty he or she chooses will define the specific functions that will be expected, personal qualities needed, and any other supplemental training required.

Hospital nurses plan, carry out, and evaluate a patient's nursing needs in conjunction with the medical care plan prescribed by the physician. This care may include observing, assessing, recording, and reporting the patient's progress; administering medications; giving injections; and implementing treatments. Registered nurses in hospitals supervise the activities of licensed practical nurses, nursing aides, and orderlies. Nurses document patients' status in the patient chart and also spend time teaching patients how to care for themselves after discharge from the hospital.

Community health nurses (or public health nurses) care for patients in community settings such as clinics and schools, and in patients' homes. They provide nursing care in conjunction with the physician's plan of care; teach patients and their families, as well as community groups, about management of health conditions, good nutrition, and preventative health care; and act as liaison between the community and the hospital. They may also arrange for and implement immunization programs and conduct treatment programs for special groups in the community (such as alcohol abusers and other groups of individuals who share a common health problem).

Private duty nurses are self-employed nurses hired directly by the patient or the patient's family to provide constant personal nursing care in a hospital setting or in the home.

Office nurses assist physicians, dental surgeons, dentists, nurse practitioners, and nurse-midwives who are in private practice or who work in clinics. In addition to nursing duties, office nurses may be expected to perform routine laboratory tests and office functions.

School nurses are hired by boards of education to provide various health and nursing services in schools or for entire school systems. They serve as consultants to the school's administration, parents, and students regarding health matters; handle school medical emergencies; implement state health code statutes (regarding immunization and communicable diseases); assist in administering physical examinations to students and reporting the findings to parents; and alert parents to any evidence of emotional problems in their children.

Occupational health nurses and *industrial nurses* are independent practitioners who, under the supervision and responsibility of a physician (usually a medical director or consultant), work in government facilities, factories, corporations, and other work sites, providing nursing care to employees (including the treatment of minor injuries and illnesses occurring in the workplace); assisting in physical examinations and carrying out educational programs designed to improve the health of workers.

Nurse educators work in schools of nursing and nursing programs providing classroom instruction for nursing students and continuing education for men and women who are already nurses. They also work in health care facilities proving self-care information to patients.

Some hospital nurses become experts in a particular clinical specialty, which means that they concentrate their efforts in one particular area of nursing. Specialization entails additional training and education.

Operating room nurses use nursing concepts and judgment, together with special scientific knowledge and technical skills, to provide a continuous cycle of patient care before, during, and after surgical procedures. Preoperatively, they assess the patient. Intraoperatively, they are responsible for maintaining an environment conducive to quality patient care (promoting effective working relationships, the smooth functioning of the department, quality control of materials and techniques, and safe and properly equipped operating rooms). Working at the patient's side, the operating room nurse must anticipate the needs of the surgical team. Postoperatively, they visit the patient to evaluate postoperative care. Some operating room nurses specialize in a particular type of surgery, such as neurosurgery, orthopedic surgery, thoracic surgery, or cardiac surgery. There are approximately 60,000 operating room nurses in the United States. To become an operating room nurse, a registered nurse must supplement his or her basic nursing education by enrolling in a formal, postgraduate operating room course or by participating in a hospital-sponsored in-service program that focuses on the development of the various skills necessary to function as an operating room nurse.

Critical care nurses are registered nurses who have special education in the care of critically ill patients that prepares them to operate highly sophisticated monitoring equipment, recognize physiological changes in the patient's condition, and administer complex nursing support to treatment being administered by physicians. Their education provides them with indepth knowledge of the physiology of the body systems and the social skills needed to deal with stress to the patient's family.

Rehabilitation nurses work with children and adults who suffer from permanent or temporary physical, mental, or emotional impairments caused by accident, illness, congenital anomaly, birth injury, surgery, or old age and who need assistance to attain an optimal level of functioning in their lives. They work with patients who are physically disabled from strokes, spinal cord injuries, brain injuries, amputation, cancer, heart or lung disease, neurological disease, and others, providing treatments, exercises, and emotional support that will help them to regain lost abilities and to adapt where loss is permanent. There are approximately 10,000 rehabilitation nurses nationwide. To become a rehabilitation nurse, a registered nurse typically completes a post-RN course in rehabilitation nursing, or he or she may obtain a master's degree in rehabilitation nursing.

Advanced practice nurse (APN) is an umbrella term given to a registered nurse who has met advanced educational and clinical practice requirements beyond the two to four years of basic nursing education required of all RNs. Under this umbrella fall four principal types of APN: nurse practitioner, certified registered nurse anesthetist, clinical nurse specialist, and certified nurse-midwife. There are more than 100,000 advanced practice nurses, and this number is rapidly growing.

Nurse practitioners (or NPs) are qualified to handle a wide range of basic health problems. Most have a specialty—for example, adult, family, pediatric, or geriatric health care. NPs conduct physical examinations, take medical histories, diagnose and treat common acute minor illnesses and injuries, order and interpret laboratory tests and X rays, and counsel and educate patients. In approximately 35 states, they may prescribe medications. Most of the approximately 150 nurse practitioner education programs in the U.S. today confer a master's degree. NPs work in clinics, nursing homes, hospitals, or in their own offices.

Certified registered nurse anesthetists (CRNAs), working either with an MD anesthesiologist or independently, administer more than 65 percent of all anesthetics given to patients each year. (In 85 percent of rural hospitals, they are the sole providers of anesthetics.) Two to three years of additional training beyond the four-year bachelor of science in nursing degree, plus national certification and recertification, are required. CRNAs work in almost every setting in which anesthesia is administered—operating rooms, dentists' offices, ambulatory surgical settings. Nurse anesthetists were the first nurses to specialize beyond general duty nursing. This specialty has been recognized for almost a century.

Clinical nurse specialists (CNSs) are registered nurses with advanced nursing degrees (master's or doctorate) who are experts in a specialized area, such as cardiac or cancer care, mental health, or neonatal health. Besides delivering direct patient care, CNSs work in a variety of consultative, research, education, and administrative roles. They provide primary care and psychotherapy; develop nursing care techniques and quality control methods; teach nurses and other health care professionals; and act as clinical consultants. CNSs work in clinical settings, community or office-based settings, and hospitals.

Certified nurse-midwives (CNMs) provide prenatal and gynecological care; deliver babies in the home, in hospitals, and in birthing centers; and follow mothers postpartum. (See Chapter 35.)

Many nursing specialties exist. Below is a list of specialty nursing organizations in the United States and their addresses:

American Academy of Nurse Practitioners
P.O. Box 12846
Austin, Texas 78711

American Association of Critical-Care Nurses
101 Columbia
Aliso Viejo, California 92656-1491

American Association of Neuroscience Nurses
224 North Des Plaines, Suite 601
Chicago, Illinois 60661

American Association of Nurse Anesthetists
222 South Prospect Avenue
Park Ridge, Illinois 60068-4001

American Association of Nurse Attorneys
720 Light Street
Baltimore, Maryland 21230

American Association of Occupational Health Nurses
50 Lenox Pointe
Atlanta, Georgia 30324

American Association of Spinal Cord Injury Nurses
75-20 Astoria Boulevard
Jackson Heights, New York 11370-1177

American College of Nurse-Midwives
1522 K Street, Suite 1000
Washington, D.C. 20005

American Nephrology Nurses' Association
North Woodbury Road, Box 56
Pitman, New Jersey 08071

American Organization of Nurse Executives
840 North Lake Shore Drive
Chicago, Illinois 60611

American Society of Opthalamic
  Registered Nurses
P.O. Box 193030
San Francisco, California 94119

American Society of Plastic and Reconstructive
  Surgical Nurses, Inc.
North Woodbury Road, Box 56
Pitman, New Jersey 08071

American Society of Post Anesthesia Nurses (ASPAN)/
  Recovery Room Nurses
11512 Allecingie Parkway
Richmond, Virginia 23235

American Urological Association Allied
  (for urological nurses)
11512 Allecingie Parkway
Richmond, Virginia 23235

Association for Practitioners in Infection Control
505 East Hawley Street
Mundelein, Illinois 60060

Association of Operating Room Nurses, Inc.
2170 South Parker Road, Suite 300
Denver, Colorado 80231-5711

Association of Pediatric Oncology Nurses
11512 Allecingie Parkway
Richmond, Virginia 23235

Association of Rehabilitation Nurses
5700 Old Orchard Road, First Floor
Skokie, Illinois 60077-1057

Association of Women's Health, Obstetric, and
  Neonatal Nurses
409 Twelfth Street S.W., Suite 300
Washington, D.C. 20024-2137

Council on Cardiovascular Nursing
American Heart Association
7320 Greenville Avenue
Dallas, Texas 72531

Dermatology Nurses Association
North Woodbury Road, Box 56
Pitman, New Jersey 08071

Emergency Nurses Association
216 Higgins Road
Park Ridge, Illinois 60068

National Association of Orthopedic Nurses, Inc.
North Woodbury Road, Box 56
Pitman, New Jersey 08071

National Association of Pediatric Nurse Associates
    and Practitioners
1101 King's Highway North, Suite 206
Cherry Hill, New Jersey 08034

National Association of School Nurses, Inc.
P.O. Box 1300
Scarborough, Maine 04074-1300

National Flight Nurses Association
6900 Grove Road
Thorofare, New Jersey 08086

National Nurses Society on Addictions
5700 Old Orchard Road, First Floor
Skokie, Illinois 60077-1057

Oncology Nursing Society
501 Holiday Drive
Pittsburgh, Pennsylvania 15220

Society of Otorhinolaryngology
    and Head/Neck Nurses
116 Canal Street, Suite A
New Smyrna Beach, Florida 32168

SETTINGS, SALARIES, STATISTICS

Slightly over half of all licensed practical nurses work in general hospitals. Other opportunities exist in nursing homes (which are the second biggest employer), HMOs, rehabilitation centers, clinics, sanitariums, day-care centers, industry, psychiatric hospitals and other long-term facilities, doctors' and dentists' offices, correctional institutions, and patients' homes (where their responsibilities may also include meal preparation and teaching the patient's family how to perform simple nursing tasks).

There are approximately 631,000 LPNs in the United States. Most of them are women. Starting salaries for licensed practical nurses begin at about $18,500 per year. An experienced licensed practical nurse working in a hospital setting may earn as much as $27,000 annually. Licensed practical nurses employed by nursing homes and the Department of Veterans Affairs tend to earn slightly less. These amounts will vary geographically, however.

Almost two-thirds of all registered nurses work in hospitals (where, on average, they make up 22 percent of the staff), and another third work in community health agencies (public health departments, visiting nurse associations, home health agencies), nursing homes, physicians' offices, and nursing schools. Opportunities also exist in business and industry, public schools, and research. Approximately 32,000 nurses are private duty nurses.

Nurses' hours and workweeks vary, and the number of hours spent on the job each week will depend on the area of nursing in which one works. If emergencies are common to a particular specialty (as is the case with nurse anesthetists), then erratic schedules may be expected. In other specialties (such as school nurse or industrial nurse), more predictable, forty-hour (or less) workweeks can be anticipated. Hospital nursing often entails rotated night and weekend shifts. About one-third of all RNs practice part time.

There are approximately 2.2 million registered nurses in the United States at this time, 1.8 million of whom are currently practicing. Of these, approximately 30,000 are nurse practitioners, 25,000 are certified registered nurse anesthetists, 40,000 are clinical nurse specialists, and 4,200 are certified nurse-midwives.

Ninety-seven percent of all RNs are female, but the number of men entering this field is increasing rapidly, and, whereas males nurses once worked almost exclusively in the emergency room, today they function in all areas of the hospital.

The average annual salary for all registered nurses nationwide is approximately $40,000. (Actual salaries vary from the low twenties to $60,000 per year or more.) Nationwide, the average starting salary is $27,700. Experienced nurses with administrative duties average approximately $48,000. Much depends on the amount of nursing education (especially if there has been graduate study), the type of position held, specialty, and geographic location.

Advanced practice nurses tend to earn more. In 1993, nurse practitioners earned an average of $47,000, certified registered nurse anesthetists earned $80,000, certified nurse-midwives earned $55,000, and clinical nurse specialists earned salaries that ranged from $30,000 to $80,000, depending on experience and geographic location. Some nurse executives who are in charge of patient care management, human resources management, and/or fiscal and human resources management for large hospitals or multihospital systems earn over $100,000 annually. Salaries are highest in the West. It should be noted, however, that in 1993, for the second year in a row, the average increase in the base pay of RNs in acute-care hospitals slipped (from 8.9 percent in 1991, to 6.1 percent in 1992, to 5.7 percent in 1993).

HOW TO BECOME A LICENSED PRACTICAL NURSE
OR A REGISTERED NURSE

In all fifty states and the District of Columbia, practical nurses must be licensed. To become licensed, a student must complete a 12 to 18-month state-approved practical nursing course and pass a written examination. At this time, there are about 1,154 state-approved practical nurse training programs nationwide. Most of the programs are offered by trade, technical, and vocational schools. Hospitals, community and junior colleges, and health agencies also offer practical nurse training. The curriculum typically includes courses in anatomy and physiology, medical-surgical nursing, psychiatric nursing (the care of mental patients), pediatrics (the care of children), obstetrics (the care of mothers and newborns), the administering of medications, first aid, nutrition and diet therapy, family living, growth and development, community health, nursing concepts and principles, and elementary nursing techniques. Supervised clinical experience (usually conducted in a hospital) is also part of the training. A high school diploma is usually, but not always, necessary for admission to a practical nurse training program. Upon successful completion of a practical nurse educational program, students are awarded a diploma or certificate and may then sit for the state board licensing exam in the state(s) in which they seek employment.

In all fifty states and the District of Columbia, a registered nurse must have a license to practice. To obtain a license, a student must graduate from a state-approved school of nursing and pass a state board examination.

There are three educational routes to becoming a registered nurse. Option one entails two academic years of education and training in an accredited program offered by a community, junior, or technical college. Upon satisfactory completion of a two-year nursing program, the student is awarded an associate of applied science or associate of science degree.

Option two entails three academic years of accredited preparation. These programs are offered by hospitals, and a diploma is awarded.

Option three entails four years of study and training. Accredited programs are offered by four-year colleges and universities, and, upon graduation, a bachelor of arts or bachelor of science in nursing degree is awarded.

All three educational options prepare candidates to sit for the state nursing board exams.

A minimum of a high school diploma and usually a minimum of a C average in high school are necessary for admission to two-, three-, and four-year nursing programs. The type of nursing program selected—two-, three-, or four-year—will affect employment potential. The more education, the greater the possibilities and, hence, the greater the salaries obtainable. The type of education will also affect the level of responsibilities assigned, and often the greater the responsibility, the greater the intellectual and emotional challenges. Public health and school nurse jobs, supervisory and administrative positions, graduate programs in nursing, and many clinical specialties and nurse practitioner training programs all require a minimum of a bachelor's degree in nursing. Exactly which type of program a student selects should depend on his or her career and personal goals, interests, and abilities. A bachelor's degree program is recommended, however, because of the trend toward upgrading criteria in this field. Sometimes, transfer from one type of nursing program to another is possible.

All two-, three-, and four-year nursing programs consist of classroom instruction plus supervised nursing practice. The curriculum (although, again, varying in depth and breadth according to the length of the program) will include courses in anatomy and physiology, psychology, English, nursing concepts and techniques, microbiology, sociology, and philosophy. In the bachelor's degree nursing program these subjects are taught in greater depth, and courses in chemistry, biology, precalculus mathematics, cultural anthropology, organic chemistry, parent-child nursing, epidemiology, nursing research, health care in the social system, community nursing, and nursing trends are added.

At this time, there are 848 associate's degree, 135 diploma, and 501 bachelor's degree nursing programs in this country. In addition, there are 243 master's degree programs and 55 doctoral degree programs, which provide the advanced nursing education necessary to carry out administrative, teaching, and research activities.

Personal qualities that are essential to success and satisfaction in the important profession of nursing include compassion, patience, good physical and emotional health, the ability to work well as part of a team, the willingness to assume responsibility, the ability to react quickly and correctly in emergency situations, a genuine love of people, the desire to help all kinds of patients in need of all kinds of medical care, and optimism.

Despite the many factors that are pressing on this profession, nursing has been and continues to be a source of great personal satisfaction for millions of individuals. When a patient leaves a hospital, it is often the help, encouragement, comfort, and kind words of a nurse that he or she takes home as a lasting image.

THE FUTURE

The recent history of employment for nurses in the U.S. has been: acute shortage, followed by a surplus, followed by another acute shortage, followed by yet another surplus. Why is the job picture for nurses so volatile?

In the late 1970s, there was a severe shortage of nurses. Job offers were plentiful, and for several years nurses' salaries rose by up to 14 percent a year.

Then, in the early 1980s, in what would be a harbinger of things to come, Diagnostic Related Groups were established and instituted. Diagnostic Related Groups (DRGs) are standards which place limits on the number of days a patient may occupy a hospital bed. The DRG philosophy is fiscal and medical. Statistically likely outcomes were applied to personal medical situations. Because a quarter of all nurses worked in hospitals at that time, one of the many side effects of DRGs was a nurse surplus; hospitals, facing the prospect of empty beds, cut or did not refill nursing jobs. Across the country, the annual rate of increase in nurses' salaries fell to 3 percent. Nursing school enrollment fell off by 30 percent, setting the state for a future shortage. By late 1987, the shortage of nurses was so acute that in January 1988, the Department of Health and Human Services of the federal government established a Federal Commission on Nursing to determine what factors were discouraging students from pursuing careers in nursing. Conditions in the workplace, salaries, competition from other professions, and educational requirements were studied. The federal government projected that by 2000 there would be a shortfall of at least a million nurses. This shortage resulted in great competition for nurses and impressive gain in nurses' salaries, with some major city hospitals sweetening their job offers with such enticements as a year's paid rent.

Today, the employment picture is again different. As nurses retire, they are not being replaced. Many nurses are being laid off. For the third year in a row, it appears that salary increases will be smaller.

What has changed in the last two or so years? Surely, the need for nursing services is as great as ever. Indeed, with an ever-growing general population; a rapidly growing elderly population, expanding technologies and techniques for nurses to apply; more people than ever being treated for and surviving traumas (burns, spinal cord injuries), diseases, and congenital conditions that until recently were thought insurmountable; and the needs of the growing number of Americans with AIDS, it would seem likely that the nurse's services would be more in demand.

Aggressive cost containment is the new and powerful factor in the patient needs/patient care equation. Part of this cost containment is in reaction to soaring medical costs during the 1980's; part is the result of the recession of the late 1980s and early 1990s. Today, the major agent of cost concerns is the health care reform movement, which holds courses of medical treatment to economic tests. For many nurses, the result of this ongoing cost containment has been unemployment. Many hospitals around the country, faced with uncertainty about future financing under health care reform, are paring their nursing staffs and relying, instead, on less qualified, unlicensed assistive personnel (UAPs), a move which many in the field fear could pose serious risks to patient care and safety. (One study found that a short-staffed hospital unit actually drove up costs because the hospital had to absorb the cost of extra patient days incurred by complications.) It should be noted that since 1985, labor costs as a percentage of total hospital expenses have declined.

What, then, is the future for LPNs and RNs? The American Nurses Association predicts that after a period of adjustment to the effects of future cost containment, the outlook for RNs should be bright. The hospital sector of the profession will continue to shrink, and more LPNs and RNs will find themselves carrying out their important duties in less expensive outpatient ambulatory settings in the community which will increase in number and scope. Remaining in hospitals will be the sickest patients, and to care for them, hospitals will need more nurse practitioners and other nurse specialists. The United States Department of Labor projects an increase of almost 40 percent in the number of RNs needed by 2005. LPNs, too, can expect a similar rate of growth in their profession. Opportunities should be particularly plentiful in nursing homes and residential care facilities. Many more men are particularly being attracted to the challenges of the clinical specialties and to the job security and relatively high pay offered by nursing. For years, men have made up 4 to 5 percent of all registered nurses, but last year they made up approximately 10 percent of all student nurses.

For more information about a career in nursing, contact the:

National Student Nurses Association
10 Columbus Circle
New York, New York 10019

National League for Nurses
350 Hudson Street
New York, New York 10014

American Nurses Association
600 Maryland Avenue S.W., Suite 100W
Washington, D.C. 20024-2571

Information is also available from the boards of nursing of the individual states:

Alabama
RSA Plaza, Suite 250
770 Washington Avenue
Montgomery, Alabama 36130-3900

Alaska
Division of Occupational Licensing
P.O. Box 110806
Juneau, Alaska 99811-0806

Arizona
2001 West Camelback Road,
   Number 350
Phoenix, Arizona 85015

Arkansas
1123 South University, Suite 800
Little Rock, Arkansas 72204

California
P.O. Box 944210
Sacramento, California 95814

Colorado
1560 Broadway,
   Suite 670
Denver, Colorado 80202

Connecticut
150 Washington Street
Hartford, Connecticut 06106

Delaware
Margaret O'Neil Building,
   Third Floor
P.O. Box 1401
Dover, Delaware 19903

District of Columbia
614 H Street, N.W., Room 904
Washington, DC 20001

Florida
111 East Coastline Drive
Jacksonville, Florida 33202

Georgia
166 Pryor Street, S.W., Suite 400
Atlanta, Georgia 30303

Guam
P.O. Box 2816
Agana, Guam 96910

Hawaii
Box 3469
Honolulu, Hawaii 96801

Idaho
280 North Eighth Street, Suite 210
Boise, Idaho 83720

Illinois
320 West Washington Street
Springfield, Illinois 62786

Indiana
402 West Washington Street,
    Room 041
Indianapolis, Indiana 46204

Iowa
1223 East Court Avenue
Des Moines, Iowa 50319

Kansas
Landon State Office Building,
    Suite 551
900 South West Jackson
Topeka, Kansas 66612

Kentucky
312 Whittington Parkway, Suite 300
Louisville, Kentucky 40222-5172

Louisiana
Pere Marquette Building, Room 907
150 Baronne Street
New Orleans, Louisiana 70112

Maine
State House Station 158
Augusta, Maine 04330

Maryland
Metro Executive Center
4201 Patterson Avenue
Baltimore, Maryland 21215-2299

Massachusetts
100 Cambridge Street,
    Room 1519
Boston, Massachusetts 02202

Michigan
905 Southland
P.O. Box 30018
Lansing, Michigan 48909

Minnesota
2700 University Avenue West,
    Room 108
Saint Paul, Minnesota 55114

Mississippi
239 North Lamar Street,
    Suite 401
Jackson, Mississippi 39201

Missouri
P.O. Box 656
Jefferson City, Missouri 65102

Montana
P.O. Box 200513
Helena, Montana 59620-0513

Nebraska
State House Station
Box 95007
Lincoln, Nebraska 68509

Nevada
1281 Terminal Way, Suite 116
Reno, Nevada 89502

New Hampshire
6 Hazen Drive
Concord, New Hampshire
   03301-6527

New Jersey
P.O. Box 45010
Newark, New Jersey 07101

New Mexico
4206 Louisiana N.E., Suite A
Albuquerque, New Mexico 87109

New York
The Cultural Education Center
Room 3013
Albany, New York 12230

North Carolina
P.O. Box 2129
Releigh, North Carolina 27602 2129

North Dakota
919 South Seventh Street, Suite 504
Bismarck, North Dakota 58504-5881

Ohio
77 South High Street, 17th Floor
Columbus, Ohio 43266-0316

Oklahoma
2915 North Classen Boulevard
Suite 524
Oklahoma City, Oklahoma 73106

Oregon
800 N.E. Oregon Street, Suite 25
Portland, Oregon 97232

Pennsylvania
P.O. Box 2649
Harrisburg, Pennsylvania 17105-2649

Puerto Rico
Call Box 10200
Santurce, Puerto Rico 00908-0200

Rhode Island
Cannon Health Building, Room 104
3 Capitol Hill
Providence, Rhode Island 02908-5097

South Carolina
220 Executive Center Drive, Suite 220
Columbia, South Carolina 29210

South Dakota
3307 South Lincoln Avenue
Sioux Falls, South Dakota
   57102-5224

Tennessee
283 Plus Park Boulevard
Nashville, Tennessee 37247-1010

Texas
Box 140466
Austin, Texas 78714

Utah
Heber M. Wells Building
P.O. Box 45805
Salt Lake City, Utah 84145-0805

Vermont
109 State Street
Montpelier, Vermont 05609-1106

Virgin Islands
P.O. Box 4247, St. Thomas
U.S. Virgin Islands, 00803

Virginia
6606 West Broad Street, 4th Floor
Richmond, Virginia 23230-1717

Washington
P.O. Box 47864
Olympia, Washington 98504-7864

West Virginia
101 Dee Drive
Charleston, West Virginia
    25311-1620

Wisconsin
P.O. Box 8935
Madison, Wisconsin 53708-8935

Wyoming
Barrett Building
2301 Central Avenue
Cheyenne, Wyoming 82202

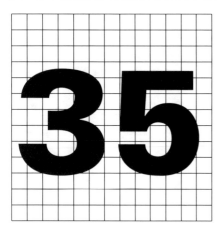

NURSE-MIDWIFE

The word "midwife" comes from Old English and means "with woman." Today's nurse-midwife is a health care professional who, in addition to being a registered nurse, has successfully completed an accredited program of study and clinical experience in obstetrics (the branch of medicine concerned with the care and treatment of women during pregnancy, childbirth, and the period immediately following), which qualify the nurse-midwife to provide professional health care to women and their babies throughout pregnancy, labor, delivery, and after birth. Nurse-midwives care for women who, after careful screening, appear likely to have uncomplicated deliveries. Patients with certain health problems and those with a history of complicated births are handled solely by a physician or in collaboration with a physician. Nurse-midwives maintain a consultative affiliation with physicians and other health care professionals so that this additional medical assistance is readily available when needed.

Although midwifery is as old as maternity, specially educated and trained nurse-midwives are relatively new members of the professional health care team. After World War I, the national trend was away from home midwife-attended births and toward in-hospital deliveries attended by an obstetrician. In recent years, although there has been only a slight increase in the number of home deliveries (99 out of every 100 American babies are born in a hospital), there has been substantial renewed interest in the use of nurse-midwives in normal deliveries.

The number of in-hospital attended births by certified nurse-midwives (these are nurse-midwives who have satisfied the educational and examination requirements of the American College of Nurse-Midwives) has grown from 20,000 in 1975 to approximately 175,000 in 1993 (that is almost 5 percent of all U.S. births), and this dramatic increase is expected to continue.

The reasons for this revival range from the practical to the philosophical. Many prospective mothers believe nurse-midwives provide more personal care during pregnancy, labor, and delivery than do busy obstetricians. Also, the nurse-midwives' philosophy of prepared, and preferably drug-free, natural childbirth is appealing to many women. Nurse-midwife-attended deliveries often take place at home, in hospital birthing rooms, or in birthing centers, and these noninstitutional, homey settings are, for many women, an appealing alternative to a hospital delivery room.

In 1993, 94 percent of all deliveries attended by certified nurse-midwives took place in hospitals, another 3 percent took place in birthing centers, less than 1 percent took place in clinics or doctors' offices, and 2 percent were at-home births. In addition, nurse-midwives promote family-centered childbirth—that is, the presence and participation in the birth not only of spouses but of other relatives, children, and friends is encouraged, and, in most cases, such a birthing experience is available only with a nurse-midwife attending. Cost is also a factor: midwife-attended births cost less.

An indication of the building interest in and acceptance of nurse-midwife care is the continuing trend toward state legislation requiring insurance coverage to be extended to include maternity care provided by certified nurse-midwives working under the guidance of a doctor and in conjunction with a hospital or clinic. At this time, 24 states have enacted such legislation. In addition, as of 1987 both Medicare and Medicaid coverage apply.

The prenatal (before birth) care a nurse-midwife typically provides includes performing physical examinations of the pregnant woman (including breast, abdominal, and pelvic examinations) and regularly monitoring the progress of the pregnancy. The nurse-midwife also educates the prospective mother regarding nutrition; exercise during pregnancy, labor, and after the baby's birth; parent-infant bonding; child care; breastfeeding; bottle feeding; preparing for the newborn; and family adjustment to the new addition. The nurse-midwife teaches and counsels the mother-to-be about preparation for labor and delivery. The woman and her spouse (or support person) are encouraged to read about childbirth and attend childbirth classes, and, prior to delivery, the nurse-midwife will discuss with them a plan of care during birthing that will accommodate their needs and desires.

Throughout labor and delivery, the nurse-midwife stays with the woman, providing emotional support and comfort measures and supervising and evaluating the progress of the labor. Should pain-relieving medications be required, the nurse-midwife may prescribe and administer them. The nurse-midwife performs the delivery of the baby and is responsible for all related procedures. Nurse-midwives do not, however, perform cesarean section deliveries. Should such a surgical situation suddenly develop, an obstetrician is called in immediately.

Immediately after delivery, the nurse-midwife examines and evaluates the condition of the newborn and provides care, including resuscitation, if needed. The nurse-midwife then provides follow-up care for mother and baby and assists the new mother with self-care, breast or bottle feeding, and infant care.

In addition, nurse-midwives perform routine gynecological checkups for nonpregnant patients and prescribe and provide various methods of contraception.

SETTINGS, SALARIES, STATISTICS

Nurse-midwives work in private practices, university teaching hospitals, and city hospitals (in their regular maternity sections and, in some cases, in specially outfitted birthing rooms), in rural outreach centers, group health maintenance organizations, the military, family planning centers, on native American reservations, in public health facilities, alternative birth centers, and, if certain criteria are met, in patients' homes. While the important contribution nurse-midwives have made in bringing professional health care to countless mothers and babies in rural America cannot be overstated, in fact, an even greater percentage of inner city women (33.7 percent) and suburban women (25.4 percent) are served by nurse-midwives.

Currently, there are approximately 4,200 certified nurse-midwives practicing in the United States. This profession is dominated by women, but the American College of Nurse-Midwives records approximately 50 male nurse-midwives among its members. It should be noted here that in addition to the 4,200 certified nurse-midwives, there is an unknown number of non-certified midwives who attend home deliveries (mostly in rural settings), many of whom have no formal training. To practice professionally, however, specific educational requirements must be met, and certification by the American College of Nurse-Midwives is generally required to obtain a state license to practice.

Salaries for certified nurse-midwives depend on practice setting and geographic location. In 1994, the mean annual salary for certified nurse-midwives in clinical practice was $55,000. Certified nurse-midwives who serve lower socioeconomic and poor rural populations do not earn as much, unless they work for a federally supported program. States where certified nurse-midwives typically earn the highest salaries include Alaska, California, New York, Pennsylvania, and Florida. In these states, some practitioners earn as much as $70,000 annually.

Nurse-midwives tend to work erratic, long hours. Most have regular office hours, patient rounds, and then are on call. And because babies are born at all hours, late-night, all-night, weekend, and holiday deliveries are routine.

HOW TO BECOME A NURSE-MIDWIFE

Certified nurse-midwives are educated in both nursing and midwifery. To become a certified nurse-midwife you must first be a registered nurse. Several education courses may be followed—certificate, master's degree, or combined RN/master's degree—all of which can lead to certification as a nurse-midwife.

A certificate program entails 9 to 12 months of intensive study and clinical experience. To qualify for a certificate program, one must currently be licensed as a registered nurse in the United States or in one of the U.S. territories.

The master's degree nurse-midwife programs are usually 16 to 24 months long and lead to a certificate in nurse-midwifery plus a master's degree. To enter these programs, one must be a currently licensed registered nurse and have a B.S. in nursing.

The third route, that is, the combined RN/master's degree program for non-nurses, requires a bachelor's degree. Combined programs typically require three years of education and training. The first intense 12 months are dedicated to nursing education, after which a candidate may sit for the RN examination. After passing this examination, the candidate then chooses a specialty, and, if that specialty is nurse-midwifery, she or he enters a nurse-midwife master's degree program.

Among the courses in a typical nurse-midwife educational program are antepartum care, intrapartum care, postpartum care, contraceptive gynecology, and childbirth education.

Most schools consider it advisable for applicants to have some clinical experience in obstetrical nursing prior to enrollment in a nurse-midwife educational program. At this time, there are 39 nurse-midwife programs that are approved by the American College of Nurse-Midwives. These programs admit small numbers of students annually, and competition for admission is strong.

Nurse-midwife educational programs attract students of all ages. While many students are in their twenties and thirties, people in their forties and fifties are regularly embarking on nurse-midwife educations, suggesting that nurse-midwifery is an appealing second career for many.

Personal prerequisites important for success and satisfaction as a nurse-midwife include good health, sensitivity, humaneness, assertiveness, decisiveness, integrity, and, perhaps, a special sense of joy. Nurse-midwives do very special work.

All graduates of nurse-midwife educational programs approved by the American College of Nurse-Midwives are eligible to take the national certification examination given by the ACNM. Upon passing this examination, an individual is entitled to use the initials CNM after her or his name.

All states recognize the legality of certified nurse-midwife practice, and most accept certification by the American College of Nurse-Midwives as the standard for licensing nurse-midwives.

THE FUTURE

The outlook for nurse-midwives is excellent. The American College of Nurse-Midwives predicts the need for at least 6,000 additional nurse-midwives by the year 2001. Interest in nurse-midwifery education is burgeoning. In 1993, ACNM accredited programs produced more than twice as many graduates as they did just three years before, in 1990. More and more prospective mothers see their pregnancies and deliveries not as infirmities requiring doctors, hospitals, and days of confinement but as natural events for which less medical intervention and more emotional and educational support is preferable. They are seeking birthing experiences that include family, care that is more personal, and birthing settings that are less institutional. Increasingly, pregnant women are choosing the nurse-midwife alternative because they see nurse-midwives as being providers not only of the type of physical care they want but also of the physical setting and overall philosophy they desire. Lower costs and the trend toward insurance reimbursement further enhance the nurse-midwife alternative and the outlook for it. Today, up to 70 percent of the care provided by certified nurse-midwives is to women from traditionally underserved communities. Well over half of the women and infants seen by CNMs have their care paid for by government sources through Medicaid, Medicare, or the Indian Health Service—more than twice the percentage seen by obstetricians. Because of the high quality of the care they provide and the lower cost of their services, and because both of these features have long and well-documented histories, it is probable that nurse-midwives will find that their profession plays prominently in health care under future reform.

For more information on nurse-midwives, including a list of accredited educational programs, write to:

> The American College of Nurse-Midwives
> 818 Connecticut Avenue N.W., Suite 900
> Washington, D.C. 20006

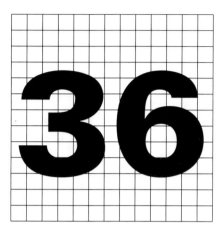

NURSING AIDE AND PSYCHIATRIC AIDE

also known as
Nurse's Aide
Nursing Assistant
Orderly
Hospital Attendant
Auxiliary Nursing Worker
Geriatric Aide
Psychiatric Nursing Assistant
Ward Attendant

Paradoxically, although nursing aides and psychiatric aides often are at the bottom of the health care personnel hierarchy in the hospitals and other institutions in which they are employed (working under the doctors, registered nurses, and licensed practical nurses; earning the least; performing almost of all of the routine patient care), they are very often the health care givers who matter the most to patients. Working under the supervision of RNs and LPNs, *nursing aides* and *psychiatric aides* feed, bathe, dress, help out of bed, and walk patients who need assistance; serve meals; take temperature and pulse readings; make beds; give massages; deliver messages; empty bed pans; provide important skin care to patients confined to bed for extended periods; escort patients to and from operating, examining, and treatment rooms; and respond when patients buzz for help. In short, aides deliver much of the human touch care that comforts and calms a patient. Nursing aides perform these duties for patients who are physically ill or disabled. Their responsibilities are much the same as those of home care aides. Psychiatric aides perform these duties for patients who are mentally impaired or emotionally disturbed. Because of their patient population, psychiatric aides must sometimes restrain violent patients.

Most nursing aides and psychiatric aides work in settings that provide long-term care. Almost half of all nursing aides work in nursing homes, where they may have contact with a patient for months or years. In nursing homes, aides are the principal care givers, and often a warm bond develops between patient and aide. The very nature of inpatient psychiatric treatment entails extended hospitalization, so psychiatric aides, too, often establish ongoing relationships with the patients they daily help. In both cases, because aides have so much close contact with a patient over what is often a prolonged period of time, they are in an important position to affect the patient's attitude, communicate to and for the patient to the rest of the health care staff, and monitor the patient's progress.

SETTINGS, SALARIES, STATISTICS

Almost 50 percent of all nursing aides are employed by nursing homes (where they are sometimes called geriatric aides). Another 25 percent of all nursing aides work in general hospitals. Opportunities also exist in special hospitals and long-term care facilities.

Over 90 percent of all psychiatric aides work in hospitals (state and county facilities, on the psychiatric floors of general hospitals, private psychiatric hospitals, community mental health centers, residential facilities for the mentally retarded, and in alcohol and drug rehabilitation facilities). Three percent work in nursing homes.

There are approximately 1,300,000 nursing aides employed in the United States at this time. There are approximately 100,000 psychiatric aides.

Salaries are not high. In 1993 they ranged from $9,200 annually for full-time aides to $26,800, with the median income somewhere around $13,500. Department of Veterans Affairs hospitals and nursing homes tend to pay slightly less than general hospitals. The mounting shortage of aides is expected to improve salaries.

A forty-hour workweek is typical. Evening, night, weekend, and holiday hours are rotated in.

HOW TO BECOME A NURSING AIDE OR PSYCHIATRIC AIDE

Educational and training requirements for employment are minimal. Some employers (especially nursing homes) require neither a high school diploma nor prior experience. Proficiency in English is not always necessary. Because the prerequisites are few, being an aide is a very accessible occupation for many individuals who want to be part of a health care community. Some aides go on to seek the additional education necessary for higher professional responsibility as LPNs or RNs. Most hospitals, however, require aides to have at least one year of experience. Often this experience is as a home care aide (see Chapter 25).

Until recently, most aides' education and training were provided on the job by employers. This preparation typically lasted six weeks to three months. In recent years, however, efforts to upgrade and standardize nursing and psychiatric aide education have resulted in the passage by half of the states of laws or regulations requiring aides to successfully complete approved training courses either before starting to work or within a specific period of time after being hired. Nursing aide training programs are offered by community colleges, vocational-technical schools, nursing homes, and hospitals. Anatomy, physiology, infection control, nutrition, and communication skills are taught. There is, however, significant latitude in the length and depth of these courses from state to state. Aides who successfully complete state-mandated programs are awarded certificates.

Once on the job, a new aide is given an orientation which may last from one week to several months.

Important personal prerequisites for this work include dependability, patience, tact, emotional stability, and physical strength.

THE FUTURE

For nursing aides, the employment forecast is excellent. Four hundred thousand new jobs for nursing aides should open up between now and 2005, according to the U.S. Department of Labor, which ranks nursing aides as the tenth fastest growing occupation requiring a high school diploma or less in the coming decade. Salaries should increase as well. Many of the reasons for this growth are the same as those that are spurring demand for more home care aides and many other types of direct care givers: our population is growing, it is growing older, and long-term care facilities and programs for the chronically ill are expanding. Specifically, employment opportunities for nursing aides should increase in nursing homes and other long-term care facilities and decrease in general hospitals which, increasingly, are focusing only on the seriously ill who require high-technology medical care.

The employment picture for psychiatric aides is not quite as bright. Cost constraints and a continuation of the thirty-year trend toward the deinstitutionalization of all but the most serious patients will result in lower-than-average growth in public mental hospital settings; but in private psychiatric facilities, the rapidly growing elderly population and ever-expanding treatment options should create employment opportunities in the coming decade.

For more information about nursing aides and psychiatric aides, write to the:

American Hospital Association,
   Division of Nursing
840 North Lake Shore Drive
Chicago, Illinois 60611

American Health Care Association
1201 L Street N.W.
Washington, D.C. 20005

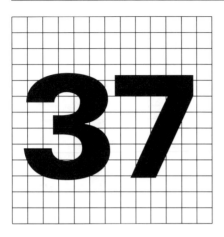

OCCUPATIONAL THERAPIST AND OCCUPATIONAL THERAPY ASSISTANT

The "occupation" in occupational therapy means "purposeful activity." Occupational therapy is the art and science of employing various educational, vocational, and rehabilitational activities for the purpose of improving the mental abilities, physical abilities, and general health of individuals suffering from developmental deficits, physical injuries or illnesses, psychological or social disabilities, the aging process, poverty and culture differences, or other conditions that threaten or impair their ability to cope with the tasks of living. Occupational therapy is the process of analyzing patients' potentials and limitations and then selecting and implementing specific activities that teach their minds and their bodies how to maximize their potentials and to minimize their limitations so that they may function more effectively and happily. The goal of occupational therapy is improvement. Whether this improvement is the acquisition of skills never before attained, the restoration of abilities lost to injury or illness, adaptation to permanent limitations, or the alleviation of pain, the objective is to help the patient attain his or her highest functional level.

Carrying out this important work are occupational therapists and occupational therapy assistants.

Occupational therapists are educated in the origin, progression, management, and prognosis of congenital and developmental impairments and deficits; diseases; and physical, emotional, and environmental stresses and traumas. They know how to recognize and identify manifestations and symptoms of wellness and illness in their patients (or clients). They work with physicians, physical therapists, vocational counselors, and other professionals in evaluating patients and developing short- and long-term goals for them. In planning an occupational therapy program, therapists consider the patient's physical capacity, developmental level, intelligence, and interests.

Because they are tailor-made to treat the patient's specific disability problems, occupational therapy's purposeful activities are as numerous and diverse as there are physical, mental, and social limitations. Occupational therapists may conduct programs designed to improve sitting and standing tolerances for patients with chronic pain; teach muscle reeducation to persons who have experienced strokes and others with neurological disabilities; monitor the heart rates and energy requirements of heart patients as they practice self-care or homemaking activities; make home evaluations to recommend modifications that will maximize the patient's function and safety at home; design and construct splints and other orthoses for injury and surgery patients; adapt daily activities for persons who need to develop skill using one hand; evaluate the developmental levels of high-risk infants and plan treatment programs to ensure their healthy growth; initiate group and individual treatment activities designed to help clients in mental health centers to learn personal and social behavior skills, to become more independent in daily life and more effective in interacting with others; teach compensatory skills to patients with perceptual deficits; help injured workers return to the job or adapt the work environment to compensate for disabling conditions; and conduct community living skills programs that prepare recovering patients for their return to the community.

There are constant innovations in the field of occupational therapy. In some institutions there are occupational therapy apartments where patients with physical impairments learn adaptive methods of cooking and other home responsibilities and where the patient and his or her family may have an overnight trial living experience prior to hospital discharge. To determine if a patient has the potential for on-the-road driving, a sophisticated driving simulator, which assesses selected component skills, may be used. Over a thousand occupational therapists around the country and a thousand volunteer magicians have joined forces in a special rehabilitation program call Project Magic. This program, which was begun by magician David Copperfield and inaugurated at Daniel Freeman Memorial Hospital, in Inglewood, California, teaches persons with disabilities how to perform magic tricks as a method of achieving improvement of gross motor skills, fine motor skills, problem-solving abilities, perception, higher cognitive skills, and psychosocial abilities. Project Magic not only works the patient's hands and minds, it gives the person with a disability a skill that most people do not have. The patient, in turn, teaches his or her magic tricks to a non-patient. Both the learning of a unique and entertaining skill and the teaching role do much to enhance the patient's self-esteem.

Many occupational therapists specialize, working with patients of a certain age group (children, the elderly) or having a certain disability. Three out of five occupational therapists work primarily with persons who have physical disabilities.

SETTINGS, SALARIES, STATISTICS

Occupational therapists serve a wide population in a wide variety of settings. Forty percent work in hospitals, and fifteen percent work in nursing homes. Opportunities also exist in schools for children and adults who have physical and mental disabilities, community mental health centers, special camps, clinics, retirement communities, senior citizen centers, rehabilitation centers, and home care programs. Occupational therapy is a career offering many part-time work arrangements. Some occupational therapists who have graduate degrees carry out research and/or teach.

Most occupational therapists work standard forty-hour weeks. Depending on the setting, evening and weekend hours may be required.

There are approximately 40,000 occupational therapists currently practicing. Earning potential for occupational therapists is very good. Salaries vary with type of employer, experience, and geographical location. Entry-level salaries range between $30,000 and $36,500 per year, and experienced occupational therapists earn between $36,500 and $43,000 annually. Occupational therapists who are in supervisory and administrative positions may earn salaries as high as $50,500 per year.

Advancement for occupational therapists usually comes in the form of promotion from staff therapist to senior therapist or specialized practitioner. Some therapists advance further, to supervisory or administrative positions in occupational therapy programs, and other experienced occupational therapists become teachers and/or researchers in occupational therapy.

HOW TO BECOME AN OCCUPATIONAL THERAPIST

To become an occupational therapist, a student must graduate from one of the many occupational therapy educational programs offered by colleges and universities throughout the United States. Approximately 66 institutions offer educational programs that are accredited by the American Occupational Therapy Association. Master's degree or certificate programs are for students who already have a baccalaureate degree. Other programs offer a four-year baccalaureate degree (bachelor of science, bachelor of arts, or bachelor of science in occupational therapy). Some programs admit students for a four-year occupational therapy curriculum. Others require two years of liberal arts and science courses, prior to admittance to an occupational therapy curriculum for the junior and senior years.

Graduate study (which is often required for teaching, research, and administrative positions in this field) is offered both to students with undergraduate degrees in occupational therapy (they may earn a master's in occupational therapy, or MOT) and to students who have undergraduate degrees in majors other than occupational therapy (who may enter programs leading to a certificate or to an MOT).

Occupational therapy students learn about the structure and function of the human body and human systems; the structure and function of human personality and cognition; the human growth process; social-cultural systems and the interrelationship with individual development functioning; developmental tasks and needs in each period of life from birth to death; the development of human relationships, roles, and values; the impact of nonhuman environment on normal growth and development; the meaning of activity in development of human potential and competency; the meaning and impact of symbols and the symbolization process throughout the life cycle; and the concepts and modes of adaptation and their relationship to performance. They are taught how to observe, identify, and analyze tasks and activities performed by others and to relate the elements of these tasks to age, psychological, perceptual-motor, cognitive, physical, social, cultural, and economic-specific needs, capabilities, and roles.

Specifically, an accredited curriculum typically includes courses that cover anatomy, neuroanatomy, physiology, pathology, neurophysiology, kinesiology (the science and study of human muscular movements), general psychology, educational psychology, sociology, anthropology, group psychology, social psychology, developmental psychology, psychoanalytic theory, neurobehavioral science, psychobiology, pediatrics, gerontology (the study of the aged), human relations, fine and applied arts, home economics, industrial and manual arts, self-care activities, physical education and recreation, vocational rehabilitation, public health, communication theory and principles, teaching/learning theory, and community resources.

Students are also required to spend six to nine months in a hospital, health agency, school, or other setting gaining experience in clinical practice.

Last year, approximately 3,000 men and women graduated from accredited occupational therapy educational programs.

In high school, interested students should take courses in biology, chemistry, health, art, and social studies. Admission to occupational therapy educational programs is highly competitive. A minimum grade of *B* in the science courses in usually necessary.

Personal qualifications for success and satisfaction in this career include patience, imagination, maturity, tact, stamina, manual and teaching skills, and a genuine love of people. Very important, too, is a balance of objectivity and empathy, professionalism and compassion. As with physical therapy and the creative arts therapies, occupational therapy is a career that provides almost constant patient contact and the opportunity to contribute to and follow the progress of patients over an extended period of time. The potential for deep personal satisfaction in this profession is great.

Graduates of accredited occupational therapy educational programs are eligible to sit for the certification examination administered by the American Occupational Therapy Certification Board. Upon passing this examination, a candidate becomes a registered occupational therapist and may use the designation OTR after his or her name. The vast majority of states regulate the practice of occupational therapy, most by licensure. Applicants for licensure must have a degree or certificate from an accredited educational program and satisfy the requirements of the state's licensing program. Successful completion of the American Occupational Therapy Association's certification examination satisfies the licensing requirements.

THE FUTURE

The employment outlook for occupational therapists is extremely favorable. Currently, there is a shortage of occupational therapists, and the growing number of older Americans (who may particularly need the special services of an occupational therapist) and the ever-expanding application of occupational therapy to various disabilities should contribute significantly to an increase in demand. Indeed, according to the U.S. Department of Labor's employment projections, for the next ten or so years, occupational therapy will be the sixth fastest-growing occupation for college graduates, with as many as 16,000 new jobs created.

For more information about occupational therapists, contact the

American Occupational Therapy Association
1383 Piccard Drive
Rockville, Maryland 20849-1725

OCCUPATIONAL THERAPY ASSISTANT

The approximately 10,000 *occupational therapy assistants* in the United States work under the supervision of occupational therapists and perform much of the routine work that an occupational therapy program entails. Like occupational therapists, they select and construct equipment that helps patients function more independently; they help plan and implement treatment activities for individuals and groups of patients; and, under supervision, they perform most of the other functions inherent to occupational therapy. Occupational therapy assistants may also be expected to order, prepare, and lay out materials and maintain equipment.

Occupational therapy assistants work in the same settings as occupational therapists. Openings for occupational therapy assistants are particularly prevalent in nursing homes and mental health facilities. Annual starting salaries for occupational therapy assistants range between $18,500 and $23,500. With experience and the assumption of greater responsibility, an occupational therapy assistant may earn $24,500 to $28,000 per year.

There are two routes to the preparation necessary to work as an occupational therapy assistant: two-year associate's degree programs that are offered by community colleges (the majority of programs) and one-year, nondegree certificate programs offered by vocational and technical schools.

Occupational therapy assistant educational programs are accredited by the American Occupational Therapy Association. The curriculum typically includes classroom study of the history and philosophy of occupational therapy; occupational therapy theory and skills; and human anatomy, physiology, and development. There is also supervised practical experience lasting several months. A high school diploma or its equivalent is required for admission to an occupational therapy assistant educational program. In high school, classes in health, the sciences, and arts and crafts are useful.

Graduates of approved occupational therapy assistant educational programs are eligible to sit for a certification examination administered by the American Occupational Therapy Certification Board. Assistants who pass this examination are designated certified occupational therapy assistants, and they may use the abbreviation COTA after their names. The employment picture for occupational therapy assistants (and especially for COTAs) should be favorable.

For more information about occupational therapy assistants, write to the:

American Occupational Therapy Association
1383 Piccard Drive
Rockville, Maryland 20849-1725

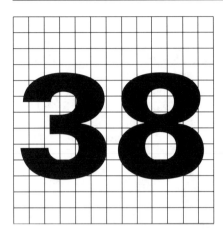

OPHTHALMIC LABORATORY TECHNICIAN

also known as
Optical Mechanic
Optical Goods Worker
Manufacturing Optician

Ophthalmic laboratory technicians fabricate eyeglasses. Working from specifications written by the customer's ophthalmologist (eye doctor), optometrist (licensed, nonmedical eye practitioner), and/or optician, the technician cuts, grinds, and finishes the prescription lenses and then assembles them in the frames selected by the customer. The process begins with standard lens blanks that are ground and polished to meet the specifications of the prescription. The ground lenses are then cut to fit the frames, their edges are smoothed, and they are inserted into the frames. In smaller ophthalmic laboratories, the same technician may perform all of these procedures. In larger laboratories, these processes may be broken down, and technicians may specialize. There will be surfacers who grind the lenses and bench technicians who finish the glasses. In some laboratories, these two functions are further specialized.

SETTINGS, SALARIES, STATISTICS

Ophthalmic laboratory technicians work in ophthalmic laboratories, in the offices of ophthalmologists and optometrists who dispense glasses directly to patients, and in opticians' shops and other retail outlets that sell eyewear (department stores, drugstores). Some ophthalmic laboratory technicians own their own laboratories. Most job opportunities in this field are in or near large cities. The workweek is typically forty hours long, much of which is spent standing. Part-time positions in this field exist.

There are approximately 31,000 ophthalmic laboratory technicians employed at this time. The majority of them are men. The average starting salary for ophthalmic laboratory technicians is approximately $18,500 per year. Some technicians earn as much as $28,000 annually.

HOW TO BECOME AN OPHTHALMIC LABORATORY TECHNICIAN

Several formal and informal education and training options exist for students interested in this field. Most ophthalmic laboratory technicians learn their skills on the job in small and medium-size laboratories. Students learn procedures gradually, and it usually takes about three years before a student has the experience and expertise to work as an all-around technician. A high school diploma is usually required for on-the-job training.

Of the formal educational routes, many optical goods companies offer three- to four-year formal apprenticeships in optical technology. Students who have superior ability may progress through an apprenticeship in less time. These programs are considered an excellent method of preparation. A high school diploma is almost always required for acceptance into an apprenticeship. Also, many community colleges around the country offer two-year associate's degree programs in optic technology (a high school diploma is usually necessary), and many vocational/technical institutes and trade schools offer shorter certificate or diploma programs in this field (a high school diploma is also necessary). Students who learn their skills in these shorter programs usually need additional on-the-job training.

In high school, students interested in ophthalmic laboratory technology should take courses in physics, algebra, geometry, and mechanical drawing.

Abilities and personal qualities that are important to effective performance in optical technology include good or good corrected vision, manual dexterity, and an appreciation for precision.

THE FUTURE

Job opportunities in this field should be only average. Our increasing population and, especially, our increasing elderly population should place greater demands on vision care services. Also, public awareness of the importance of proper eye care and vision correction is greater than ever before. And the public today is more able to pay for vision care, thanks largely to more widespread insurance coverage. Simultaneously, however, automation and computerization of ophthalmic laboratory procedures threaten technicians' jobs. The computerized grinding and polishing machines that many laboratories now use can mass produce more lenses faster, and this productivity is reducing the demand for personnel.

For more information about ophthalmic laboratory technicians, contact the:

National Association of Manufacturing Opticians
13140 Coit Road
Dallas, Texas 75240

Commission on Opticianry Accreditation
10111 Martin Luther King Jr. Highway, Suite 110
Bowie, Maryland 20720-4299

National Academy of Opticianry
10111 Martin Luther King Jr. Highway, Suite 112
Bowie, Maryland 20720-4299

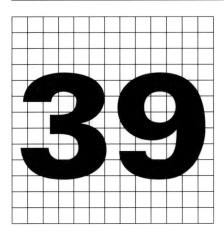

OPHTHALMIC MEDICAL PERSONNEL

including
Ophthalmic Medical Assistant
Ophthalmic Technician
Ophthalmic Technologist

An ophthalmologist is a physician who treats eye defects, diseases, and injuries. Ophthalmologists prescribe medications, perform eye surgery, and provide other types of treatment (including the fitting of contact lenses). *Ophthalmic medical assistants*, *ophthalmic technicians,* and *ophthalmic technologists* are skilled persons qualified by academic and clinical training to render support services to ophthalmologists. Working under the supervision, direction, and responsibility of the ophthalmologist, they carry out various diagnostic and therapeutic procedures inherent to the practice of ophthalmology. They are always dependent practitioners.

Depending on the worker's experience and level of education, the specific functions may include taking the patient's medical history; administering diagnostic tests; making anatomical and functional ocular measurements; testing visual acuity, visual fields, and sensorimotor function; administering topical ophthalmic medication; instructing the patient about home care and the use of contact lenses; care and maintenance of optical instruments; care, maintenance, and sterilization of surgical instruments; maintenance of ophthalmological office equipment; assisting in ophthalmic surgery in the ophthalmologist's office or in the hospital; making optical measurements; administering orthoptic procedures; performing ocular electroneurological procedures; assisting in the fitting of contact lenses; fitting, adjusting, and making simple repairs on glasses; and clinical photography.

The term *ophthalmic medical personnel* actually represents three levels of skill and preparation. An *ophthalmic medical assistant* is qualified by education and training to perform the entire range of tasks required to provide continuous assistance to the physician. Ophthalmic medical assistants typically take detailed medical histories, administer eye drops, change dressings, and give simple vision tests. An *ophthalmic technician* is qualified to do everything an ophthalmic medical assistant can do, only in greater detail, plus certain special, more complex tasks. An *ophthalmic technologist* has the most education and assists the ophthalmologist in advanced areas of microbiology, advanced color vision, ophthalmic photography, and surgery, using the most sophisticated instruments and diagnostic techniques.

SETTINGS, SALARIES, STATISTICS

Ophthalmic medical personnel may be involved with patients of an ophthalmologist in any setting for which the ophthalmologist is responsible. Most ophthalmic medical assistants, technicians, and technologists work in ophthalmologists' offices. Opportunities also exist in hospitals, clinics, medical centers, and in research settings. The workweek is usually forty hours long, and those hours tend to be predictable. There are approximately 13,000 certified ophthalmic medical assistants, technicians, and technologists in the United States.

Starting salaries in these fields range between $14,000 and $25,000, with assistants earning the least and technologists earning the most.

HOW TO BECOME AN OPHTHALMIC MEDICAL ASSISTANT, TECHNICIAN, TECHNOLOGIST

There are 24 educational programs in the United States and Canada for ophthalmic medical personnel. These programs are located in universities, colleges, and hospitals. All of these programs require a high school diploma. Two years of college and experience working with the public are useful, however. For many years, the accrediting body for these programs was the American Medical Association's Committee on Allied Health Education Accreditation (CAHEA). However, since July 1, 1994, accreditation of educational programs in this, and 21 other allied health professions formerly accredited by CAHEA, is granted by CAHEA's successor, the Commission for the Accreditation of Allied Health Education Programs (CAAHEP). (CAAHEP is an independent body in which the AMA participates as one sponsor among many.) Eleven of these programs for ophthalmic medical personnel are accredited at this time.

An ophthalmic technology curriculum typically covers anatomy and physiology, medical terminology, medical law and ethics, psychology, ocular (eye) anatomy and physiology, ophthalmic optics, microbiology, ophthalmic pharmacology and toxicology, ocular motility, diseases of the eye, and diagnostic and treatment procedures (including ophthalmic surgery, contact lens fitting, visual field testing, care and maintenance of ophthalmic instruments and equipment). Supervised clinical practice is also part of the program of instruction.

Personal qualifications for a career in ophthalmic medical work include good vision, manual dexterity, good communication skills, maturity, common sense, and concern for accuracy and neatness. In addition, ophthalmic medical personnel have a lot of patient contact, so they must enjoy working with and helping a wide variety of people.

Certification in this field is available through the Joint Commission on Allied Health Personnel in Ophthalmology. Although voluntary, certification has become an important credential documenting competence. Certification is awarded upon successful completion of a written examination plus a practical test at the technician and technologist levels. To qualify for the written examination, candidates must fulfill a basic educational requirement and a work experience requirement.

THE FUTURE

The employment outlook for ophthalmic medical personnel is very favorable. At present, there are more positions available than there are applicants to fill them. Older individuals are traditionally major consumers of ophthalmic care, and as "the graying of America" (the bulge in the over-sixty-five population anticipated in the coming four decades) continues, the demand for ophthalmic medical personnel should increase. Individuals with the best academic credentials will have the widest range of opportunities.

For more information about careers in ophthalmic medical assisting and technology, write to the:

> Joint Commission on Allied Health Personnel
>   in Ophthalmology
> 2025 Woodlane Drive
> St. Paul, Minnesota 55125-2995

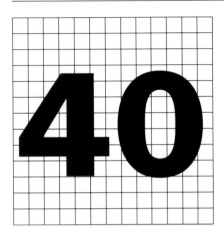

OPTICIAN

also known as
Dispensing Optician

An *optician* fits, adjusts, and dispenses glasses and other optical devices on the written prescription of an ophthalmologist or optometrist. The optician interprets the prescription, assists the customer in the selection of frames that complement facial features and hairstyle and that can accommodate the thickness and weight of the lenses prescribed, and measures the distance between the centers of the customer's pupils to determine where the lenses should be positioned in relation to them. The optician then writes the orders (containing the lens prescription, lens size, frame style, and lens tint) from which an ophthalmic laboratory technician will work. When the glasses are ready, the optician adjusts them with optical pliers, files, and screwdrivers so that they fit comfortably and properly.

In some states, opticians may also fit contact lenses, a process that is more demanding than fitting conventional glasses. Again, the optician works from a prescription written by the customer's ophthalmologist or optometrist. He or she will examine and measure the customer's corneas and then write specific orders from which the contact lens manufacturer will work. After the lenses are made, the optician teaches the customer how to insert, remove, and care for them.

Some opticians specialize in the fitting of optic prostheses (artificial eyes) or cosmetic shells that conceal defects in the appearance of the eye.

SETTINGS, SALARIES, STATISTICS

Opticians work in retail optical stores, ophthalmologists' and optometrists' offices, and in hospital eye clinics. Many opticians open their own retail optical shops. The average workweek is 45 hours long. If the optician works in a retail situation, Saturday and evening hours may be expected. Part-time positions in this field are available.

There are approximately 65,000 opticians working in the United States at this time.

Starting salaries range from $20,000 to $27,000 annually. Experienced opticians who own and operate their own shops earn an average of $40,000 per year, and many earn far more.

HOW TO BECOME AN OPTICIAN

Most opticians learn their skills on the job, a process that may last up to four years and that typically includes instruction in optical mathematics, optical physics, the use of precision measuring instruments and other optical apparati, sales, and office management. In small establishments, this training may be conducted informally. In large optometric dispensing companies, the on-the-job training is usually a structured apprenticeship lasting from two to four years. To prepare for such on-the-job training, applicants usually need a high school diploma. In high school, student should take courses in physics, algebra, geometry, and mechanical drawing.

Approximately 20 community colleges in the country offer two-year associate's degree programs in optical fabricating and dispensing (half of which are accredited by the Commission on Opticianry Accreditation). Other formal programs in this field are offered by vocational/technical institutes, trade schools, and manufacturers, and these programs, which vary in length from six months to one year, award certificates or diplomas. In addition, short nondegree courses in contact lens fitting are offered by some medical schools, contact lens manufacturers, and professional societies.

In almost half of the states, opticians must be licensed to dispense eyeglasses. To obtain a license, an optician must meet certain educational and training criteria established by the state and pass a written and/or practical examination. In many states, to maintain this license, the optician must accumulate a specific number of continuing education credits in this field. Although voluntary, certification is an important enhancement to employment. Certification is offered by the American Board of Opticianry, which administers two examinations: the National Opticianry Competency Examination, which attests to entry-level competence (candidates who pass this examination are awarded a certified optician certificate); and the Master in Ophthalmic Optics Examination, which is for experienced opticians (a master in ophthalmic optics certificate is awarded). The National Commission of Contact Lens Examiners administers the Contact Lens Registry Examination, which tests competency in the fitting of contact lenses.

Abilities and personal qualities that can enhance performance in this career include manual dexterity, sharp vision, mathematical aptitude, patience, tact, good communication skills, and a pleasant personality.

THE FUTURE

With more than half of all Americans already wearing glasses or contact lenses to correct their vision and with the older segment of the American population expanding (older individuals typically require more vision care), the demand for opticians—and particularly for opticians who have an associate's degree—should be better than average. Openings for as many as 7,000 new opticians may develop before 2000. However, because of its retail nature, opticianry is an occupation easily affected by fluctuations in the general economy.

For more information about opticians, contact the:

Opticians Association of America
1250 Connecticut Avenue, N.W.
Washington, DC 20036

National Academy of Opticianry
10111 Martin Luther King Jr. Highway
Suite 112
Bowie, Maryland 20720-4299

Commission on Opticianry Accreditation
10111 Martin Luther King Jr. Highway
Suite 110
Bowie, Maryland 20720-4299

National Federation of Opticianry Schools
10111 Martin Luther King Jr. Highway
Suite 112
Bowie, Maryland 20720-4299

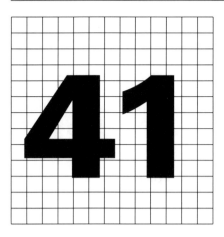

OPTOMETRIC TECHNICIAN AND OPTOMETRIC ASSISTANT

also known as
Paraoptometric

Optometric technicians and *optometric assistants* (also sometimes called paraoptometrics) perform certain routine optometric patient-care functions. Their duties include taking preliminary medical histories, preparing patients for eye examinations, conducting simple vision tests, recording the results of eye examinations, measuring patients for correct and comfortable fit of glasses, suggesting appropriate eyeglass shape and size, making minor adjustments and minor repairs on finished eyeglasses, assisting the optometrist in teaching the patient how to use and maintain contact lenses and how to carry out programs of vision therapy exercises, and cleaning and caring for optometric instruments. Technicians and assistants handle these routine functions so that the optometrist is free to carry out the more technical aspects of his or her practice. Optometric assistants and technicians may also be expected to carry out certain clerical duties, including keeping patient records; maintaining the schedule book; handling bookkeeping, correspondence, and filing; and maintaining the inventory of optometric materials. In theory, optometric technicians handle the more complex duties (conducting the more technical basic vision tests, recording pressures in the eye) and have more extensive training, while optometric assistants perform the less demanding tasks and have less preparation. In reality, the specific division of labor may not be sharply defined and will vary according to setting, employer, and the size of the practice for which the paraoptometric works.

SETTINGS, SALARIES, STATISTICS

Most optometric assistants and technicians work in optometrists' offices. Opportunities also exist in health clinics, health maintenance organizations, government agencies, the armed forces, and optical companies. A forty-hour workweek is common, with Saturday and evening hours often expected. Part-time positions also exist.

There are approximately 50,000 paraoptometrics in the United States, most of whom are female.

The average salary for optometric assistants is approximately $15,400 per year. For optometric technicians, the average is approximately $19,700 per year.

HOW TO BECOME AN OPTOMETRIC ASSISTANT OR AN OPTOMETRIC TECHNICIAN

Most paraoptometrics are trained on the job by the optometrists for whom they work. There are also formal education and training programs in this field. For prospective optometric assistants, there are one-year courses offered by community colleges and technical institutes. For prospective optometric technicians, there are two-year associate's degree programs offered by community colleges and colleges of optometry. The Council on Optometric Education of the American Optometric Association has accredited five of the technician programs. Many employers give preference to graduates of accredited programs.

Formal training for paraoptometrics typically includes courses in ocular anatomy and physiology, vision training, contact lens theory and practice, as well as secretarial and office procedures. Students learn in the classroom, in the laboratory, and in supervised clinical settings (clinics, private offices).

Registration of paraoptometrics is available through the National Paraoptometric Registry. An optometric assistant who satisfies certain training and experience criteria may become a registered optometric assistant (Opt.A.,R.). An optometric technician who meets the appropriate criteria may become a registered optometric technician (Opt.T.,R.). Though voluntary, registration can be an important advantage in seeking employment.

Abilities and personal qualities that can contribute to success as a paraoptometric include accuracy, neatness, the ability to put patients at ease, and good verbal and written communication skills.

THE FUTURE

Several factors should contribute to an increased demand for paraoptometrics. First, the demand for eye care services should increase. The population, in general, is growing larger, and, in particular, the senior citizen population, which traditionally accounts for a major segment of all optical service consumers, is growing disproportionately larger. Second, optometry students today are taught in school to work with paraoptometrics, so when they open their offices, they tend to hire assistants and technicians. Delegating certain responsibilities is a fairly recent development. The employment outlook for all assistants and technicians is bright, and for those paraoptometrics who graduate from formal training programs, opportunities should be even brighter.

For more information about optometric assistants and optometric technicians, write to the:

American Optometric Association,
   Paraoptometric Section
243 North Lindberg Boulevard
St. Louis, Missouri 63141

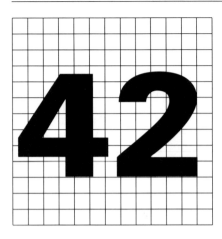

ORIENTATION AND MOBILITY INSTRUCTOR FOR THE BLIND

also known as
Orientation and Mobility Specialist
O & M Instructor

Each year, an estimated 50,000 Americans lose their sight, and hundreds of thousands of others suffer serious vision impairment. *Orientation and mobility instructors* (formerly called peripatologists) help the visually impaired (young children who have never seen, newly blinded adults, and people with multiple disabilities) to achieve independence with regard to traveling. The orientation and mobility instructor (or O & M instructor) evaluates the nature and extent of the patient's visual impairment and plans and implements an individualized program of instruction.

In actual and/or real travel situations, the patient is taught how to become oriented to physical surroundings so that eventually he or she may safely and effectively travel alone, with or without a cane, in familiar and unfamiliar environments. Gradually, the world in which the patient may safely travel independently expands from his or her own neighborhood to a larger area—from quiet residential streets to urban situations and the use of mass transit.

Often, this training is conducted on a one-to-one basis. Sometimes orientation and mobility instructors teach group activities such as swimming, dancing, and adapted versions of popular sports. As the patient acquires these new skills, he or she also gains important social contact.

Communication skills are stressed. The instructor teaches the patient how to maximize his or her unaffected senses, especially hearing and touch. The patient is taught how to be an especially effective listener. In the course of the education and training necessary to become an orientation and mobility instructor, students spend time blindfolded so as to better appreciate the physiological and psychological changes visual impairment may bring and better understand the implications of nonvisual travel.

Depending on the patient's needs, an orientation and mobility instructor may collaborate with other health care professionals—teachers of the visually impaired, occupational therapists, rehabilitation counselors—to help that patient become more competent and independent. Clearly, helping the visually impaired toward full and happy lives is very important and potentially very satisfying work.

SETTINGS, SALARIES, STATISTICS

Orientation and mobility instructors work in hospitals (mostly Department of Veterans Affairs facilities), residential and public schools, rehabilitation centers, public and private community-based agencies, nursing homes, and in the homes of their students. A forty-hour workweek is typical. Because O & M is mostly taught on a one-to-one basis and six hours of teaching per day is the prescribed maximum of the National Accreditation Council for Agencies Serving the Blind and Visually Handicapped, the mean daily caseload is under six persons and the mean annual caseload is about 30 individuals.

There are approximately 1,800 orientation and mobility instructors in the United States. Until fifteen years ago, this was a male-dominated profession. Today, more than half of all practicing O & M instructors are women. As a group, O & M instructors are paid on a scale that is roughly equivalent to the pay scale for teachers in the U.S.; however, salaries range widely depending on the setting and degree attained. The average salary earned is approximately $25,500 per year. Instructors holding master's degrees and having experience may earn as much as $40,000 per year. Generally, salaries paid by private agencies are not as competitive as those offered by public institutions.

HOW TO BECOME AN ORIENTATION AND MOBILITY INSTRUCTOR FOR THE BLIND

Although, until recently, a master's degree in orientation and mobility was the standard level of education expected by employers, an acute shortage of O & M instructors caused the opening up of job opportunities to holders of bachelor's degrees. Today, while the master's degree is still preferred and expected, and although more master's graduates than bachelor's graduates are being produced in this field, a bachelor's degree is sufficient for employment. Master's degree programs combine academic and clinical training with an internship in a clinical setting. At this time there are 16 master's degree O & M training programs in the U.S. and two bachelor's degree programs.

Instructors who satisfy certain education and experience requirements may become certified by the Association for the Education and Rehabilitation of the Blind and Visually Impaired. There are no state licensing requirements in this field.

Abilities and personal qualities that can enhance performance and satisfaction in this career include patience, compassion, excellent verbal communication skill, warmth, and perseverance.

THE FUTURE

The employment picture for orientation and mobility instructors is excellent. At present there is a serious shortage of qualified instructors which will, most likely, grow as the number of older Americans grows.

For more information about a career as an orientation and mobility instructor, contact the:

> National Consultant in Orientation & Mobility
> American Foundation for the Blind
> 15 West Sixteenth Street
> New York, New York 10011

> Association for the Education and Rehabiliation
>   of the Blind and Visually Impaired
> 206 North Washington Street, Suite 320
> Alexandria, Virginia 22314

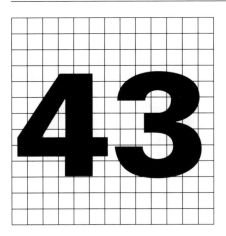

ORTHOPTIST

Orthoptics means straight (ortho) eyes (optics). An *orthoptist* is an eye muscle specialist who, working under the supervision of an ophthalmologist, diagnoses and treats conditions affecting ocular motility (eye movement) and binocular vision (vision using both eyes at the same time). Most of the patients seen by orthoptists are children who have an ocular defect known as strabismus. Strabismus is the misalignment of the eyes. The eyes do not work in tandem. The patient's vision is not fused; one eye will focus properly, but the other strays, sometimes creating a crossed-eye appearance. As the patient strains to use both eyes together, he or she may experience discomfort. Strabismus is often psychologically uncomfortable as well. Two to four percent of all children suffer from some degree of this problem, which is typically present and detected early in the first few years of life. In addition to children, many adults have uncorrected strabismus.

To repair most cases of strabismus, corrective surgery is performed. Eyeglasses are also frequently prescribed to correct focusing errors and to improve eye alignment. Orthoptic therapy is a third, less common option. An orthoptist teaches the patient special exercises that gradually improve the control of eye movement so that vision, comfort, and appearance are improved. Treatment of strabismus improves not only patients' ability to see the world but also the way they see themselves.

Orthoptics is still a relatively new health care profession in the United States. During the late nineteenth and early twentieth centuries, orthoptic treatments were carried out in Europe and Great Britain, and the first orthoptic clinic was opened in England in 1930. Although the first orthoptic clinic in America opened in 1932, this field has become a recognized and organized auxiliary to ophthalmology only in the past 45 years.

In addition to diagnosing and treating eye coordination defects, an orthoptist may, under the supervision of an ophthalmologist, conduct visual field and other ancillary ophthalmic tests. New and exciting in this field is the preferential looking test, or PLT, which is a simple method of testing visual acuity in children under the age of three. An orthoptist presents to the child cards that are part blank and part striped and then observes the child's reaction. Seventy-five percent of all young children tested display a preference for the patterned portion. Their eyes become fixed on the stripes, suggesting that they can detect them and that normal infant vision includes a preference for pattern. Because PLT testing requires neither verbal reliability nor verbal response on the part of the child, assessment of younger children is possible.

SETTINGS, SALARIES, STATISTICS

Orthoptists work in clinical settings, in the private offices of ophthalmologists (some orthoptists work for more than one private practice), in hospitals, in eye clinics, and in the departments of ophthalmology of teaching hospitals. Many orthoptists teach and conduct research in their particular settings. Opportunities for orthoptists exist nationwide.

There are approximately 360 certified orthoptists in the United States. Interestingly, Australia, with a population one-fourteenth the size of America's, has approximately 400 practicing orthoptists. Orthoptics is practiced extensively in Europe.

Salaries for certified orthoptists range between $25,000 and $50,000 per year.

HOW TO BECOME AN ORTHOPTIST

To become an orthoptist, a person must successfully complete a 24-month-long training program. These programs, located in training centers, combine practical and theoretical training. Most training centers charge a nominal or no tuition fee. The American Orthoptic Council presently accredits 12 training center programs in the United States and Canada. At this time there are no graduate programs in orthoptics, but there are graduate-level courses offered in this field.

To qualify for admission to a training center program, a candidate must have successfully completed a baccalaureate degree. High school and college courses in biology, physics, psychology, and anatomy provide a useful background for the study of orthoptics.

Personal qualities that can enhance performance and enjoyment as an orthoptist include patience, kindness, sound judgment, emotional maturity, and scientific curiosity. And, because they often work with young children, orthoptists should like children and be able to relate well to them. A good rapport with the patient is essential. Good vision and good health are also necessary.

Orthoptists who have successfully completed an accredited orthoptic education program and who pass written, oral, and practical examinations administered by the American Orthoptic Council are awarded certification. Certification is required for most hospital, institutional, and office positions. The American Orthoptic Council also offers continuing education credits annually.

One-third of all ophthalmic technologists are orthoptists.

THE FUTURE

The employment picture for orthoptists is very positive. At present, the number of positions for orthoptists far exceeds the number of orthoptists available to fill them. Because there are so few training programs for orthoptists (in 1990 there were 22, in 1994 there were 12) and because they graduate so few new orthoptists each year (not even enough to fill the openings created by retirement), this trend will continue well through the 1990s.

For more information about a career as an orthoptist, contact the:

American Orthoptic Council
3914 Nakoma Road
Madison, Wisconsin 53711

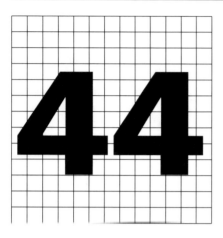

ORTHOTIST, PROSTHETIST, AND ORTHOTIC-PROSTHETIC TECHNICIAN

Orthotists design, fabricate, and fit braces and strengthening devices for patients with disabling conditions of the limbs or spine. Such a device is technically called an orthosis, from the Greek work *orthos*, meaning straight. Orthoses support weakened body parts and help to correct physical defects. Persons requiring orthoses include those whose limbs or spine have been affected by stroke, polio, muscular dystrophy, spinal cord injury, congenital musculoskeletal disorders, fracture, or other orthopedic impairment. The Milwaukee back brace worn by many adolescents to correct scoliosis (curvature of the spine) is a common example of an orthosis.

An orthotist formulates the design of the orthosis; selects the appropriate materials (wood, polyester resin, polyethylene and other plastics, fabric, steel, aluminum, and leather are used predominantly); makes the necessary casts, measurements, model modifications, and layouts; performs fittings; evaluates the fit and function of the orthosis; and teaches the patient how to use and care for the device. Usually the orthotist follows a prescription for the orthosis that has been written by a physician, but in some cases the orthotist may be called in by the physician to examine and evaluate the patient's orthotic needs and to consult on the formulation of the prescription.

Orthotists are also responsible for maintaining accurate patient records and for keeping abreast of new developments in the field. In addition, they supervise the functions of support personnel and laboratory activities related to the development of orthoses. Some orthotists teach and conduct research.

There are several new and exciting developments in this field. Recently, research orthotists have developed the first all-carbon, fiber knee-ankle-foot-orthosis (KAFO). This revolutionary brace, intended for patients with post-polio syndrome, spina bifida, cerebral palsy, and other lower-extremity disorders, is one-third the weight of traditional KAFOs. This sophisticated orthosis is also more cosmetically pleasing and less cumbersome for the patient to wear because it is contoured to the entire length of the affected leg. Experts expect this development to lead to other advancements in carbon-graphited orthotics.

The title certified orthotist, or CO, is awarded to practitioners who satisfy specific educational, training, and examination requirements established by the American Board for Certification in Orthotics and Prosthetics, Inc. (ABC).

Prosthetists are practitioners who design, fabricate, and fit artificial limbs for patients who, because of illness, accident, or congenital condition, are missing part or all of their own limbs. These artificial limbs are technically called prostheses, and they are made out of various plastics, metals, woods, and fiberglass. The prosthetist's goal is a prosthesis that the patient will find functional, comfortable, and aesthetically acceptable.

In prosthetics, the most advanced technology is myoelectrics. *Myoelectric* is the technical term for an electro-mechanical prosthesis. Myoelectric technology utilizes electronic sensors (electrodes) to detect small electric signals emitted during the contraction of muscles in the residual limb. These signals are electronically processed and used to control a motor within a prosthesis. The prosthesis, in turn, activates a simulated body part, such as an arm, wrist, or hand.

Another new development in prostheses is the use of computers to design and manufacture artificial limbs. The patient's body measurements are fed into a computer, which then produces a detailed, three-dimensional blueprint of the prosthetic joint needed. This blueprint, in turn, is fed into a manufacturing machine that sculpts the prosthesis.

Prosthetists formulate the design of the artificial limb; select the best materials; make the necessary casts, measurements, models, alignments; evaluate the prosthesis on the patient; and instruct the patient on its use. In some cases the prosthetist fills a prescription for the artificial limb that has been written by the attending physician. In other cases, the prosthetist is called in to consult on the formulation of the prescription, and he or she will examine the patient and personally evaluate his or her prosthetic needs.

Like orthotists, prosthetists are also expected to maintain patient records, supervise the functions of technicians and other support personnel, and keep up to date on new developments in the field. Prosthetists also engage in teaching and research.

The title certified prosthetist, or CP, is awarded to practitioners who satisfy specific educational, training, and examination requirements established by the American Board for Certification in Orthotics and Prosthetics, Inc. (ABC).

Because the fields of orthotics and prosthetics are so closely related, many prosthetists study orthotics, and vice versa. When sufficient additional education, training, and examination requirements are achieved in the complementary discipline, the professional designation certified prosthetist/ orthotist, or CPO, is used.

SETTINGS, SALARIES, STATISTICS

Orthotists and prosthetists work in privately owned facilities and laboratories, hospitals, rehabilitation centers, university teaching and research programs, and government agencies.

The average starting salary for orthotists and prosthetists holding bachelor's degrees is $24,000 per year. In both fields, practitioners with experience earn an average of $35,000 per year, and individuals who go into private practice can earn well beyond that figure. Advancement in these fields may come in the form of promotion to supervisory and administrative positions. A significant number of orthotists become owners or managers of private facilities.

There are approximately 2,900 ABC-certified orthotists, prosthetists, and prosthetists/orthotists in the United States. The majority of them are men, but in recent years an increasing number of women is entering these fields. 1993 figures from the American Orthotic and Prosthetic Association (which is the trade association for these fields) show that about a third of its active members are certified orthotists, another third are certified to practice prosthetics, and the remaining third are certified prosthetist/orthotists.

HOW TO BECOME AN ORTHOTIST OR A PROSTHETIST

There are several educational routes to a career in orthotics and prosthetics. One route is to receive a bachelor's degree with the major emphasis in orthotics or prosthetics from a college or university having a program accredited by the National Commission on Orthotic and Prosthetic Education (NCOPE) in conjunction with the American Medical Association's Commision for the Accreditation of Allied Health Education Programs (CAAHEP). In addition, a minimum of one year of clinical experience is necessary. The candidate is then eligible to take the American Board for Certification in Orthotics and Prosthetics (or ABC) Practitioners Certification Examination, which is a three-part, written, clinical, and written simulation test of competence in the field. At this time, five colleges and universities across the country offer accredited bachelor's degrees in orthotics and/or prosthetics.

Undergraduate preparation in prosthetics and orthotics typically includes courses in psychology (and specifically, the psychology of the physically disabled), chemistry, physics, biology, anatomy, physiology, mathematics, biostatistics, mechanics, biomechanics, properties of materials, mechanical drawing, metalworking, prosthetic and orthotic techniques, orthopedic and neuromuscular conditions, lower and upper limb prosthetics, lower and upper limb orthotics, and spinal orthotics. It also includes extensive clinical training.

Students holding bachelor's degrees in majors other than orthotics or prosthetics may prepare for these careers by successfully completing an NCOPE-accredited postgraduate certificate program in orthotics and/or prosthetics. These educational programs are one to two years in length, at the end of which a certificate is awarded. Currently, there are seven accredited certificate programs nationwide. A minimum of one year of acceptable experience is also required before the candidate may take the ABC Practitioners Certification Examination.

Candidates possessing a unique combination of qualifications that may not comply with the specific requirements set forth but that demonstrate a unique combination of education, clinical experience, and professional training qualifications at least equivalent to the specific requirements set forth are also eligible to apply to take the Practitioners Certification Examination.

To maintain certification, individuals must satisfy certain ABC requirements for continuing education.

There are also many orthotists, prosthetists, and prosthetist/orthotists who are not certified. Salaries and opportunities tend to be greater for certified practitioners, however.

To prepare for any of the educational routes, high school classes in biology, physics, chemistry, mathematics, and shop courses in metal, wood, and plastics are recommended.

Also working in these fields are *orthotic-prosthetic technicians*. Orthotic-prosthetic technicians work in a laboratory fabricating, preparing, and maintaining braces, surgical supports, artificial limbs, and other orthotic and prosthetic devices under the supervision of a prosthetist/orthotist. They work directly with the materials and are responsible for ensuring that the workmanship is of high quality. Using precision measuring instruments and various tools, they shape and assemble the plastic, wood, and metal to meet the specifications of the prescription.

The ABC registers orthotic-prosthetic technicians who meet specific requirements. To become certified, students must (1) complete a formal education program in orthotics or prosthetics that is approved by NCOPE (at this time there are three in the United States) and then pass the ABC's technical examination, or (2) possess at least a high school education and accumulate a minimum of two years of work experience in the making of orthoses and/or prostheses under the supervision of a certified orthotist, certified prosthetist, or certified prosthetist/orthotist and then pass the ABC Technical Examination. A registered technician (orthotics), or RT(O), is a person who has passed the technical examination in orthotics; a registered technician (prosthetics), or RT(P), is one who has passed the Prosthetic Technician Examination; and a registered technician (orthotics-prosthetics), or RT(OP), is someone who has passed the combined examination for orthotic-prosthetic technicians.

Again, there are many orthotic-prosthetic technicians who are not certified, and there are many junior and community colleges across the country offering technical training. However, salaries for registered orthotic-prosthetic technicians are higher and job opportunities greater.

Personal qualities and talents that a student would do well to bring to these professions include skillful hands, mechanical ability, concern for detail, patience, good communication skills, and a genuine desire to help individuals who are disabled.

THE FUTURE

It is an exciting time to be working in the fields of orthotics and prosthetics. Advances in technology and materials are allowing prosthetists and orthotists to design and fabricate devices that provide greater comfort, safety, and freedom than ever before possible. The use of myoelectrics, hydraulics, and biofeedback to provide mobility are just a few of the new directions being pursued.

Employment prospects in the United States and overseas are very favorable. The demand for professionally trained prosthetists, orthotists, prosthetist/orthotists, and orthotic-prosthetic technicians is growing.

For more information about orthotists, prosthetists, prosthetist/orthotists, and orthotic-prosthetic technicians and for a list of approved educational programs and certification requirements, write to the:

> O & P National Office
> 1650 King Street, Suite 500
> Alexandria, Virginia 22314

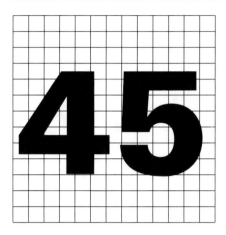

PATIENT REPRESENTATIVE

also known as
Patient Advocate
Health Advocate
Ombudsman

Patient representatives—also known as patient advocates, health advocates, ombudsmen, and a dozen other similar titles denoting the liaison nature of the work—help patients understand hospital procedures, services, and policies; obtain solutions to patients' problems and address their concerns; and sensitize hospital personnel to patients' perceptions of the hospital experience. A patient representative is a listener, a communicator, and a catalyst for change from within the system. He or she is an open line between the patient (and often the patient's family) and the institution, who is there to help the patient deal not only with his or her health problem but with the personnel, procedures, and policies working to resolve that health problem.

Health care today is better and more accessible than every before. Age-old illnesses are being cured, infirmities once thought hopeless are being corrected, and life spans are lengthening. Yet sometimes the very things that enable our modern hospitals to deliver an ever-improving level of health care—the huge, rotating staffs of specialized professionals; the myriad sophisticated diagnostic and therapeutic procedures; the complicated, and expensive, options now possible because of new technology—can confuse and distress a patient in pain who is already feeling disoriented, worried, and vulnerable. If that patient is also economically and socially disadvantaged, elderly, or not fluent in English, the confusion and distress may be compounded. Although physically benefiting from all of the new advancements in modern medicine, the patient may feel victimized by the very complexity and fragmentation that make them possible. The personal, individual needs of the patient may be overshadowed or perceived to be forgotten. The person who is the patient may be neglected, and, sometimes, amidst all that complexity and fragmentation, a person who is a patient may not receive the proper health care.

The patient representative's job is to humanize and individualize health care for the patients—assisting them by acting on their behalf in securing appropriate medical care, evaluating problem areas in patient care, and serving as a catalyst for improvement. By displaying a personal interest in the patient and by working to resolve that patient's problems, a patient representative can bring that vast, busy medical staff in that huge, impersonal hospital down to a one-to-one scale. The patient representative is a caring constant in a fast-changing scene; an unhurried listener to the patient's concerns; an articulate—and heard—voice for the patient's needs, wishes, and complaints; a sensitive and compassionate translator of the medical team's treatment plans, goals, concerns, and the hospital's policies; and a defender of the patient's legal, social, and human rights. In fact, many states and health care institutions have established a "Patient's Bill of Rights," which is given to and/or read to and explained to each patient upon admission. Some typical rights are considerate and respectful care at all times; complete and current information concerning diagnosis, treatment, and outcome, presented in understandable terms; every consideration of privacy; an interpreter if language barrier or hearing impairment presents a continuing problem to the patient's understanding of care and treatment; confidentiality; continuity of care; notification if the institution proposes to engage in or perform human experimentation affecting the patient's care or treatment; and the right to refuse treatment to the extent permitted by law. Patient representatives also work to sensitize health care professionals to the need for humanizing patients' hospital experiences by conducting new employee orientation programs and ongoing training programs.

The exact responsibilities of the patient representative differ from hospital to hospital. This is still a relatively new health career, and specific duties, education and training requirements, criteria for employment, and even the name are not sharply defined. The National Society for Patient Representation and Consumer Affairs (formerly the National Society of Patient Representatives) has developed a list of functions and goals for patient representatives which it calls "Elements of Patient Representatives Programs in Hospitals," and this list is available to guide hospitals in initiating such programs. Depending on the institution and the situation, a patient representative will be an advocate (working for change on behalf of an individual patient or for changes in the health care delivery system), a facilitator, a bilingual translator, an ombudsman, an educator, a troubleshooter, a negotiator, a spokesperson, and—always—someone ready to listen, care, and work for the patient's safety and well-being.

SETTINGS, SALARIES, STATISTICS

Approximately 3,200 hospitals (or roughly 47 percent of all U.S. hospitals) have patient representative services. Small and average-size hospitals often employ one part-time patient representative, while a large teaching hospital may have several patient representatives on its staff. Of all new patient representative programs, 60 percent are initiated by individuals who already work for the hospital. Health maintenance organizations, government and private programs for the elderly, nursing homes, schools, programs for the physically and mentally disabled, community and rural health centers, disease-related foundations, and industry also employ patient representatives.

Annual salaries for patient representatives begin at about $15,000 and may go as high as $51,000. The mean salary for patient representatives with between one and five years of experience is $35,000.

HOW TO BECOME A PATIENT REPRESENTATIVE

Criteria for employment is this field are flexible. There are no official, specific requirements. Instead, hospitals and other employers establish their own educational and work experience requirements to meet the specific needs of their institution and community. Patient representatives come from a variety of backgrounds, bringing with them educations ranging from high school diplomas to graduate degrees. However, a significant number of people now entering the profession have backgrounds in the health field, and many employers are requiring a bachelor's degree.

The schools of human services at several universities across the country offer undergraduate courses in patient representation, and, since 1980, one school, Sarah Lawrence College, in Bronxville, New York, has offered a unique master's degree in health advocacy. The curriculum for this program can be completed in 18 months, two years, or part-time in three years and includes courses in the history of health care in America, health care organization and concepts for change, human anatomy and physiological systems, the language of patient care, the psychology of stress and the coping process, health law, and the economics of health and health advocacy and includes 600 hours of practical fieldwork.

Prerequisites for admission to the Sarah Lawrence Health Advocacy Program include a bachelor's degree, introductory biology, a course in microeconomics, and intermediate-level work in the social sciences. Facility in a second language, especially Spanish, is considered advantageous.

In its guidelines, the National Society for Patient Representation and Consumer Affairs suggests that persons selected to coordinate patient representative programs understand the health care system and have education or experience in human relations, communications, supervision, management, conflict negotiation, and medical terminology.

Personal qualities that are important to effective and satisfying performance in this job include empathy, tact, objectivity, maturity, the ability to cope with stress and pressure, tenacity, a sense of humor, and sound judgment. A patient representative must be able to relate to a wide variety of patients as well as to the hospital staff and be the type of person in whom a patient can quickly and justifiably place his or her trust.

No certification or licensing requirements exist for patient representatives.

THE FUTURE

Predicting the future for patient representatives is difficult. Certain important trends may work against each other. Cost containment efforts may inhibit some institutions from inaugurating patient representative programs. At the same time, however, patient consumerism is increasing, and as results from these still-new programs come in, more and more health care institutions, health care personnel, and patients should become aware of the important benefits of health advocacy. Health advocacy services are among the benefits proposed in several of the 1994 health care reform plans, including the plan promoted by the White House.

Also affecting the job outlook will be the increasing American population and the increasing percentage of elderly persons in that population. Weighing these factors, it is expected that over the next ten years, the number of job opportunities for patient representatives should grow steadily.

For more information about patient representatives, write to the:

> National Society for Patient Representation
>   and Consumer Affairs of the American
>   Hospital Association
> 840 North Lake Shore Drive
> Chicago, Illinois 60611

For more information about a master's degree in health advocacy, write to the:

> Health Advocacy Program
> Sarah Lawrence College
> Bronxville, New York 10708

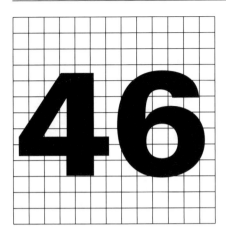

PERFUSIONIST

also known as
Cardiovascular Perfusionist
Clinical Perfusionist
Extracorporeal Perfusionist
Extracorporeal Technologist
Perfusion Technologist/Technician
Pump Technician

A heart-lung machine is the crucial piece of biomedical equipment that temporarily maintains proper oxygen and carbon dioxide levels and blood circulation outside of the human body (or extracorporeally) during heart-lung bypass procedures, such as open heart surgery and surgery of the large blood vessels and during respiratory failure and other medical situations where it is necessary to support or temporarily replace the patient's circulatory or respiratory functions. The heart-lung machine continuously drains blood by gravity from the patient's venous system, reoxygenates it, and pumps it back into the patient's arterial system. This revolutionary machine was developed by Dr. John H. Gibbon, Jr., who used it in 1953 in the first successful human open-heart surgery. Assisting Dr. Gibbon in that landmark operation was a nurse (Dr. Gibbon's wife, Mary) who had been specially trained to operate the new heart-lung machine and monitor the oxygenation of the patient's blood during the operation. Mary Gibbon was the first extracorporeal perfusionist.

A *perfusionist* (this is the preferred occupation title now in wide use) is a skilled person, qualified by academic and clinical education, who operates extracorporeal circulation equipment. Perfusionists provide consultation to the physician in the selection of the appropriate equipment and techniques to be used during extracorporeal circulation. During cardiopulmonary bypass, the perfusionist may, on prescription, administer blood products, anesthetic agents, and drugs through the extracorporeal circuit.

Perfusionists are also involved in the blood salvaging (or blood conservation) techniques that are so critical in light of today's diminishing blood bank supplies and fear of AIDS. Blood salvaging is the effort to use as much of a patient's own blood and as little bagged (donated) blood as possible during and after surgery. (The predepositing of a person's own blood for his or her own use several weeks prior to surgery is an example of salvaging.)

Perfusion technology helps to conserve blood in the cases of preoperative and intraoperative phlebotomies performed on bypass patients. After anaesthesia is administered, before or during the operation, one or two units of the patient's blood are drained and stored, to be given back—through the heart-lung pump—to the patient at the end of the procedure, when blood volume is needed.

Perfusionists also operate Cell-Savers, which are machines that use centrifugal force to separate out from whatever blood is still in the pump after surgery all of the plasma, damaged platelets, and saline that should not be returned to the patient's body. After washing from the reclaimed red blood cells the clotting inhibitor heparin and other drugs, the perfusionist can then return the patient's blood, again via the pump. In both situations, the need for bagged blood can be radically reduced, if not eliminated.

A perfusionist must also be in attendance when extracorporeal membrane oxygenation (ECMO) is being carried out. ECMO is a procedure for premature infants experiencing respiratory distress, certain post-op heart patients, heart patients awaiting transplant organs, and others needing extra heart and respiratory support. The patient is placed (by a surgeon) on a heart-lung pump that is then operated and monitored by a perfusionist. The pump buys the patient the time needed for additional development, healing, or, in the case of the transplant recipient, the time until a donor can be matched.

New applications for perfusion techniques are developing constantly. Today, perfusionists can also be found in the operating room when liver transplants, orthopaedic surgery, and cancer surgery are being performed, using rapid infusion techniques to quickly replace lost or lowered blood volume with warmed blood, thereby minimizing trauma and maximizing the opportunity for healing.

Perfusion procedures involve specialized instrumentation and/or advanced life-support techniques and may include a variety of related functions. The perfusionist is educated to conduct extracorporeal circulation and to ensure the safe management of physiologic functions by monitoring the necessary variables. Final medical responsibility for extracorporeal perfusion rests with the surgeon in charge, however.

SETTINGS, SALARIES, STATISTICS

Perfusionists usually work in a hospital setting, and the vast majority are employed directly by hospitals. Perfusionists work outside of their hospitals when they are engaged in efforts to procure and transport organs for transplant. Specifically, in heart-lung transplant cases, a perfusionist will travel to the donor's hospital and maintain the donor's respiration and heart rates until the optimal time for removal of the organs prior to transport, or throughout the trip if the donor's body is transported. The perfusionist maintains respiration by placing the donor on the coronary bypass machine, and then, on the receiving end, the perfusionist puts the recipient on the machine during surgery.

Some perfusionists work for individual surgeons or surgical groups, and health care corporations also employ perfusionists. Perfusionists work long hours. Emergencies frequently necessitate working back-to-back shifts, and eighty-hour workweeks are not uncommon. Most job openings are in cities and other high population areas.

There are approximately 3,000 perfusionists currently practicing in the United States. While historically this field has been dominated by men, rapidly increasing numbers of women (some of them nurses) are becoming perfusionists.

Salaries range greatly. New graduates of accredited educational programs in perfusion start at about $40,000 or more per year. The annual average for all experienced perfusionists is between $50,000 and $80,000. However, the potential for earnings in this field is great. Some perfusionists who are in private practice and who are very busy earn salaries in the six figures.

HOW TO BECOME A PERFUSIONIST

Until the mid-1970s, most perfusionists came to the field from other disciplines (nursing, respiratory therapy, biomedical engineering, surgical technology, and laboratory) and trained on the job. Of the 3,000 or so perfusionists presently practicing, perhaps 40 to 50 percent were educated this way. Today, students embarking on a career in cardiovascular perfusion are encouraged to attend one of the 32 formal educational programs in perfusion, which are accredited by the Commission for the Accreditation of Allied Health Education Programs (CAAHEP), which, on July 1, 1994, succeeded the American Medical Association's Committee on Allied Health Education and Accreditation (CAHEA) in granting accreditation for this and 21 other allied health professions. CAAHEP is an independent body in which the AMA participates as one sponsor among many. Last year, 218 men and women graduated from accredited programs.

Perfusionist educational programs are generally one to two years in length, depending on the program design, its objectives, prerequisites, and the student's qualifications and prior experience. Because there are so few perfusionist educational programs, admission is highly competitive. Almost all of the programs require a bachelor's degree as a prerequisite. Several of the programs require candidates to have backgrounds in medical technology, respiratory therapy, or nursing.

Early in the development of this field, most perfusionist educational programs were offered by community colleges or were hospital based. Today, as is the case with other allied health professions, larger universities are initiating educational programs. A perfusionist's education typically includes classroom work in anatomy, physiology, pathology, chemistry, pharmacology, and courses covering heart-lung bypass for adults, pediatric and infant patients undergoing heart surgery, long-term supportive extracorporeal circulation, and special applications of perfusion technology. Clinical experience incorporating performance of an adequate number and variety of circulation procedures is also a required part of the formal education.

A perfusionist should have high intelligence, skillful hands, mechanical aptitude, and be able to concentrate intensely for long periods of time. Other important personal qualities include a strong sense of responsibility, the ability to work well with people, and, especially, the ability to work correctly and quickly in emergency situations. Perfusionists work under very stressful conditions. The hours are long, and the situations are life-and-death. A perfusionist must be emotionally stable and able (mentally and physically) to react efficiently and effectively to all situations within the hospital.

Certification in this field is available through the American Board of Cardiovascular Perfusion (ABCP). Although certification is voluntary, most employers will hire only perfusionists who are certified or certifiable. To become certified, a candidate must satisfy the ABCP's education and clinical experience requirements and pass a rigorous oral and written examination. A perfusionist who satisfies all of these requirements is known as a certified clinical perfusionist and may use the letters CCP after his or her name. There are, at this time, approximately 2,300 certified perfusionists.

THE FUTURE

The demand for experienced certified perfusionists far exceeds the present supply, and several studies have identified cardiovascular perfusion as an emerging occupation that should experience significant relative growth in the near future. The high earnings potential in this allied health profession makes it especially attractive, and interest in this field is high. The high number of bypass procedures performed annually plus the many new applications for perfusion technology discussed earlier in this chapter (blood salvage techniques, ECMO) should cause strong continued demand for perfusionists in the coming decade.

For more information about perfusionists, write to:

> The American Society of Extra-Corporeal Technology (AmSECT)
> 11480 Sunset Hills Road, Suite 100E
> Reston, Virginia 22090

For information about perfusionist certification, contact:

> The American Board of Cardiovascular Perfusion
> 123 South 25th Avenue
> Hattiesburg, Mississippi 39401

And for a list of accredited educational programs for perfusionists, contact:

The Accreditation Committee for Perfusion Education
20 North Wacker Drive, Suite 900
Chicago, Illinois 60606

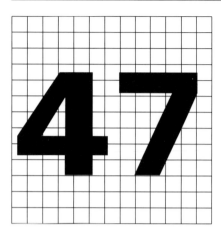

PHARMACIST

The principal goal of pharmaceutical care is improvement in the quality of patients' lives through the use of medications that have been developed and prescribed to achieve definite outcomes. *Pharmacists* are the health care professionals who serve patients, as well as other health care professionals, in assuring the appropriate use of these medications and in achieving optimal therapeutic results from their use. Specifically, they are responsible for the professional interpretation and review of the prescription orders written by physicians, dentists, and other authorized prescribers and for the accurate dispensing of the medications ordered. They are educated in the composition, uses, and interactions of medicines and in how they change biological function.They maintain detailed patient medication profiles listing vital health information (allergies, other medications also being taken), advise people on the use of prescription and nonprescription (over-the-counter) medications, and act as an information resource to physicians and other health care professionals. As opposed to the early days of pharmacy, when the pharmacist measured, mixed, and assembled ingredients to form the capsules, solutions, and ointments prescribed, most medications today are mass manufactured in the form in which they will be used by the patient. For this reason, the majority of the community pharmacist's activity is in the maintaining and dispensing (counting, decanting, packaging, and careful labeling) of medications, not in the compounding of them.

SETTINGS, SALARIES, STATISTICS

Two-thirds of all pharmacists work in community pharmacies. Of these approximately 100,000 pharmacists, one-quarter are owners. The rest are salaried employees. Opportunities for pharmacists also exist in hospital and government pharmacies; in the laboratories of pharmaceutical companies and other settings where research in this field is conducted; in health maintenance organizations; in consulting (to nursing homes, other health care facilities, and pharmaceutical manufacturers); and in teaching, marketing, and sales. Pharmacists who work in community pharmacies average 45-hour workweeks, some of which are evening and weekend hours. Some pharmacists work part-time.

There are approximately 160,000 pharmacists in the United States. The number of women enrolling in pharmacy schools has grown dramatically, and last year women accounted for 60 percent of all pharmacy students.

Salaries for pharmacists vary considerably depending on the type of setting, experience, duties, and geographical location. Experienced hospital pharmacists earn an average of $45,000 annually. The average salary for a federally employed pharmacist is about $40,000. Average salaries of pharmacists employed in academic settings is $46,233 per year, and industrial pharmacists average $58,900 annually. Pharmacists in management positions in all areas of pharmacy may earn considerably more.

HOW TO BECOME A PHARMACIST

Because of the critical nature of the work, a license to practice pharmacy is required in all fifty states, the District of Columbia, and Puerto Rico. To become a licensed pharmacist, a student must graduate from one of 74 pharmacy programs that are accredited by the American Council on Pharmaceutical Education; pass a state board examination; and either serve as an intern under the supervision of a licensed pharmacist for a specific period of time (usually in a community or hospital pharmacy) or accumulate a specific amount of practical experience (this will vary from state to state). Most states accept licenses granted by other states, and many pharmacists are licensed in more than one state.

Colleges of pharmacy award two professional degrees in pharmacy: the bachelor of science in pharmacy (B.S. pharmacy) and the doctor of pharmacy (Pharm.D.). However, in July 1992, a majority of the nation's schools and colleges of pharmacy voted to move toward awarding the doctor of pharmacy (Pharm.D.) degree as the only professional degree in pharmacy. As schools make plans to offer the Pharm.D. degree and modify their curricula accordingly, some will continue to offer the B.S. in pharmacy during the foreseeable future. Either degree fulfills the degree requirements to take the licensure examination of a state board of pharmacy in order to practice pharmacy. A Pharm.D. degree requires four years of professional study, following a minimum of two years of pre-pharmacy study, for a total of six academic years following high school. Including pre-pharmacy study, the minimum educational program for a B.S. in pharmacy is five academic years.

A pharmacist who wishes to do administrative work, teach, or carry out research in this field may go on to study in an advanced professional program leading to a master of science degree in pharmaceutical science or a doctor of philosophy (Ph.D.). Although many pharmacists who seek advancement continue on to graduate study in pharmacy, some go on to medical school, dental school, law school (leading to jobs as pharmaceutical patent attorneys or consultants on pharmaceutical and drug laws), or to graduate education in pharmacology, toxicology, pharmaceutical bacteriology, or other related fields.

As undergraduates, pharmacy students study medicinal chemistry (the study of all aspects of chemicals used as medicinal agents); pharmacognosy (examines the nature and sources of pharmaceuticals obtained from plants or animals, such as the heart stimulant digitalis, which comes from the plant foxglove, and some types of insulin, which are extracted from the pancreas of cattle and hogs); pharmacology (the medicine science which involves all aspects of the actions of drugs on living systems and their constituent parts, including the intermolecular reactions of chemical compounds in a cell with drugs, the evaluation of a drug's effectiveness, and the effects of chemicals in our environment on entire populations); pharmaceutics (the physical and chemical properties of medicinal agents with respect to dosage forms and their impact on pharmacological activity); clinical pharmacy (drug management problems in the care of patients); pharmacy practice (the skills involved in compounding and dispensing prescriptions and professional ethics); and pharmacy administration. From six months to one year of the curriculum is spent in clinical experience rotations in various pharmacy practice settings.

Personal qualifications for a career in pharmacy include accuracy, orderliness, honesty, and for the majority of pharmacists who are self-employed, good business sense. A pharmacist who works in a community pharmacy must be the kind of person the public can trust. Often patients want more than their prescriptions properly filled; they want a thoughtful and pleasant explanation of the medication's use and of any side effects. To be effective in a patient-care setting, a pharmacist must have good communication skills and be patient and friendly.

THE FUTURE

The employment outlook for pharmacists is good. In some areas of the country, competition for jobs has developed. Older individuals are major consumers of medical services and medicines, and as the percentage of older Americans in the population grows (as it is expected to do), the demand for the services of pharmacists will grow as well.

For more information about a career in pharmacy, contact the:

American Association of Colleges of Pharmacy
Office of Student Affairs
1426 Prince Street
Alexandria, Virginia 22314

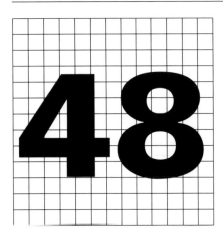

PHYSICAL THERAPIST AND PHYSICAL THERAPIST ASSISTANT

Physical therapy is the assessment, evaluation, treatment, and prevention of physical disability, movement dysfunction, and pain resulting from injury, disease, disability, or other health-related conditions through the use of physical therapeutic measures, as opposed to the use of medicines, surgery, or radiation. Specifically, it is the science and art of applying the therapeutic properties of exercise, heat, cold, water, electricity, ultrasound, massage, education, and other modalities for the purposes of restoring function, relieving pain, preventing disability, and promoting healing following disease, injury, or other disabling condition of the muscles, nerves, joints, or bones, or loss of body part. Where physical therapy cannot restore, relieve, or heal, it teaches adaptation. Fundamental to the practice of physical therapy is consideration of the "whole person" in whom the affected muscles and nerves are contained. Individuals with disabilities (and especially those with permanent afflictions and those in pain) are often emotionally distraught and feel victimized and hopeless. In physical therapy emphasis is placed on psychologically preparing the patient for therapy and rebuilding confidence.

Physical therapy is a direct form of professional patient care that can be applied in almost all of the medical specialties—neurology, neurosurgery, orthopedics, general surgery, family practice, pediatrics, geriatrics, rheumatology, internal medicine, obstetrics-gynecology, cardiovascular medicine, cardiopulmonary medicine, psychiatry, and sports medicine.

Those helped by physical therapy include individuals who have experienced strokes, head injury, and others suffering form hemiplegia and/or hemiparesis (paralysis and weakness of one side of the body); individuals who are paralyzed and other spinal cord injury patients; people who have arthritis (who experience loss of joint motion and muscle strength and, often, experience great pain); patients who have lost limbs; sustained burns; been injured in sports activities; postoperative patients; children with congenital disabilities; and children with muscular dystrophy and cerebral palsy. Each day, 200,000 Americans are helped in physical therapy sessions.

Physical therapists are health care professionals who test and evaluate patients and then plan, provide, and monitor customized physical therapy treatment programs. The physical therapist evaluates the patient's problem using a variety of assessment procedures that measure joint range of motion and mobility, skeletal muscle strength, posture and gait, limb length and circumference, performance in activities of daily living, cardiopulmonary (heart-lung) function, sensation and sensory perception, reflexes and muscle tone, sensory and motor nerve conduction velocity, and sensorimotor performance. Where appropriate, the physical therapist assesses the fit and function of orthoses, prostheses, and other assistive devices (crutches, canes, wheelchairs). The results of these and other assessments and the physical therapy plan of care are then reported back to the physician.

Specifically, the patient's plan may include shortwave or microwave diathermy; massage; ultrasound; infrared and ultraviolet radiation; cold; electrical stimulation (including transcutaneous electrical nerve stimulation for pain control); intermittent venous compression; cervical and lumbar spine traction; joint mobilization; therapeutic exercise (including the use of biofeedback); and iontophoresis and phonophoresis, which are the use of electrical current and sound waves, respectively, to deliver, through the skin, a topically applied medication, such as cortisone, to relieve the pain and inflammation of arthritis, tendonitis, and other joint problems.

For the person who has experienced a stroke and others with head trauma resulting in temporary paralysis and weakness on one side of the body, the physical therapist will implement an exercise program to restore lost muscle control and strength. For the individual who is paralyzed, the physical therapist will promptly initiate exercises to maintain joint motion in the legs and to strengthen muscles in the arms and shoulder girdle. The physical therapist also teaches the proper use of wheelchairs, braces, and crutches.

The physical therapist will help the patient with serious arthritis and other, often painful, joint immobility conditions to move, rotate, and otherwise exercise the affected limb(s). When necessary, the physical therapist will visit the patient's home to evaluate the need for special equipment and any modifications in living areas that will facilitate independence and ensure safety. Individuals who have lost limbs are taught how to use their prostheses effectively and how to adapt to new ways of performing everyday personal and work skills.

For individuals who have sustained burns, the physical therapist will administer whirlpool treatments that ease movement, and assist in exercises. Physical therapists work in hospital nurseries testing and examining newborns to detect congenital conditions so that physicians can start remedial therapy early.

Patients who have coronary artery disease are referred to physical therapists for graded exercise stress testing and carefully planned outpatient exercise programs. Special breathing exercises taught by the physical therapist can prevent pulmonary complications following open heart surgery.

In schools, physical therapists design athletic training regimens and plan special physical education programs for children with disabilities.

Some therapists specialize in one area of physical therapy, such as ortho-pedics, pediatrics, sports, cardiopulmonary, geriatric, or neurologic physical therapy. The trend toward specialization is growing.

A major change in the way physical therapy is practiced today is direct access. Patients may now seek physical therapy directly, without the physi-cian's referral that was necessary in the past. This change is partly the result of the evolution of much of physical therapy from the institutional setting to the private practice setting. Direct access has resulted in increased profes-sional responsibility and autonomy in practice for physical therapists.

Physical therapists do important, respected "people work." They give the individual who is disabled his or her old abilities—and new hope. And for the baby with a disabling orthopedic congenital disability, physical therapy can "educate" muscles and neural pathways so that a more complete, inde-pendent, normal, and happy life lies ahead. Some of the biggest miracles in medicine take place in the physical therapy room.

SETTINGS, SALARIES, STATISTICS

Most physical therapists (25 percent) work in the rehabilitation departments of hospitals (93 percent of all hospitals with a hundred or more beds provide physical therapy services). Opportunities also exist in nursing homes (ap-proximately 8 percent of all physical therapists work in this setting), schools for children who have physical disabilities, private offices, rehabilitation centers, community health centers, and research centers. Twenty-five percent of all physical therapists are in private practice. Others are physical therapy educators and consultants to public schools and community and government agencies. There are approximately 88,000 physical therapists in the United States. Seventy-five percent of them are women.

Starting salaries for physical therapists range between $33,000 and $35,000 annually. Physical therapists with five years of experience earn an average of $45,000, and physical therapists who have supervisory responsi-bilities may earn as much as $60,000 annually. Self-employed physical ther-apists who work full time earn an average of $100,000 annually.

Advancement in this field can come in the form of elevation to therapy positions of greater responsibility (to senior therapist or department supervi-sor) or to administrative positions (to coordinator of rehabilitation services or facility administrator).

Increasingly, physical therapy is becoming a second career for many indi-viduals. Women who are returning to the paid work force after raising fami-lies, teachers looking for new challenges, and other older students are enrolling in physical therapy education programs. Competition for places in physical therapy education programs is so great that only the most clearly motivated students are accepted. Older students often fit this description.

HOW TO BECOME A PHYSICAL THERAPIST

In all 50 states, the District of Columbia, and Puerto Rico, a license to practice physical therapy is necessary. To become licensed, a physical therapist must have a degree or certificate from an accredited physical therapy education program and pass the licensure examination of the state(s) in which he or she intends to practice. Currently, 21 states and jurisdictions require continuing education.

For students holding only a high school diploma or its equivalent, there are four-year professional bachelor's degree programs in physical therapy offered by 66 colleges and universities around the country. For students who already hold a bachelor's degree in a field other than physical therapy, there are three options: earning a (second) bachelor's degree in physical therapy, earning a certificate in physical therapy, or completing a professional master's degree program in physical therapy. There is only one certificate program in the United States at this time, and it entails two to three years of study and clinical experience. There are 69 professional master's degree programs, and they typically also entail two to three years of study. In addition, there are many other graduate programs (master's degree and doctorate) providing advanced study and training for persons already in the field. These entry-level graduate programs emphasize the various physical therapy specialties (such as neurology, pediatrics, and orthopedics). The Commission on Accreditation in Physical Therapy Education (CAPTE) accredits physical therapy educational programs.

A physical therapy curriculum typically includes courses in human anatomy and physiology; neuroanatomy; neurophysiology; biomechanics of motion; human growth and development; manifestations of diseases and trauma; psychology; biology; physics; chemistry; clinical medicine; tests and measurements; therapeutic exercise and assistive devices; and physical agents. The curriculum will also include supervised clinical experience applying physical therapy theory in a hospital or other practice setting.

In high school, prospective physical therapy students should take courses in health, biology, chemistry, physics, mathematics, and social studies. There is strong competition for admission to most physical therapy educational programs. Very good grades in high school and in any other post-high school education are usually required. A good way to learn about what physical therapists do and to see if you have the personal qualities necessary to work in this field is to serve as a summer or part-time volunteer in a physical therapy practice setting.

Personal qualities and abilities that are important to career-long success and satisfaction as a physical therapist include optimism, tact, manual dexterity, good communication skills, imagination, and stamina. Perhaps most important is patience. Physical therapy is often a long, slow process. The personal rewards are frequently delayed but almost always very satisfying.

THE FUTURE

All indications lead to spectacular growth in this field. Older people comprise a large percentage of the patients served by physical therapy, and as the number of older Americans increases (as experts predict), the demand for physical therapy should increase. Also, lower mortality rates for babies with disabilities are resulting in a greater need for newborn evaluation and rehabilitation programs. In addition, as awareness of the potential benefits of physical therapy grows, more people with disabilities each year seek out physical therapy—or are brought to it. Physical therapy is projected to grow by 52 percent between now and the year 2005—that means an additional 46,000 job openings. Demand will be great.

For more information about physical therapists, write to the:

American Physical Therapy Association
1111 North Fairfax Street
Alexandria, Virginia 22314-1488

PHYSICAL THERAPIST ASSISTANT

The approximately 11,400 *physical therapist assistants* in the United States are educated health care providers who, functioning under the direct supervision of licensed physical therapists, assist in patients' treatment programs. The scope of the physical therapist assistant's responsibilities is defined by state law, rules, and regulations, as well as by the policies of the practice setting in which he or she works. The physical therapist assistant's duties may include training patients in exercises and activities of daily care (dressing, undressing, moving about); preparing for and carrying out treatments utilizing special equipment; assisting in the carrying out of tests, evaluations, and more complex treatment procedures; observing and reporting patients' progress; and cleaning and preparing the work area for the next activity and/or patient. The physical therapy assistant also teaches patients how to use and care for orthoses, prostheses, and assistive apparatus.

Most states license physical therapist assistants, and in these states physical therapist assistants must be graduates of accredited two-year associate's degree programs and pass a state examination. There are 140 physical therapist assistant educational programs that are accredited by the Commission on Accreditation in Physical Therapy Education (CAPTE), and most of them are offered by community colleges.

It is important to note that the transition from physical therapist assistant to physical therapist is a difficult one to make. Assistant education stresses techniques. Therapist education includes theory. Very little of the assistant education is convertible to therapist credit. An assistant who decides that he or she wants to be a therapist may well have to take one year of biology, chemistry, and physics before proceeding with therapy education. For this reason, it is very important for a person to assess his or her career goals before embarking on the training and education necessary for practice in this field.

New physical therapist assistants earn about $19,000 per year, and experienced assistants usually earn up to $26,000 annually. As with physical therapists, employment for physical therapist assistants is projected to grow significantly in the next ten years. The U.S. Department of Labor projects approximately 43 percent growth, which means that almost 20,000 new jobs for physical therapy assistants should be created by 2005.

For more information about physical therapist assistants, contact the:

American Physical Therapy Association
1111 North Fairfax Street
Alexandria, Virginia 22314-1488

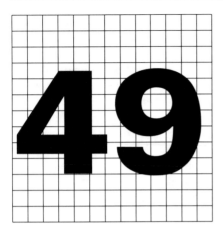

PHYSICIAN ASSISTANT

including
Surgeon Assistant

The *physician assistant* (PA) is a health care professional who, having successfully completed an accredited program of academic and clinical training, is qualified to work under the supervision of a physician performing certain diagnostic, therapeutic, and preventative activities and services that, until the mid-1960s, were carried out almost exclusively by physicians themselves. The physician assistant is a dependent practitioner working with the supervision of a doctor of medicine or osteopathy who is responsible for the PA's performance. Various laws, regulations, and rules specifically define the functions a PA may carry out. These limits have been developed by the medical community and by the various states. Also, the physician assistant is subject to the limitations established by his or her supervising physician.

Typical of the functions a PA may be expected to carry out are interviewing patients and taking detailed medical histories, conducting physical examinations, ordering and/or interpreting selected diagnostic studies (common laboratory procedures and radiologic studies), making tentative diagnoses, performing certain therapeutic procedures (administering injections and immunizations, applying casts, suturing wounds), following up on patient care, teaching and counseling patients (regarding nutrition, disease prevention, family planning), assisting the physician by conducting rounds and recording patient progress in inpatient settings, and responding to emergencies (from severe drug reactions to psychiatric crises to heart attacks to uncomplicated deliveries) but always under the direction of a supervising physician. In 35 states, PAs may even prescribe medications. PAs also assist in delivering health services to patients requiring continuing care at home, in nursing homes, or in other extended care facilities.

Studies have shown that PAs have the training to care for eight out of ten people who visit a family practitioner's office in any one day.

PAs came into being during the 1960s when there was a critical doctor shortage. This shortage was the most acute in rural areas (almost 20 percent of all Americans live in counties with less than 50,000 people, but only 8 percent of all actively practicing physicians are located in these areas) and in the inner city. Almost everywhere in the country, primary care physicians—general practitioners, general internists, and general pediatricians—were struggling to deliver medical services to large patient loads. Primary care physicians and their patients particularly felt the crunch because of the nature of the primary care practice. Primary care physicians are the doctors that patients tend to turn to first when they have health concerns. They are very different from the specialists who deal with only one part of the body or one particular type of health problem. Primary care physicians deal with the whole body. They are expected to handle a wide range of medical situations, from treating injuries and illnesses to handling emergencies and emotional problems. The primary care physician traditionally has a heavy workload, treating whole patients and, often, whole families. Passing through his or her office are patients suffering from everything from the sniffles and sprains to serious physiological and emotional disorders. Until the advent of the physician assistant profession, the primary care physician was the first line of defense in coping with health situations, with referral to a specialist as a subsequent course of action when necessary. Today, in many health care situations in many states, it is the PA who is the first line of defense. He or she is often the first health professional with whom many Americans now come in contact when they seek medical attention. But, again, the supervising physician is ultimately in charge of the patient's care.

During the doctor shortage of the 1960s, nurses were also in short supply because of a pattern of high turnover. Coinciding with this demand for health practitioners was the influx of former medical corpsmen, trained during the Vietnam War, who were returning to civilian life and seeking employment. Many of them hoped to utilize their military medical training in their new civilian careers. An idea was born. The physician assistant profession developed from the hope that, with additional training, these exmedics (and others with patient-care experience, such as nurses) might be able to fill the health care gap.

In 1965, at the Duke University Medical Center, the first physician assistant educational program began. The student body consisted of four exmilitary corpsmen. Today, there are approximately 23,000 PAs in clinical practice, performing medical services with the supervision of a licensed physician in all fifty states and the District of Columbia. Last year, the 58 accredited physician assistant educational programs in this country graduated 1,750 new PAs ready to step into a variety of health care situations.

The physician and the physician assistant form a health care team that offers benefits all around. First, the diagnostic and therapeutic patient care provided by the PAs frees the supervising physicians to devote more time to those patients with more serious illnesses. The PA's work allows the doctor in charge more time to practice the sophisticated medicine for which he or she was trained. PAs are providing more health care than ever before available in rural areas and the inner city. In rural and remote areas, PAs sometimes keep in contact with their supervising physicians via telephone, radio, or television. In 1993, 34 percent of all PAs practiced in towns of fewer than 50,000 people, and 33 percent practiced in cities of more than 500,000. Other traditionally underserved geographical areas are today benefiting from the presence of these 23,000 new health care practitioners. In many cases, patient waiting times have been reduced, examinations are less hurried, and there is more time for the patient to ask questions and to be answered. Sixty percent of all doctors responding to a recent national survey stated that they felt delegation of certain responsibilities to PAs would increase the quality of health care. It is felt by many that PAs have brought better and more personalized vital health care to populations that, until recently, had limited access to medical care.

Also, as had been hoped for when the PA concept was begun, PAs are offering strong support to primary care physicians. Approximately 70 percent of all PAs in clinical practice assist physicians who are in primary care practices, such as family and general internal medicine, emergency medicine, pediatrics, and obstetrics and gynecology. There are PAs working wherever doctors are working, in a full spectrum of specialties—allergy, dermatology, endocrinology, gastroenterology, hematology, psychiatry, public health, physical rehabilitation, radiology, anesthesiology, infectious diseases, geriatrics, preventative medicine, and neurology. In addition, 17 percent of all PAs work in surgical specialties, including general surgery, orthopedic surgery, thoracic surgery, cardiovascular surgery, urologic surgery, neurosurgery, plastic surgery, otolaryngology, and ophthalmic surgery. In Alabama, PAs who work in surgical specialties are known as surgeon assistants, or SAs (see page 230).

And, too, the people working in the physician assistant profession have benefited. PAs do important and respected work in our society. That work is well remunerated both financially and emotionally. As with other medical paraprofessions, by virtue of the shorter training time and smaller dollar commitments required and the fact that less educational preparation is necessary, the PA field is attractive to many people who are interested in serving in a medical profession but who are unable or unwilling to attend medical school. In the academic year 1992–1993, the average age of students admitted to PA training programs was 26. This statistic suggests that a career as a physician assistant is something that one can begin later in life, perhaps as a second career. While 56 percent of these students had a baccalaureate degree prior to beginning their programs, 9 percent had no college experience at all. Prior to their enrollment, 15 percent of all PAs were nurses, 14 percent were emergency medical technicians, 13 percent were medical corpsmen, 9 percent were emergency room technicians, 7 percent were medical laboratory technicians, 5 percent were medical assistants, and 19 percent had previous health care experience in occupational therapy, physical therapy, and other health professions.

SETTINGS, SALARIES, STATISTICS

Because physician assistants help physicians, they can be found working wherever physicians are working—in private practices, comprehensive health clinics, hospitals, satellite clinics, prisons, the military, nursing homes, health maintenance organizations, industrial clinics, student health services, and urban community centers. Approximately 32 percent work mostly in hospital settings (including those of the Department of Veterans Affairs and the public health service), 24 percent work in nonhospital clinic settings, 37 percent work for single practitioners or for groups of doctors, and 7 percent work in the military. There are even physician assistants in the White House who work with the president's physician in treating the president, vice-president, their families, and their staffs.

A normal workweek for a physician assistant ranges between 40 and 50 hours. Depending on the specific nature of the practice and the duties assumed, a PA may be expected to be on call or to work additional and evening hours. Nearly half of all PAs now spend some hours on call per week. Some emergency room PAs work 24-hour shifts twice per week; others work three 12-hour shifts per week. PAs in clinics often have more predictable, five-day, 40-hour workweeks.

There are, at this time, over 23,000 PAs working in the United States, more than 40 percent of whom are male.

Salaries for PAs vary because of state, specialty, and practice differences. Generally, starting salaries range in the mid-thirties, and more experienced PAs earn incomes ranging from $50,000 to $55,000 annually. Salaries are highest in the eastern states.

HOW TO BECOME A PHYSICIAN ASSISTANT

Requirements for admission to physician assistant educational programs vary. Four-year programs will accept applications from students with only a high school diploma or its equivalent, and two-year programs require a bachelor's degree. Two years of undergraduate study in a science or health profession program is the common prerequisite today. Some work experience in personal health care is preferred. In 1993, the typical PA student had a bachelor's degree and over four years of health care experience before being accepted into a program.

PA educational programs also differ in length, but most call for 24 months of training. The typical PA educational program is a two-year bachelor's or associate's degree program with a prerequisite of two years of college. Other programs are three or four years in length, with the prerequisite built in. Some programs award certificates instead of associate's degrees.

Physician assistant educational programs are most often offered by medical centers, but programs also exist in liberal arts colleges.

Typically the course of study is divided into two segments. The first, the didactic segment, can last from 6 to 12 months and covers anatomy, physiology, chemistry, biochemistry, clinical medicine, clinical pharmacology, electrocardiography, human behavior, medical terminology, microbiology, pathology, physical diagnosis, and radiology.

The second stage of the program, which typically lasts from 9 to 15 months, is made up of clinical rotations and preceptorships in hospitals, clinics, and physicians' offices. These rotations offer intensive clinical learning experiences in the disciplines of ambulatory medicine, emergency medicine, family practice, general surgery, inpatient surgery, internal surgery, obstetrics and gynecology, outpatient medicine, pediatrics, primary care, and psychiatry, with the emphasis on primary care and family practice.

In recent years, as the physician assistant concept and physician assistant programs have become more accepted and popular, a number of postgraduate training experiences have been developed. These PA residencies provide additional clinical experience in such areas as emergency medicine, surgery, and neonatology (the care of newborns).

Competition for admission to PA educational program is strong. For every position available, at least six applications from qualified candidates are received.

Among the personal qualities important to success in this very people-oriented occupation are intelligence, compassion, patience, and the capacity for calm and good judgment when confronted with emergency situations. The willingness to carry out instructions and the ability to work with others are essential.

The activities of PAs are regulated by nearly every state, but requirements for practice vary. In approximately 47 states, PAs must be certified by the National Commission on Certification of Physician Assistants (NCCPA). To become certified, a PA must pass the National Certifying Examination for Primary Care Physician Assistants, which was developed and is administered by the National Board of Medical Examiners. This day-long examination (consisting of a written test and an assessment of practical skills) is administered nationwide once a year. To take the certifying examination, a student must graduate from a physician assistant program that is accredited by the Commission for the Accreditation of Allied Health Education Programs (CAAHEP), which, on July 1, 1994, succeeded the Committee on Allied Health Education and Accreditation (CAHEA) of the American Medical Association. There are currently 57 accredited PA programs. (CAAHEP, which certifies education programs for most allied health professions, is an independent body in which the AMA participates as one sponsor among many.) Candidates who successfully satisfy the certification requirements may use the designation physician assistant-certified or the initials (PA-C) after their names. To maintain certification, a PA must log 100 continuing medical education credits every two years and retake the national certification exam every six years.

Licensure varies from state to state. The most common requirements are proof of graduation from an approved educational program, proof of NCCPA certification, letters of reference, and a statement from the supervising physician assuring proper supervision.

THE FUTURE

The employment outlook for PAs is excellent. The validity and effectiveness of PAs' contributions to health care have been clearly demonstrated, and patient acceptance of this still relatively new health profession has been strong. PAs did, in fact, help to alleviate the strains on both physicians and patients created by the doctor shortage, and they have succeeded, as well, in providing more health care and health education than ever before. This profession, though still relatively new, has grown amazingly fast. In 1970, there were fewer than 100 PAs nationwide. Today, there are approximately 27,000, and they are practicing in every state, the District of Columbia, and in several foreign countries. Most certified PAs have several employment offers from which to choose. Sometimes locating a satisfactory position requires relocating to a medically underserved area, but a large percentage of PA students have expressed a preference for a small-town setting.

One long-standing barrier to major expansion in this field fell in the mid-1980s. While almost every study has shown that the use of PAs lowers medical costs without compromising medical care—not a small consideration considering the staggering medical bills this nation annually rings up—this advantage was, until recently, largely lost because most health insurance plans, including Medicare and Medicaid, would not provide reimbursement for treatment performed solely by a PA. Today, reimbursement by third-party payers exists for many patients, and physicians may bill Medicare for services provided to their hospital and nursing home patients by their PAs. This change in Medicare policy has spurred the increased use of PAs by office-based physicians.

Opportunities should also open up in hospitals and health maintenance organizations (HMOs). These attitudinal and economic changes, set against a backdrop of an aging population needing more health care, should create a job situation where the demand for PAs outstrips the supply. The U.S. Department of Labor predicts a 44 percent growth rate in this profession by 2005.

For more information on physician assistants, write to the:

American Academy of Physician Assistants
950 North Washington Street
Alexandria, Virginia 22314

The academy's book, *1994 Physician Assistant Programs Directory*, gives state-by-state listings of accredited educational programs and detailed information about application procedures and financial aid.

SURGEON ASSISTANT

Seventeen percent of all physician assistants specialize in surgery. The term *surgeon assistant* (SA) is used by one state, Alabama, for physician assistants who, having successfully completed an accredited program of specialized academic and clinical training, are qualified to work under the direction, supervision, and responsibility of a licensed surgeon, providing certain patient services formerly performed only by surgeons. (In the other 49 states these specialists are simply called physician assistants, and the vast majority of them prepare for this profession by supplementing their accredited physician assistant educations with on-the-job training in surgery.) Like all physician assistants, surgeon assistants are dependent practitioners who work with a supervising surgeon as an integral part of a surgical team, helping the surgeon to serve his or her patients.

Also, as is the case with other physician assistants, the specifics of the job are defined by the extent of the SA's training, the legal limitations imposed by the state in which he or she practices, and the arrangement the SA has with his or her supervising surgeon. Fundamentally, SAs gather the data necessary for the surgeon to make a diagnosis and assist the surgeon in carrying out the patient's therapy.

Typical of the functions a surgeon assistant may be expected to perform are the interviewing of patients and taking of accurate medical histories, performing physical examinations, ordering and/or performing routine laboratory tests and other diagnostic procedures, organizing the data from these tests and making preliminary interpretations of these results for presentation to the supervising surgeon, performing certain therapeutic procedures, carrying out preoperative procedures that prepare the patient for surgery, assisting the surgeon during operations, helping the supervising surgeon in making hospital rounds, participating in the care and evaluation of the patient during the postoperative period, and dealing with minor injuries and emergency situations.

SAs working for general surgeons routinely perform a wide variety of procedures. SAs who work under the supervision of a surgeon who specializes (such as an orthopedic surgeon or plastic surgeon) will assist in carrying out procedures inherent to that specialty.

SETTINGS, SALARIES, STATISTICS

Surgeon assistants work wherever surgeons work: in the surgeon's office, the hospital operating rooms, recovery rooms, intensive care units, emergency rooms, and in hospital outpatient clinics. A typical workweek for an SA ranges between 40 and 50 hours, with additional hours and on-call hours often added.

Seventeen percent of all physician assistants are surgeon assistants. Surgery is the second largest physician assistant specialty after primary care. There are approximately 2,000 practicing surgeon assistants at this time.

As with other physician assistants, salaries vary from state to state and region to region and will depend, too, on the specifics of the work performed and of the particular working arrangement. Generally, starting salaries begin around $30,000, and experienced surgeon assistants may earn $46,000 or more per year.

HOW TO BECOME A SURGEON ASSISTANT

There are several routes to a career as a surgeon assistant. One alternative is graduation from one of the two special surgeon assistant educational programs in the United States that are accredited by the Commission for the Accreditation of Allied Health Education Programs (CAAHEP), which on July 1, 1994, succeeded the Committee on Allied Health Education and Accreditation (CAHEA) of the American Medical Association. (CAAHEP, which accredits education programs for this and twenty-one other allied health professions, is an independent body in which the AMA participates as one sponsor among many.) One of the surgeon-assistant programs is at the University of Alabama at Birmingham, and the other is at Cuyahoga Community College in Ohio. These programs require a minimum of a high school diploma or its equivalent and at least two years of college course work. (These two years of college work should include courses in general biology, general chemistry, physics, algebra, geometry, organic chemistry, microbiology, and the behavioral sciences.) Also, some experience in the medical field is preferred.

The second route to a career as a surgeon assistant is to satisfactorily complete one of the 54 physician assistant educational programs accredited by CAAHEP, become certified, and then accumulate additional, specialized training and experience in one of the many postgraduate programs offered by institutions accredited to teach surgeon assistants. For these students, then, the prerequisite for embarking on the training necessary for a career as a surgeon assistant are those admissions prerequisites established by the various physician assistant educational programs. These standards range from a high school diploma to four years of college.

A third route to surgeon assistant status is also for men and women who are already graduates of physician assistant programs. They may accept a position on a surgical service and, over the course of approximately a three-month period, be oriented to the role.

Like the educational regimen for physician assistants, surgeon assistant educational programs are divided into a didactic phase followed by a clinical practicum. In the surgeon assistant program, however, the emphasis is on those clinical and technical skills related to surgical patient care as well as on basic medicine sciences. Surgeon assistant students gain the necessary clinical experience in general and specialty surgical services and in the emergency room.

Surgeon assistant educational programs are typically 24 months long. The first segment of the curriculum consists of courses in gross anatomy, neuroanatomy, physiology, physiological chemistry, management of medical and surgical disorders, medical history and physical evaluation procedures, pharmacology, roentgenogram and electrocardiogram interpretation, sterile technique, assisting at surgical procedures, administration of parenteral fluids via venipuncture or venous cutdown, the administering of injections, ventilation therapy, cardiopulmonary resuscitation, and urethral catheterization.

After this didactic phase, surgeon assistant candidates rotate in general surgery and in the various surgical specialties under the supervision of a surgical resident or surgeon-in-charge. At this time, the student directly participates in the surgical patient care. Among the specialties a surgeon assistant student might rotate in are cardiovascular surgery, neurologic surgery, oncologic surgery, plastic surgery, orthopedic surgery, pediatric surgery, renal transplant surgery, thoracic surgery, trauma surgery, and urologic surgery. Again, there is variety in approach and in the course work required from program to program.

Upon successful completion of a surgeon assistant educational program, a candidate is awarded a certificate. In some cases, the course work necessary for the awarding of this certificate may be applied toward satisfying the requirements for a bachelor of science degree. Competition for places in surgeon assistant educational programs and postgraduate surgeon assistant training programs is strong.

Personal qualities one would do well to bring to a career as a surgeon assistant include intelligence, strong motivation, dedication, dexterity, the ability to remain calm and effective in emergency situations, and the ability to follow orders and to work for and with others.

The National Commission on Certification for Physician Assistants (NCCPA) no longer offers certification specifically for surgeon assistants. Rather, SAs may apply for physician assistant certification (see page 228).

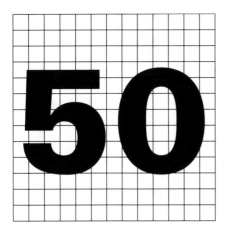

PULMONARY TECHNOLOGIST

also known as
Pulmonary Technician
**Pulmonary Function Technologist/
    Technician**
**Pulmonary Physiology Technologist/
    Technician**
**Cardiopulmonary Technologist/
    Technician**
**Physiological Monitoring
    Technologist/Technician**
**Stress Testing Technologist/
    Technician**
ICU Technologist/Technician
**Medical Machine Technologist/
    Technician**

Pulmonary means pertaining to the lungs. Pulmonary disease (which includes lung cancer, emphysema, and environmental damage) is a leading cause of death and disability in America today. The use of new and sophisticated medical instruments to screen for medical problems related to pulmonary function has become an integral part of modern preventative medicine and comprehensive health care. Operating these machines and evaluating the diagnostic data they produce are specially trained, newly defined and recognized allied health professionals called pulmonary technologists. The support services they perform are called pulmonary technology.

Working under the supervision of a physician, a *pulmonary technologist* conducts diagnostic evaluations of normal and abnormal pulmonary parameters by administering a variety of tests to the patient. These tests include blood gas studies, bronchial challenge studies, bronchoscopic examination, exercise tolerance testing, gas diffusion studies, and sleep studies. Some of these tests are invasive, others are noninvasive. Some use video apparatus, scans, and computerized interpretation. The pulmonary system and the cardiovascular system (heart and arterial) are closely related in the human body; therefore, the functions of a pulmonary technologist often overlap with or call upon the functions of another health care professional, the cardiovascular technologist. In pulmonary exercise testing, for example, an electrocardiograph monitor is used to observe the patient's heart activity while lung function is being studied. Other tests call for the administering of certain medications which help in evaluating the patient's pulmonary status.

The pulmonary technologist is responsible for selecting and setting up the appropriate equipment, explaining the procedure to the patient and eliciting his or her cooperation, carrying out the test, supervising other personnel who are assisting, monitoring the patient's response, calculating the test results, evaluating their reliability, and evaluating the patient's performance and its clinical implications. From the data gathered from these various tests, a picture of the patient's pulmonary health emerges. Using this picture, the physician can make a diagnosis and determine a course of treatment.

Pulmonary technology has just in recent years been defined as a specific, formal field, and it is expanding rapidly. As a result, job descriptions, requirements, and even titles for pulmonary technologists vary widely. Many pulmonary technologists specialize in performing a specific diagnostic procedure, and in some situations, they have been given position titles that identify them with the machine or test that they handle instead of the field of which they are a part (hence, stress testing technologist, for example).

SETTINGS, SALARIES, STATISTICS

Pulmonary technologists work in hospitals, clinics, private practice offices, home care facilities, environmental institutions, diagnostic centers, rehabilitation centers, mobile units, research facilities, and government facilities. Cardiopulmonary testing is usually performed within a hospital setting.

Pulmonary technologists may occasionally work irregular hours, and, as with many other health care professionals, moderate exposure to infectious diseases exists.

Salaries depend on level of training. Generally, they range from $18,000 to $31,500 annually for experienced technologists.

HOW TO BECOME A PULMONARY TECHNOLOGIST

Although a bachelor's degree is preferred for students applying for pulmonary technology training, it is not always necessary. There are four paths to education and training in this field. A student may: (1) enroll in a postcollege program offered by a medical center; (2) receive an associate's degree in pulmonary technology from a community college; (3) receive a bachelor's degree with a major in pulmonary technology from a college or university; (4) receive a high school diploma and then receive extensive on-the-job training.

Personal qualities important to satisfying and satisfactory performance in this field include precision, dexterity, dependability, and good communication skills.

At this time, there is no state or federal licensure for pulmonary technologists. Certification and registration (which are voluntary) are offered by the

National Board for Respiratory Care (NBRC). A written examination is part of the certification process. To sit for the NBRC certification examination, a candidate must be a graduate of, or expect to graduate from one of the 300 respiratory therapy educational programs accredited by the Commission for the Accreditation of Allied Health Education Programs, or CAAHEP, (CAAHEP succeeded the American Medical Association's Committee on Allied Health Education and Accreditation, or CAHEA, on July 1, 1994 and is an independent body in which the AMA participates as one sponsor among many); be a graduate of a pulmonary technology program accredited by the National Society for Pulmonary Technology (there are five); be a certified or registered respiratory therapist; have 62 semester hours of college credit which include courses in chemistry, biology, and mathematics, plus six months of clinical experience in pulmonary functions; or have a high school diploma and two years of clinical experience in pulmonary functions. Upon successful completion of this examination, the letters CPFT, which stand for certified pulmonary function technologist, may be used after one's name. At this time, there are over 7,500 CPFTs in the United States. Last year, nearly 1,000 men and women took the NBRC certification examination.

THE FUTURE

Future employment opportunities in this field are very promising. A shortage of trained, qualified personnel currently exists. As more hospitals and other health care institutions establish cardiopulmonary laboratories, this shortage should grow.

For more information about pulmonary technologists, write to the:

> National Society for Pulmonary Technology, Inc.
> 120 Falcon Drive, Unit #3
> Fredericksburg, Virginia 22408

and for certification information, contact the:

> National Board for Respiratory Care
> 8310 Nieman Road
> Lenexa, Kansas 66214

and for information about accredited education programs, write to the:

> Joint Review Committee for Respiratory Therapy
>   Education
> 1701 West Euless Boulevard, Suite 300
> Euless, Texas 76040

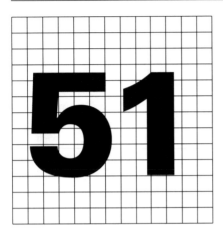

RADIATION THERAPIST

Radiation therapy is the use of high-energy X rays, gamma rays, electron beams, and other forms of radiation in the treatment of diseases, especially certain forms of cancer. It is one of the most sophisticated tools of modern medicine. Radiation can kill cells, but it is indiscriminate, killing normal as well as abnormal cells. Radiation therapy is the careful and controlled application of radiation to cancerous cells while shielding the adjacent normal cells from exposure and possible damage. Radiation is directed to the patient's malignant tumor for just a few seconds from the outside, through the skin and other tissues overlying the tumor. Because of the potential for damage to normal cells, the exact location of the tumor must be pinpointed. Physical examinations and diagnostic X rays as well as CT scans, magnetic resonance imaging, ultrasound, and the use of radioisotopes may be required to determine its exact position and dimensions. The frequency of the treatments, duration of the therapy, dosages, and type of radiation therapy must be carefully planned and the treatment skillfully administered. Depending on the nature and extent of the cancer, radiation therapy treatment (used alone or in combination with chemotherapy and/or surgery) can ease the pain caused by this disease, prolong life, and, in a growing number of cases, bring about a permanent cure.

In most hospitals, a team of health care professionals plans and carries out radiation therapy. The radiation oncologist is a physician who has specialized training in the use of radiation and who evaluates the patient and writes the radiation therapy prescription and instructions for its administration. The radiation physicist has extensive experience in planning radiation treatments, as well as in calibrating and maintaining the equipment. The dosimetrist is an expert in designing specialized treatment plans for each patient. Computers are used to produce the elaborate plan necessary for a course of treatment. The radiation therapy nurse is trained to care for the cancer patient as he or she undergoes and recuperates from therapy.

The *radiation therapist* carries out various phases of the actual treatment. Using sophisticated therapeutic equipment, such as high-energy linear accelerators and X ray machines, the radiation therapist exposes specific areas of the body to the prescribed doses of ionizing radiation, accurately delivering, with a minimum of supervision, the planned course of radiotherapy. The therapist will check the physician's prescription and will help the radiation physicist in calibrating and preparing the equipment, assist in tumor localization and dosimetric procedures, help to maintain the equipment so that it will function effectively and safely, and assist in the preparation and handling of the various radioactive materials used in the procedures. In addition, the radiation therapist observes the clinical progress of the patient undergoing radiotherapy, watches for any signs of complications, keeps accurate detailed records of the specifics of the treatment administered and the patient's reactions to that treatment, provides psychological support to the patient and family at what can be a very stressful time, applies surgical dressings as required, assists in minor surgical procedures related to the therapy, and cares for any surgical instruments used, following the principles of aseptic technique. And because radiation can have dangerous effects on the patient and the user when mishandled, the radiation therapist carries out all these duties while strictly adhering to the principles of radiation protection. Lead blocks are used to "shape" the treatment field and protect adjacent tissues, the controls on the machinery are carefully maintained and used so that only the specific area is exposed, and only the designated amount of radiation is administered. The radiation therapist knows how to detect any defects in the equipment that might become a radiation hazard and what steps to take should a radiation accident occur.

Radiation therapists do very important, responsible, exacting work. They routinely deal with patients who are experiencing pain and anxiety, and the treatment they provide offers hope, relief from pain, and, for many millions of these patients, a future.

SETTINGS, SALARIES, STATISTICS

Most radiation therapists work in hospitals. Radiation therapists also work in clinics, research laboratories, in veterinary medicine, in commercial sales applications, for government agencies, and in educator and management capacities. There are approximately 9,000 radiation therapists. The majority of them are female.

Salaries very depending on geographical location, experience, and ability. Entry-level salaries average about $25,000 per year. Experienced radiation therapists earn $32,000 to $36,000 annually on average. Radiation therapists who have reached administrative and managerial positions in their departments earn approximately $40,500 annually. Salaries are significantly higher on the West Coast.

HOW TO BECOME A RADIATION THERAPIST

There are fundamentally four educational routes to a career in radiation therapy: there are one-year, hospital-based certificate (or diploma) programs, two-year, hospital-based certificate programs, two-year associate's degree programs, and baccalaureate degree programs. Within each of these options, specific prerequisites and program lengths vary. Each of these options is sufficient for employment at this time. Administrators, instructors, and researchers often work for their bachelor's degrees and then go on to graduate studies. However, a resolution was passed in 1993 at the American Society of Radiologic Technologists house of delegates session, stating that "all students entering radiation therapy programs in the year 2000 and thereafter will be required to complete a baccalaureate degree for entry into the profession."

The Joint Review Committee on Education in Radiologic Technology (JRCERT), an independent accrediting agency for radiation therapists and radiographers which is recognized by the U.S. Department of Education, currently accredits a total of 123 educational programs for radiation therapy technologists. (For many years, accreditation was granted by the American Medical Association's Committee on Allied Health Education and Accreditation—CAHEA—of which JRCERT was a sponsor. However, as of 1994, JRCERT is the sole accrediting body.) Accredited programs are offered by hospitals, universities, four-year colleges, and community colleges throughout the country. Several institutions offer more than one program. Last year, 921 men and women graduated from approved radiation therapy programs. The one-year, hospital-based certificate programs, of which there are 84, are open only to graduates of accredited radiography programs and, in some cases, to registered nurses and students holding bachelor's degrees in certain areas or specialties. The two-year, hospital-based certificate programs usually require only a high school diploma or its equivalent. (In high school, courses in the basic sciences and mathematics are strongly advised.) Two-year associate's degree programs, of which there are 30, also typically require a high school diploma, and 9 programs offer a bachelor of science degree (one of which is specifically called a bachelor of science in radiologic technology). The bachelor's degree programs vary somewhat in length and requirements, but all entail a minimum of approximately four years of post–high school education.

Radiation therapy education entails classroom settings, laboratory work, and supervised clinical experience. The professional curriculum typically includes courses in medical ethics and law, methods of patient care and health education, medical terminology, human structure and function, pathology, clinical radiation oncology, radiobiology, mathematics, radiation physics, radiation protection, technical radiation oncology, medical imaging, brachytherapy, quality assurance, introduction to computers, introduction to hyperthermia and venipuncture, and clinical dosimetry.

Personal qualities that are important to success and satisfaction as a radiation therapist include a genuine desire and willingness to help others, compassion, a mechanical inclination, aptitude in math, aptitude in the physical sciences, and attention to detail.

Almost all employers today require their radiation therapists to be certified by the American Registry of Radiologic Technologists (ARRT). To be certified, a candidate must be a graduate of an accredited radiation therapy educational program (there are rare cases where graduates of nonaccredited programs appeal for waiver) and must pass a four-hour competency examination. This examination is administered by the ARRT three times yearly in approximately 100 locations (including Puerto Rico) at the same time as the examinations for radiographers and nuclear medicine technologists. Graduates of accredited programs who pass the ARRT examination and are of good moral character may call themselves registered radiation therapists and use the letters R.T.(T)(ARRT)—which stand for registered technologist in therapy certified by the American Registry of Radiologic Technologists—after their names.

At this time, 23 states require their radiation therapists to be licensed. Several other states are currently considering adopting licensure. In some of these states, certification by the American Registry of Radiologic Technologists is accepted in lieu of satisfactory completion of the state's licensure examination.

THE FUTURE

There is, at this time, a geographical shortage of registered radiation therapists. The American Society of Radiologic Technologists, which is the professional association for radiation therapists, radiographers, nuclear medicine technologists, and sonographers, estimates that there are several thousand more openings than there are therapists. This demand should continue, spurred by such factors as a growing American population, longer life spans, the growing number of older Americans, and the widening application of new radiological technologies to an expanding range of conditions. The U.S. Department of Labor projects a 45 percent increase in the number of job openings in this profession by 2005.

For more information about radiation therapists, write to the:

American Society of Radiologic Technologists
15000 Central Avenue, S.E.
Albuquerque, New Mexico 87123-3917

American Registry of Radiologic Technologists
1255 Northland Drive
St. Paul, Minnesota 55120-1155

And for information about accredited programs, contact the:

>Joint Review Committee on Education in Radiologic
>   Technology
>20 North Wacker Drive, Suite 900
>Chicago, Illinois 60606-2901

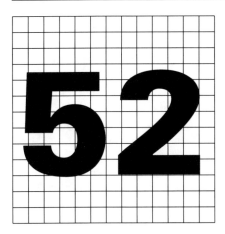

RADIOGRAPHER

Radiographers (formerly called X ray technologists) are specially trained health care professionals who perform radiographic examinations. Radiography is the use of radiation to provide images of various body parts (bones, organs, tissues, vessels) and of various body functions (digestion, circulation, the action of the heart's valves) to facilitate the diagnosis and, in some cases, the treatment of certain injuries and illnesses. These images are recorded on film (these are the black-and-white translucent images with which most of us are familiar), video tape, motion picture film, or they are displayed on a video monitor.

Radiography is an invaluable diagnostic tool that is used by almost every medical specialty. Using radiography, fractures and other orthopedic problems, tumors, ulcers, deposits and foreign matter in the body, and diseased and malfunctioning organs and vessels can be uncovered and assessed without having to perform surgery on the patient. It is estimated that last year 210 million medical diagnostic X rays and other radiologic examinations were performed in the United States. (Chest X rays continue to be the most common, accounting for 50 percent of all X rays.) Seventy percent of all Americans had radiologic examinations of one kind or another in 1993. When a physician must know what is happening inside a patient's body, he or she orders X rays, or one of their new, sophisticated cousins—computerized tomography (CT scans), mammography, and digital subtraction angiography. Perhaps the most revolutionary new breakthrough in this profession has been magnetic resonance imaging (MRI). This imaging modality uses magnetic impulses instead of radiation; among other things, it can actually allow a physician to observe the course of a disease at the cellular level. Using MRI, the physician is able to see and evaluate the effect a therapeutic drug has on a diseased cell so that he or she can modify or eliminate the therapy accordingly. As these new technologies make visible conditions in the body that until now were inaccessible, earlier and better diagnoses are becoming possible (often with less discomfort, inconvenience, and cost to the patient), and new perspectives on the body and its workings are opening up.

When radiographic examinations are ordered by a physician, radiographers are primarily responsible for the operation of radiologic equipment and for the preparation of the patient. The radiographer positions the patient, adjusts the equipment to the correct setting for the particular examination, administers any chemical tracing mixtures that are needed (often, to make an organ or other body part visible for radiological examination, liquids are swallowed by or injected into the patient), and makes the required number of radiographs, all the while adhering to the principles of radiation safety so as to protect the patient, him or herself, and others. When used by persons uneducated in its characteristics and potential hazards, radiation can be dangerous to the patient and to the user. The radiographer understands radiation and will carefully position the part of the body being imaged, protect other body parts with lead aprons and other coverings, and use only the amount of radiation necessary to produce a quality image.

A radiographer may also be expected to maintain the equipment, process the film, keep patient records, and be prepared to recognize emergency patient conditions and initiate lifesaving measures.

SETTINGS, SALARIES, STATISTICS

Three-quarters of all radiographers work in the radiology departments of hospitals. When necessary, they bring mobile equipment to the patient's bedside or into the operating room.

Radiographers also work in clinics, private offices, industrial and experimental laboratories, in commercial sales and applications, and on the teaching staffs of hospitals, colleges, and universities. Approximately 5 percent of all radiographers are employed by the federal government, primarily in the Department of Veterans Affairs.

Radiographers usually work 40 hours per week, some of which may be weekend or evening hours. Sometimes, radiographers are expected to be on call. Part-time opportunities exist, particularly in clinics and physicians' offices.

There are approximately 173,000 radiographers in the United States. Sixty-five percent of them are female, but the number of men in this profession is steadily increasing.

Advancement to teaching, supervisory, and managerial positions is possible. Salaries vary according to geographical location, experience, ability, and employer. In 1993, entry-level salaries ranged from $22,000 to $26,000.

HOW TO BECOME A RADIOGRAPHER

There are several routes to a career as a radiographer. All begin with a minimum of a high school diploma or its equivalent. In high school, courses in physics, chemistry, biology, algebra, and geometry are strongly recommended. Almost all radiography students receive their education at institutions offering programs accredited by the Joint Review Committee on Education in Radiologic Technology (JRCERT), an independent accrediting agency for radiographers and radiation therapists which is recognized by the U.S. Department of Education. (For many years, accreditation was granted by the American Medical Association's Committee on Allied Health Education and Accreditation, or CAHEA, of which JRCERT was a sponsor. However, as of July 1, 1994, JRCERT is the sole accrediting agency.) At this time, there are 692 JRCERT-accredited educational programs for radiographers, most of which are offered by hospitals and clinics. Radiographer educational programs are also located in junior and community colleges, vocational/technical schools, medical schools, four-year colleges and universities, and in the military.

Accredited programs vary in specific requirements, length, and the credentials awarded upon successful completion. Fifty-four percent of the accredited programs are two-year, mostly hospital-based certificate or diploma programs; 43 percent are two-year associate's degree programs; and 3 percent are four-year baccalaureate programs. Of the baccalaureate programs, several offer a specific bachelor of science in radiologic technology degree, or BSRT. Some of the institutions offer more than one of these educational options for radiography students. Certain degree programs require one or two years of college credit. All three levels of educational preparation are sufficient for employment as a radiographer. However, educators and administrators in this profession usually have their bachelor's or master's degrees.

Last year, 10,061 new radiographers were graduated from accredited programs. The education for radiographers is rigorous and entails classroom study, laboratory work, and clinical experience. The professional curriculum for an accredited program includes: introduction to radiography, ethics in the radiological sciences, introductory law in the radiological sciences, medical terminology, radiologic science patient care, human structure and function, radiographic procedures, medical imaging and processing, imaging equipment, evaluation of radiographs, radiation physics, radiation protection, radiation biology, radiographic pathology, introduction to quality improvement, computers in radiologic science, and pharmacology and drug administration.

There are, across the country, a few nonaccredited educational programs teaching radiography. However, by and large, only graduates of accredited programs are eligible to take the American Registry of Radiologic Technologists' (ARRT) certification examination, and certification is important, because most institutions consider it a requirement of employment. This four-hour examination is administered three times a year in approximately 100 locations nationwide as well as in Puerto Rico. Passing this examination entitles a radiographer to use the letters R.T.(R)(ARRT)—which stand for registered technologist in radiography certified by the American Registry of Radiologic Technologists—after his or her name. The American Registry of Radiologic Technologists also certifies radiation therapists and nuclear medicine technologists and administers the certification examinations for these professions at the same times in the same testing locations. Certification is recognized in all fifty states. The ARRT also offers advanced qualification examinations in cardiovascular-interventional technology and mammography. As of 1994, advanced qualification examinations in computed tomography and magnetic resonance imaging are also offered.

At this time, twenty-seven states plus Puerto Rico have specific licensing requirements for radiographers (which are usually satisfied by passing the ARRT exam), and the trend toward licensing should continue because of recent federal legislation directing states to license.

Personal qualities that are important to the successful and satisfying execution of this job include compassion, emotional stability, good health, attention to detail, and the ability to communicate well. A radiographer must have a genuine interest in helping people with all kinds of medical conditions.

THE FUTURE

Employment opportunities in radiography are expected to remain stable in the coming decade, partly because of the spreading use of new X ray and related equipment in diagnosing and treating an ever-expanding range of health conditions and because the American population is growing larger and older and will, therefore, demand more medical care. Acute shortages of radiographers currently exist in some parts of the country.

For more information about a career in radiography, write to the:

American Society of Radiologic Technologists
15000 Central Avenue S.E.
Albuquerque, New Mexico 87123-3917

For information about certification, contact the:

American Registry of Radiologic Technologists
1255 Northland Drive
St. Paul, Minnesota 55120-1155

And for information about accredited programs, contact the:

Joint Review Committee on Education in Radiologic
Technology
20 North Wacker Drive, Suite 900
Chicago, Illinois 60606-2901

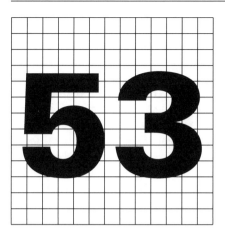

REHABILITATION COUNSELOR

also known as
Vocational Rehabilitation Counselor
including
Psychiatric Rehabilitation Counselor
Vocational Rehabilitation Therapist

To rehabilitate means to put back in good condition. *Rehabilitation counselors* are experts at putting men and women whose lives have been side-tracked by physical and/or mental disabilities back in good condition and back on the track as functioning, working members of society. Whereas the physician rehabilitates a patient with treatment, medications, or surgery, a counselor rehabilitates a patient with personalized counseling, emotional support, and rehabilitation therapy that typically entails learning useful work activities. Disability can take many forms. Patients include men and women with psychiatric problems or mental disabilities who have histories of institutionalization; workers disabled by disease or accident who, as a result, can no longer perform their old jobs; veterans; and individuals recovering from alcohol and drug abuse.

As soon as the injury or illness is stabilized, the patient is referred to the rehabilitation counselor, who will observe the patient and test his or her motor ability, skill level, interests, and psychological makeup. Hundreds of different test batteries are available for these purposes, and the counselor is educated to know which tests are most appropriate for a particular patient. Sometimes, new interests and talents are uncovered in the process. Over a period of several months, the counselor develops a profile of the patient, especially noting how the patient adapts to the disability. The counselor looks at the "whole person" and learns about what the patient's life was like prior to the disabling trauma. The rehabilitation counselor consults with the patient's family, physicians, psychologists, and other therapists and then, using this information, he or she formulates a plan of rehabilitation. Sometimes this program entails retaining the patient in a new vocation. For individuals who have physical and/or mental disabilties and who have never worked, rehabilitation may entail the learning of vocational and social skills necessary to function in a work setting. Training typically takes place in a sheltered workshop, where the trainee may learn his or her new occupation and test his or her new abilities and social skills in a controlled, noncompetitive environment. When the training is completed, for many patients a job in the community (often arranged by the rehabilitation counselor) is possible.

Psychiatric rehabilitation counselors specialize in helping psychiatric patients prepare for greater participation in the community. They also help the community prepare for the rehabilitated patient. Psychiatric rehabilitation counselors test and evaluate psychiatric patients, and on the basis of the results, they teach the patient how to perform suitable productive activities that can be used in the marketplace. Patients who have been institutionalized for many years are often out of touch with society and can easily be frightened by the daily demands of life in a noninstitutional, nonstructured setting. Years of psychological progress can quickly unravel if the patient is unprepared to reenter the community. The psychiatric rehabilitation counselor acts as the patient's supervisor, helping him or her adjust gradually. Patients are slowly eased from the institutional setting to a less protected, dormitory setting. The patient's new skills are gradually put to use in an actual work situation—perhaps first in a sheltered work setting and then in private industry. Counselors teach the patient the rules of society and offer practical lessons in how to handle money, use public transportation, and complete other everyday tasks required to function in the community.

Simultaneously, the psychiatric rehabilitation counselor works to educate the community about rehabilitated psychiatric patients. To dispel any misconceptions, calm any fears, and counter any prejudices that might exist regarding former psychiatric patients, the counselor may conduct community meetings and send out educational literature in the community in which the patient will be living and working. The counselor also works with local and national companies, educating them about the productivity and societal benefits of hiring men and women with physical and psychological disabilities who have been rehabilitated.

After the patient is placed in a vocation, be it in the community or in a long-term sheltered situation, the rehabilitation counselor provides follow-up counseling and support.

Manual arts therapy programs, which formally began at the end of World War II in response to the large number of returning soldiers who were in need of rehabilitation, are important providers of vocational rehabilitation counseling. In addition to the traditional manual arts vocations (woodworking, photography, appliance repair, graphic arts, welding, sheet metal work, drafting, gardening, automobile repair, jewelry making), clerical work, accounting, and other office skills are often introduced in these rehabilitation programs. But there are no lists of functions that rehabilitation patients are taught. The goal of rehabilitation counseling is to work with the specific patient's mental and physical abilities, interests, education, and experiences and then to tailor the training program to meet the needs of the whole person.

Also taking part in the nonmedical assessment and rehabilitation of individuals who are disabled are education therapists, who use educational activities (typing; shorthand; computer skills; bookkeeping; painting; the study of mathematics, science, and English) to evaluate and treat patients. In educational therapy, mastering the subject matter is not as important as mastering one's emotions; acquiring knowledge of the course work is subordinate to acquiring knowledge of one's own potential. Rehabilitation therapy is the "umbrella" profession in nonmedical rehabilitation, providing counseling, vocational assessment, psychiatric assessment, and job placement in all the areas of rehabilitation.

SETTINGS, SALARIES, STATISTICS

Rehabilitation counselors work in rehabilitation centers; mental hospitals; federal, state, and local government agencies; private agencies; and in public schools where they counsel troubled and disabled youths.

There are approximately 20,000 rehabilitation counselors in the United States, three-quarters of whom work for the various states. Slightly more than half of them are female. Salaries very depending on experience, education, agency, and function. Generally, rehabilitation counselors who hold bachelor's degrees start at between $18,000 and $22,000 per year, and those with master's degrees begin at annual salaries ranging between $22,500 and $28,000. Generally, private, nonprofit agencies pay the least, and private, for-profit agencies pay the most. Government salaries for rehabilitation counselors fall somewhere in between. Veterans Administration salaries begin at about $32,000 per annum. Experienced rehabilitation counselors earn an average of $35,000 yearly. Doctoral level counselors who work as college professors of rehabilitation counseling typically earn salaries starting around $35,000 for nine months. Across the board, salaries tend to be higher on the East and West coasts than elsewhere in the United States. Starting salaries as high as $40,000 per year have been reported for master's degree holders working for private, for-profit agencies in southern California.

HOW TO BECOME A REHABILITATION COUNSELOR

Although the minimum educational requirement for most entry-level rehabilitation counseling jobs is a bachelor's degree, many rehabilitation counselors go on to obtain their master's degree (which entails 18 months to two years of additional study) or their doctorate degree (which entails four to six years of postgraduate study). Gradually, the master's degree is becoming the minimum standard preferred by many employers. The largest professional association serving this field, the National Rehabilitation Counseling Association (or NRCA), encourages counselors to pursue the master's degree. Rehabilitation counseling students study psychiatric rehabilitation problems, techniques of counseling, vocational guidance, testing and statistics, public relations, public speaking, community resources, and occupational and medical subjects.

Although voluntary, certification in this field is an important and respected indication of proficiency. Certification is offered by the Commission on Rehabilitation Counselor Certification (CRCC). There are several combinations of education and experience that qualify a counselor to sit for the CRCC competency examination. Option A requires candidates to hold a master's degree in rehabilitation counseling from an educational program that is accredited by the Commission on Rehabilitation Education (CORE) and to complete 600 semester hours of internship under the supervision of a certified rehabilitation counselor.

Option B requires that a candidate holding a master's degree from a rehabilitation education program not accredited by CORE accumulate 600 semester hours of supervised, on-site internship plus 12 months of acceptable employment is this field.

Option C is for holders of master's degrees in rehab counseling from nonaccredited educational programs who have no internship semesters. These candidates for the examination must have two years of work experience, one of which has been appropriately supervised.

Under option D, individuals who have received master's degrees in related fields that have included certain required course work may sit for the examination by accumulating three to five years of work experience (some of which must be supervised) and successfully completing certain supplemental course work, depending on the specifics of their prior course work.

In addition, there are certification options for doctorate holders. These options similarly call for additional course work, internship, and/or acceptable employment experience, as needed, to supplement the doctorate.

At this time, CORE accredits 88 educational programs for rehabilitation counselors. Students who satisfy the eligibility requirements may sit for the CRCC examination, and those who pass the examination are designated certified rehabilitation counselors and may use the letters C.R.C. after their names. There are over 13,000 certified rehabilitation counselors in the United States. CORE also offers specific certification for rehab counselors who have the education, experience, and other requirements to be case managers (the formal designation is Certified Case Manager, or C.C.M.) and for rehab counselors who are specially educated and experienced in substance abuse counseling (the formal designation is C.R.C.-S.A.C.).

As of April 1, 1994, forty states, plus the District of Columbia, require some form of licensing for rehabilitation counselors. Requirements vary from state to state, and the trend toward licensure is strong.

Personal qualities that can enhance performance and satisfaction as a rehabilitation counselor include empathy, patience, sincerity, good listening skills, good observing skills, warmth, imagination, and a genuine interest in people and the willingness to help them.

THE FUTURE

The employment outlook for rehabilitation counselors is good. The present supply of counselors is not adequate to meet the needs of the disabled, and as rehabilitation services expand this shortage will intensify. Opportunities in this profession should be favorable for the next decade or more. Some experts in this field see state licensing as a step towards the assumption of ever greater responsibilities for rehabilitation counselors. Under some health care reform proposals, rehabilitation counselors may eventually do some of the work of doctorate level psychologists and master's level social workers.

Although the employment outlook is favorable for most rehabilitation counselors, for two professions under this umbrella—educational therapy and manual arts therapy—the future is questionable.

In 1990, there were over 600 educational (or academic) therapists practicing in the U.S. Today there are only about three hundred, 26 of whom work for the Department of Veterans Affairs. Salaries for these professionals, who hold a minimum of a bachelor's degree and have at least six months of clinical experience in professional educational therapy before they may begin practicing, have remained relatively static in recent years (ranging from $20,000 to $35,000 annually). The very effective and valid work performed by educational therapists is still being carried out in Veterans Administration and other public and private hospitals, residential facilities, schools, adult learning centers, and prisons, but the specific job title is slowly disappearing, and the educational therapist's functions are gradually being absorbed by other related rehabilitation professionals—psychologists, occupational therapists, and vocational rehabilitation therapists (vocational rehabilitation therapist is a professional designation established in 1989 to encompass a wide variety of rehabilitation personnel, from substance abuse therapist to manual arts therapist to case manager—the specific personnel in a given setting being a function of the needs of the community served). As educational therapists are retiring, they are not being replaced.

The fate of manual arts therapy as a specific rehabilitation profession is also clouded. Manual arts therapists (also known as industrial therapists, industrial arts therapists, industrial rehabilitation therapists, compensated work therapists, incentive therapists, sheltered workshop supervisors, and vocational rehabilitation therapists) have also seen their ranks dwindle. In 1983, there were 800 manual arts therapists working in VA hospitals and centers, other public and private hospitals, sheltered workshops, workers' compensation rehab centers, mental health centers, and rehabilitation centers for the visually impaired. By 1990, there were fewer than 400 manual arts therapists still practicing, and in 1994 there are only 200 to 250. As the first generations of manual arts therapists, the oldest of whom were educated and trained to help soldiers returning from World War II (many of them in programs provided by Department of Veterans Affairs hospitals) retire, they are not being replaced. Here, too, salaries have remained flat in recent years.

The average is $30,000 per year. As with educational therapists, many of the therapeutic modalities once exclusive to this profession gradually have been adopted and assumed by other rehabilitation personnel, including vocational rehabilitation therapists. But in the case of manual arts therapy, there is an additional limiting factor, and it is perhaps best described as "generational". It appears, from the dwindling numbers, that perhaps the hands-on manual arts are not as relevant to younger patients as they were in the 1940s to 1960s. In settings serving older populations, the demand for manual arts therapists is still solid, but in other settings, often these programs are being phased out. Innovations such as the introduction of computers to the manual arts (for drafting, woodworking, and even for self-evaluation) may renew interest in this specialty, and health care reform's emphasis on preventative medicine and wellness may result in a positive reassessment of the very important work of the manual arts therapist.

On July 1, 1993, the American Association of Rehabilitation Therapists and Specialists (AART), which was the professional association serving educational and manual arts therapists, ceased operations.

For more information about rehabilitation counselors, contact the:

National Rehabilitation Association
633 South Washington Street
Alexandria, Virginia 22314

Commission on Rehabilitation Counselor Certification
1835 Rohlwing Street, Suite E
Rolling Meadows, Illinois 60008

American Counseling Association
5999 Stevenson Avenue
Alexandria, Virginia 22304

National Association of Rehabilitation
  Professionals in the Private Sector
P.O. Box 697
Brookline, Massachusetts 02146

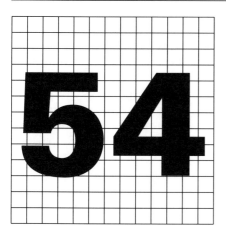

RESPIRATORY THERAPIST, RESPIRATORY THERAPY TECHNICIAN, AND RESPIRATORY THERAPY AIDE

Respiratory therapy (formerly called inhalation therapy) is the diagnostic evaluation and emergency and long-term treatment of patients suffering from cardiorespiratory (heart-lung) abnormalities and deficiencies (such as chronic asthma, pneumonia, bronchitis, emphysema, and breathing difficulties resulting from heart failure, drowning, drug poisoning, stroke, shock, surgery, and head and chest injuries) through the use of such specialized equipment as mechanical ventilators, resuscitators, heart monitors, and blood-gas analyzers, and such respiratory treatments as intermittent positive pressure breathing (IPPB), humidity/aerosol therapy, medical gas administration, broncho-pulmonary drainage, continuous ventilation, and airway management. Respiratory therapy also includes pulmonary function testing, cardiorespiratory rehabilitation, infection control, and cardiorespiratory drug administration.

Respiratory therapists and *respiratory therapy technicians* are the health care specialists who, working under the supervision of a physician, perform the tests that aid in the diagnosis and evaluation of these respiratory problems. They treat patients with the respiratory apparatus, administer the various respiratory therapies, monitor patients' progress, teach patients how to use the prescribed respiratory treatment methods and aids, and provide emergency respiratory care. In some hospitals, respiratory personnel routinely visit surgical patients prior to their operations to teach them certain respiratory exercises that can reduce the incidence of postoperative respiratory complications. Respiratory therapists and respiratory therapy technicians are also responsible for the maintenance of the respiratory equipment.

Respiratory therapy patients range in age from very premature babies with underdeveloped lungs who are experiencing respiratory distress, to the very old suffering from the cumulative effects of chronic lung disease. Respiratory therapists and respiratory therapy technicians play a crucial role. If a patient stops breathing and the brain is deprived of oxygen for longer than three to five minutes, serious brain damage will almost certainly follow. If oxygen is cut off for more than nine minutes, death usually results. Respiratory therapists and respiratory technicians are among the first medical specialists on the scene in emergencies where head injuries or drug poisoning threaten respiration.

But performing emergency resuscitation accounts for only a small part of the respiratory therapist's or respiratory therapy technician's functions. Respiratory therapy is used mostly to improve the quality of the lives of patients with chronic lung ailments. It can prevent or postpone certain complications and allow patients with respiratory conditions to feel better and function better longer.

Technically, there are three types of respiratory worker—respiratory therapists, respiratory therapy technicians, and respiratory therapy aides. Respiratory therapists and respiratory therapy technicians carry out many of the same functions; however, therapists have more in-depth education and training and are expected to carry out more complicated respiratory procedures. Their educations include courses in anatomy, physiology, pharmacology, and clinical medicine, which prepare them to exercise more independent clinical judgment and to accept greater responsibility in performing therapeutic procedures based on their own observations of the patient. Further, an experienced respiratory therapist is capable of serving as a technical resource person to the physician and other members of the hospital staff with regard to current practices and procedures in respiratory care. Some respiratory therapists conduct research. Respiratory therapists also supervise and train respiratory therapy technicians. It is the respiratory therapy technician who delivers most of the respiratory patient care, however.

Respiratory therapy aides (formerly called respiratory therapy assistants) differ from respiratory therapists and respiratory therapy technicians in that they have little patient contact. Their major responsibilities include maintaining (cleaning, sterilizing, storing) the respiratory equipment and record keeping.

SETTINGS, SALARIES, STATISTICS

Most respiratory therapy practitioners work as members of teams along with physicians, nurses, and other health care specialists in the respiratory therapy, anesthesiology, and pulmonary medicine departments of hospitals. Other respiratory therapy personnel work in physicians' offices, nursing homes, clinics, for ambulance services, and for commercial companies that provide emergency oxygen equipment and other services to home-care patients. Sometimes respiratory therapists and respiratory therapy technicians go to patients' homes to provide treatment, check equipment, and instruct the patient and the patient's family. Most respiratory therapy personnel work forty hours per week. Because this lifesaving and life-supporting therapy may be needed at any hour of any day, evening, weekend, and holiday work hours may be expected.

Currently there are approximately 100,000 respiratory care practitioners (that is respiratory therapists, respiratory therapy technicians, and respiratory therapy aides) in the United States. Sixty-two percent of them are female.

Salaries for respiratory therapy personnel vary according to education, experience, geographical location, and place of employment, but some general figures are available. The mean salary for experienced respiratory therapists is approximately $31,500. For experienced technicians, the mean is $25,500. Department directors in this field may earn as much as $78,000 per year.

There is potential for advancement for all three types of respiratory personnel. Respiratory therapy technicians and aides can progress to the therapist level by satisfying certain educational and credential requirements, and therapists can advance to supervisory status (specifically, to assistant chief or chief of the respiratory therapy department). Therapists with graduate educations may also become instructors of respiratory therapy at the college level. The American Association for Respiratory Care (AARC), the professional association for respiratory care practitioners, reports that an increasing number of people are turning to respiratory therapy as a second career. Many of these individuals are women who have completed raising their families as well as other adults who seek careers in health and who find the educational requirements, work schedules, and nature of the work in respiratory therapy to be compatible with their needs and goals. These older students often bring to the job excellent life experiences in dealing with people, and this experience tends to enhance their performance.

HOW TO BECOME A RESPIRATORY THERAPIST, RESPIRATORY THERAPY TECHNICIAN, OR RESPIRATORY THERAPY AIDE

As respiratory equipment and treatments have become more sophisticated, the education and training necessary to become a respiratory therapist or respiratory therapy technician have become more formalized and demanding. To become a respiratory therapist, a candidate must graduate from a respiratory therapy training program. These programs range from two-year associate's degree programs to four-year bachelor's degree programs. Several hundred junior colleges, four-year colleges, vocational/technical schools, and a few hospitals offer training programs. Approximately 300 of these programs are accredited by the Commission for the Accreditation of Allied Health Education Programs (CAAHEP), which on July 1, 1994 succeeded the Committee on Allied Health Education and Accreditation (CAHEA) of the American Medical Association in accrediting respiratory therapy educational programs. (CAAHEP is an independent body in which the AMA participates as one sponsor among many.) Last year, approximately 4,300 men and women graduated from accredited respiratory therapist educational programs.

Respiratory therapy technician educational programs range from 12 to 18 months in length, and a certificate is awarded upon successful completion. Of the several hundred technician programs nationwide, approximately 190 are accredited. Of these programs, several require some college credit prior to admission, and the rest require students to have only a high school diploma or its equivalent. Last year, approximately 4,050 men and women graduated from accredited respiratory therapy technician educational programs.

Although differing greatly in length and, therefore, in the depth and breadth of material covered, the curricula for respiratory therapists and respiratory therapy technicians cover basically the same ground. Typically the programs contain course work and clinical work in general science (biology, chemistry, physics, mathematics), general anatomy and physiology, cardiopulmonary-renal anatomy and physiology, microbiology, pharmacology, cardiovascular diseases, diseases of the respiratory system and disorders of breathing, general medicine and medical subspecialties, general surgery and surgical subspecialties, pediatrics, anesthesiology, patient psychology and communication, gas therapy, humidity therapy, aerosol therapy, airway management, mechanical ventilation therapy, blood-gas analysis and interpretation, cardiopulmonary resuscitation, chest physiotherapy, general patient care, cardiovascular evaluation and testing, pulmonary function testing, pulmonary rehabilitation and home care, and the ethics of respiratory therapy and medical care.

Respiratory therapy aides are trained on the job, and this training varies from institution to institution.

In high school, interested students should take college preparatory courses, including biology, physics, chemistry, health, mathematics, English, and, where possible, psychology. The academic record necessary for acceptance into respiratory therapy educational programs varies from institution to institution.

A high school diploma is usually also required for employment as a respiratory therapy aide.

Personal qualities that are essential for a successful and satisfying career in respiratory therapy include interest and aptitude in science, initiative, sound judgment, mechanical ability, physical stamina, compassion and sensitivity, and the ability to function effectively in extreme emergency situations and when working with the gravely sick and dying. Those interested in the field should keep in mind that some of the electronic equipment and high pressure gases with which respiratory therapy personnel routinely work can be dangerous. Therefore, respiratory therapists must adhere to strict safety measures and must perform regular equipment safety checks.

Certification in this field is voluntary but highly desirable. The National Board for Respiratory Care (NBRC) has established criteria for certified respiratory therapy technicians (CRTTs) and for registered respiratory therapists (RRTs). To become a certified respiratory therapy technician, a candidate must graduate from an accredited respiratory therapy technician educational program and pass a three-hour-long written examination. Upon satisfying these requirements, the candidate is eligible to use the designation CRTT after his or her name. To become a registered respiratory therapist, a candidate must graduate from an accredited respiratory therapy educational program, satisfy the requirements for certified respiratory therapy technician, and then go on to pass a two-part, written and clinical simulation examination. Upon satisfying these requirements, the candidate is eligible to use the designation RRT after his or her name. At this time, there are approximately 64,000 CRTTs and 42,000 RRTs. Licensing requirements exist in twenty states at this time, and legal credentialing is being considered in several other states. Eleven states administer an examination as part of the licensing procedure, and the test given by all of these states is the NBRC certification examination.

THE FUTURE

The employment outlook for respiratory therapists and respiratory therapy technicians is excellent. The Bureau of Labor Statistics of the U.S. Department of Labor projects an increase of 52 percent in requirements for respiratory practitioners by the year 2005. Several factors are at play here: the American population is not only growing, it is growing older, and as this occurs, it is likely that more chronic lung disease will appear. In addition, the spread of AIDS is contributing to the demand for respiratory therapy care because lung disease is common among patients with AIDS. Advances in the diagnosis and treatment of cardiopulmonary disorders and in respiratory technology should further broaden the functions of respiratory care practitioners. Greater health consciousness, accessibility of health care, and the ability to pay for health care (through private and public health insurance) will also contribute to keeping the demand for respiratory personnel high.

For more information about careers in respiratory therapy, write to the:

> American Association for Respiratory Care
> 11030 Ables Lane
> Dallas, Texas 75229-4593

> National Board for Respiratory Care
> 8310 Nieman Road
> Lenexa, Kansas 66214-1579

For information about accredited education programs for respiratory therapists and respiratory therapy technicians, contact:

> Joint Review Committee for Respiratory Therapy Education
> 1701 West Euless Boulevard, Suite 300
> Euless, Texas 76040

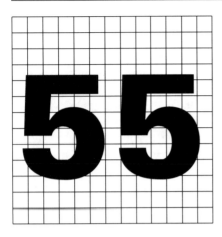

SPECIALIST IN BLOOD BANK TECHNOLOGY

including
Blood Bank Technologist

Blood is a living tissue made up of cellular elements (red blood cells, white blood cells, and platelets) that are suspended in a watery fluid called plasma. The red blood cells, or erythrocytes (the average adult has thirty trillion), carry oxygen from the lungs to the body's cells and then bring carbon dioxide back to the lungs, where it is exhaled. The white blood cells, or leukocytes (there are approximately fifty billion), protect the body against disease and infection by surrounding and destroying invading bacteria and providing immunity. Platelets help blood to clot when a person bleeds. (The average body contains two trillion platelets.) Approximately 7 percent of a person's weight is blood—the average male has about twelve pints of blood circulating through his body; the average female has about nine pints.

Transfusion of blood (both as red blood cells and as whole blood) is performed to replace blood lost during surgery, or as a result of accident, or in situations where the patient is in severe shock, and in the treatment of certain conditions and diseases (including anemia, low blood protein, hemophilia, leukemia, and cancer). The first successful transfusions of human blood were performed in 1818 by the English physician Dr. James Blundell, who used his new technique to control hemorrhaging in women who had just given birth. But success in transfusing was erratic, and it was not until 1900 that the Austrian physiologist Karl Landsteiner discovered why some transfusions did, indeed, help the patient, while others were fatal to the patient. Dr. Landsteiner discovered that not all blood is the same. He identified three different types of human blood and observed that they are not always compatible. To give a successful whole blood transfusion from one person to another, the blood from the donor must be compatible with the blood of the recipient. Dr. Landsteiner determined that blood is incompatible when certain factors in the donor's red blood cells and plasma differ from those in the recipient's red blood cells and plasma. All living cells—including our own cells, bacteria, and viruses—have as part of their surfaces protein molecules that have their own unique characteristics. Our bodies are able to recognize bacteria, viruses, or cells differing from our own by detecting these foreign proteins (which are called antigens) when they enter our body. When this occurs, our immunization mechanism sets to work producing protein molecules (called antibodies) that help to destroy or eliminate the invading cells. But just as this natural immunization mechanism protects us from invading bacteria, it also "protects" us from blood that is of a foreign—or incompatible—type, by rejecting it, and this is why early blood transfusions sometimes failed. An antigen-antibody reaction caused by incompatibility can result in a condition in the recipient known as hemolysis—or disruption of the donor cells. Hemolysis can lead to jaundice, kidney damage, and even death. For example, early in the life of a person with group A blood, an antibody against B blood cells (anti-B) develops. If that person received group B blood in a transfusion, the B cells from the transfused blood and the donor's B antibodies would combine to destroy the B red blood cells, resulting in a potentially dangerous situation for the recipient. Dr. Landsteiner's Nobel Prize-winning discovery was that there are three different major blood types—A, B, and O. In 1902, a fourth major blood group, AB, was discovered and added to the ABO, or Landsteiner, Blood Group.

Today, many other blood systems and more than three hundred blood factors (the most common being the Rh factor) have been identified. To ensure compatibility, when possible, the donor's blood is carefully crossmatched with the recipient's blood.

Transfusing is also a far more sophisticated technology today. Blood component therapy is an important advance. In the blood bank, whole blood can be separated into red blood cells, platelets, plasma, and cryoprecipitate. The plasma component of the whole blood is used for the manufacture of proteins (including albumin and gamma globulin) and coagulation factors (including Factor VIII, which is used to treat hemophilia, and Factor IX). Transfusions are even being performed on babies before birth through a process know as intrauterine transfusion. Last year, approximately 14 million units (a unit is slightly less than a pint) of blood were collected to meet the transfusion needs of 4 million Americans. Recruiting, collecting, processing, storing, testing, and typing that blood were various blood bank personnel working in public and private hospital blood banks, community blood banks, American Red Cross blood banks, and privately owned blood banks. These blood bank personnel include medical laboratory technicians, who perform daily tasks under supervision and who may also perform specialized tests that provide data for use in diagnosing diseases and evaluating treatment; medical technologists, who have general laboratory backgrounds and perform routine and certain specialized procedures in conjunction with the attending pathologist, physician, and/or scientist (in addition to supervising the laboratory and teaching other technologists); and specialists in blood bank technology.

A *specialist in blood bank technology* (SBB) is qualified by education and experience to perform all functions of the blood bank and to serve as supervisor, educator, administrator, technical consultant, and/or research specialist in this field. An SBB demonstrates a superior level of technical proficiency and problem-solving ability in selecting donors, drawing blood, typing (or classifying) blood, running pretransfusion tests to ensure the safety of the patient, detecting and identifying any unexpected antibodies in the blood that might make transfusion dangerous or impossible, investigating hemolytic diseases in newborns, and supporting the physician in transfusion therapy. An SBB may also study transfusion reactions, perform and evaluate quality assurance programs, establish programs to preserve and store blood by freezing, and operate reference laboratories to solve blood banking problems. A specialist in blood bank technology is skilled in all blood bank operations and may follow virtually any career path within this profession.

SETTINGS, SALARIES, STATISTICS

Specialists in blood bank technology work in public and private hospital blood banks and transfusion services; community blood banks; university-affiliated blood banks and transfusion services; independent laboratories; privately owned, profit-making blood banks; and university-, government-, and industry-related research laboratories. Some SBBs teach blood bank technology to medical students and medical technology students. The workweek often includes night duty, weekend hours, and emergency calls.

There are approximately 4,200 certified specialists in blood bank technology in the United States, 80 percent of whom are female. In 1993, the average starting salary for specialists in blood bank technology was $32,500 annually. Advancement in this field to supervisory or administrative positions is possible. Qualified specialists may also move into teaching and/or research.

HOW TO BECOME A SPECIALIST IN BLOOD BANK TECHNOLOGY

To become an SBB, a person must first be certified as a medical technologist and hold a baccalaureate degree (with a minimum of 16 semester hours each of biology and chemistry, with one semester of organic or biochemistry and one semester of mathematics) or hold a baccalaureate degree in a biological or physical science and accumulate a minimum of one year of full-time acceptable clinical laboratory experience following the acquisition of the baccalaureate degree. Students satisfying these prerequisites may then apply to one of the 27 year-long blood bank technology educational programs accredited by the Committee on Education of the American Association of Blood Banks (AABB) and by the Commission for the Accreditation of Allied Health Education Programs (CAAHEP), which on July 1, 1994, succeeded the American Medical Association's Committee on Allied Health Education and Accreditation (CAHEA). (CAAHEP, which accredits education programs for this and twenty-one other allied health professions, is an independent body in which the AMA participates as one sponsor among many.) Accredited programs are offered by hospital blood banks, community blood banks, universities, and American Red Cross facilities across the country. Last year, approximately 50 men and women were graduated from accredited blood bank technology programs.

A blood bank technology education consists of didactic activities covering all theoretical concepts of blood bank immunohematology plus practical experience in a blood bank setting. The curriculum typically contains courses and training in immunology, genetics, blood products, blood group systems, serology, physiology and pathophysiology, transfusion practices, and laboratory operations.

All of the accredited programs accept very limited numbers of students per class , and competition is stiff.

Personal qualities and aptitudes that can contribute to success and career-long satisfaction as a specialist in blood bank technology include intelligence, a strong interest and ability in the sciences, dependability and a sense of duty, good organizational skills, good psychomotor skills, good health, and a genuine desire to help the ill. Also, blood bank work is hectic, and SBBs must be willing and able to function effectively at that hectic pace.

Certification in blood bank technology is offered by the American Society of Clinical Pathologists (ASCP) in conjunction with the American Association of Blood Banks. ASCP administers a written examination to eligible candidates. To be eligible to sit for this examination, a candidate must (1) have a baccalaureate degree from a regionally accredited college or university and successfully complete an accredited specialist in blood bank technology program, or (2) hold BB (ASCP) certification or be an ASCP-certified medical technologist and have a baccalaureate degree plus five years of full-time acceptable clinical laboratory experience in blood banking that has been appropriately supervised, or hold a master's or doctorate in immunohematology or a related field and have three years of experience. Upon satisfying the requirements for certification, a candidate may use the designation SBB (ASCP)—which stands for specialist in blood bank who is certified by the Board of Registry of the American Society of Clinical Pathologists—after his or her name.

In 1982, the Board of Registry of the ASCP established certification at the *blood bank technologist* level in response to a perceived need for credentialling, particularly for two groups of laboratory workers: (1) individuals employed in blood bank or transfusion services who have baccalaureate degrees but are not certified medical technologists, and (2) medical laboratory technicians who work in blood banks or transfusion services who have completed a baccalaureate degree. This generalist examination was offered for the first time in 1983. The test consists of a written section only and is administered in numerous test centers throughout the United States. Upon passing this competency examination, a candidate is designated as a BB (ASCP), which stands for blood bank technologist certified by the American Society of Clinical Pathologists. Although this level of certification is new, great interest has been shown in it, and there are already approximately 1,800 certified blood bank technologists in the United States.

THE FUTURE

Although the demand for specialists in blood bank technology and other blood bank personnel presently exceeds the supply, in the future demand is expected to be stable or to decrease slightly.

For more information about a career in blood bank technology, write to the:

> American Association of Blood Banks
> 8101 Glenbrook Road
> Bethesda, Maryland 20814

And for information regarding certification, write to the:

> Board of Registry
> American Society of Clinical Pathologists
> P.O. Box 12277
> Chicago, Illinois 60612

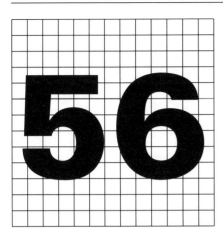

SPEECH-LANGUAGE PATHOLOGIST AND AUDIOLOGIST

Approximately 42 million people in the United States (or one American in nine) is unable to speak and/or hear clearly. According to the National Health Statistics Center, 28 million people in the United States have a hearing impairment; 14 million have a voice, speech, or language disorder. Twenty-one in every thousand children under the age of 18 have some degree of hearing loss. Six million children have a speech or language disorder. One baby in every 1,000 is born deaf. Speech and hearing impairments can affect more than a person's ability to communicate effectively—they can imperil the ability to learn, to play, to work, and to relate to others. Left uncorrected, they can seriously reduce the quality of life and cause behavioral and other emotional problems.

Speech-language pathologists and *audiologists* are health professionals who provide specialized help to children and adults who have such speech and hearing impairments.

Speech-language pathologists are health professionals who are concerned with the identification, assessment, and treatment of speech, language, and voice disorders caused by total or partial hearing loss, cleft palate or other anatomical anomaly, mental retardation, cerebral palsy, brain damage, emotional problems or foreign dialect. Children who fail to learn to talk at the usual age, those who improperly pronounce certain letters or combinations of letters, individuals who stutter, people recovering from strokes, and others suffering from partial or temporary aphasia (loss of the power to use or understand words), and other patients whose ability to communicate verbally is impaired are helped by this form of therapy.

In diagnosing and evaluating the patient's speech and language abilities and in planning and implementing a treatment program to restore and/or develop the patient's verbal communication skills, the speech-language pathologist may work closely with audiologists; physicians; psychologists; social workers; counselors; and educational, physical, and occupational therapists.

Audiologists are health professionals who specialize in the identification, assessment, and nonmedical treatment of hearing problems caused by certain otological or neurological disorders. Their goals is the prevention of hearing impairment and the conservation of hearing in children and adults.

The audiologist assesses the type and extent of the hearing impairment and supplements his or her findings with medical, educational, social, behavioral, and other data supplied by the patient's physician and other health professionals. The audiologist will then plan and implement a program of aural rehabilitation designed to meet the patient's needs. When deemed necessary, a hearing aid is dispensed.

Because speech and hearing are so interrelated, competency in one field necessitates knowledge of the other.

Speech-language pathologists and audiologists do very important "people work." Because of their skills, insights, and dedication, many hearing- and speech-impaired individuals who have felt isolated by their disabilities can, at last, understand and be understood. Whole worlds of information are suddenly opened to them, and their ideas, dreams, personalities, and futures are freed.

SETTINGS, SALARIES, STATISTICS

Audiologists and speech-language pathologists work in hospitals and medical centers, schools, rehabilitation centers, colleges and universities, and state and federal government agencies. Some are in private practice. Speech-language pathologists are also often employed by long-term health care facilities and home health programs.

There are approximately 80,000 audiologists and speech-language pathologists practicing in the United States. Salaries in these fields vary significantly, depending on setting, experience, and location. Salaries for those with one to three years of experience range between $27,000 and $30,000, and between $41,000 and $50,000 for audiologists and speech-language pathologists with 16 or more years of experience.

Advancement to administrative positions is possible in both audiology and speech-language pathology; however, the assumption of administrative duties usually curtails practice and direct patient activities. Teaching and/or research options are also available. Graduate study is usually required for such advancement.

HOW TO BECOME AN AUDIOLOGIST OR A SPEECH-LANGUAGE PATHOLOGIST

To practice as a speech-language pathologist or audiologist, a master's degree in speech-language pathology or audiology is necessary. Undergraduate programs in these two fields do exist, but they are considered preprofessional and prepare students only to function as technicians or aides. As an undergraduate studying audiology or speech-language pathology, a student will learn anatomy, biology, physiology, physics, sociology, linguistics (the science of language), semantics (the branch of linguistics concerned with the nature, structure, and, especially, the development and evolution of speech forms), phonetics (speech sounds), and child psychology.

After obtaining a bachelor's degree in speech-language pathology or audiology, the candidate proceeds to graduate school. There are approximately 235 colleges and universities offering a master's degree or a Ph.D. in these two majors. A master's degree program (which typically entails two years of study) provides advanced course work in anatomy; physics; acoustics; normal development and function of speech, language, and hearing; the nature of speech, language, and hearing disorders; the psychological aspects of communication; the mechanisms and processes of hearing and speech; the evaluation and correction of speech, language, and hearing disorders; and will also include supervised clinical experience.

A master's degree is an important enhancement to employment because Medicare and Medicaid will pay only for the services of audiologists and speech-language pathologists who hold a master's degree in these fields. In addition, a master's degree is necessary for certification. Speech-language pathologists and audiologists who hold a master's degree in these fields and who have completed a minimum of one year as an intern in an approved setting are eligible to sit for a certification examination administered by the American Speech-Language-Hearing Association (ASHA). Upon passing this national examination, the candidate earns a certificate of clinical competence (or CCC). Some audiologists and speech-language pathologists hold a certificate in both fields. Although voluntary, this credential is usually necessary for professional advancement. Most speech-language pathologists and audiologists who work in public schools must have a state-issued practice certificate, and in many states a CCC is necessary to obtain this state certificate. In many states, all audiologists and speech-language pathologists must be licensed to work.

Personal qualities that are essential to career-long success and satisfaction in the fields of audiology and speech-language pathology include the ability to concentrate intensely; a warm, friendly personality that inspires trust and confidence; and a genuine desire to help. And, because audiology and speech-language pathology are often slow processes that produce gradual results and, amid moments of deep satisfaction, moments of frustration as well, large helpings of patience and perserverence are required.

THE FUTURE

Greater than average employment growth in both of these fields is expected in the coming decade. Contributing to the increase in demand for audiologists and speech-language pathologists are two major factors: first, the population is expanding and the number of older Americans (who tend to comprise a large percentage of the hearing impaired—one out of three people over age 60 has a hearing problem) is expanding even faster; second, awareness of the importance of early detection of hearing and language problems has resulted in legislation mandating the creation of elementary school speech-language-hearing programs. (In 1993, almost 5 million American children between the ages of 6 and 21 were served through public schools.) There will be many openings for audiologists and speech-language pathologists before 2005.

For more information about audiologists and speech-language pathologists, contact the.

American Speech-Language-Hearing Association
10801 Rockville Pike
Rockville, Maryland 20852

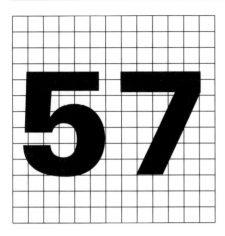

SURGICAL TECHNOLOGIST

formerly known as
Operating Room Technician

A *surgical technologist* is a member of the surgical team who works primarily in the operating room performing tasks that provide for a clean, safe surgical environment; contributing to the efficiency of the operating room team; and supporting the surgeons, surgeon assistants, anesthesiologists, nurse anesthetists, registered nurses, licensed practical nurses, and any other personnel who may be involved in the operative procedure. This allied health professional provides these services under the supervision and responsibility of the operating room supervisor, who is an RN, or under a surgical technology supervisor. A *scrub technologist* is the surgical technologist who checks supplies, equipment, sterile linens, and fluids needed for the procedure; sets up the sterile table with instruments, sutures, blades, cautery, suction, and any prostheses and solutions needed for the procedure; helps drape the sterile field; gowns and gloves the surgeons and assistants; and counts sponges, needles, and instruments prior to surgery and after the incision is closed. During surgery he or she passes instruments and other sterile supplies to the surgeons and surgeon assistants; holds retractors; cuts sutures; prepares sterile dressings; cleans and prepares instruments for sterilization; operates sterilizers, lights, suction machines, and EKG monitors; and assists in the use of electrosurgical equipment, pacemaker equipment, and sophisticated fiberoptic equipment (laparoscopes, esophagoscopes, bronchoscopes, resectoscopes). The scrub technologist may also help in cleaning the operating room and readying it for the next patient. He or she must be able to anticipate the surgeons' needs, understand the procedures being performed, and be constantly vigilant that asepsis (sterile technique) is maintained.

A *circulating surgical technologist* is the surgical technologist who is the primary unsterile member of the surgical team who obtains instruments, supplies, and equipment required while the surgical procedure is in progress. The circulating surgical technologist checks the patient's chart; identifies the patient and brings him or her to the operating room; transfers the patient to the operating table; positions the patient; washes, shaves, and disinfects the incision site; and otherwise prepares the patient. This technologist also applies electrosurgical pads and tourniquets before the procedure begins; opens the sterile field (the packages of sterilized instruments); supplies the sterile field with anything necessary during the procedure; keeps accurate records throughout the procedure; assists the anesthesia personnel; handles specimens; takes the sponge, needle, and instrument count; makes certain that dressings are secure after surgery; transports the patient to the recovery room; and assists in the cleaning and preparation of the operating room for the next patient. Surgical technologists with additional specialized education and training may also act in the role of the *surgical first assistant*. The surgical first assistant provides aid in exposure, hemostasis, and other technical functions under the supervision of the surgeon.

From region to region, institution to institution, and operation to operation, there is, of course, variation in the specific functions carried out by a surgical technologist. Some surgical technologists become highly trained and specialize in one or several related areas of surgery. A *private scrub* is a surgical technologist who is employed directly by a surgeon or group of surgeons to assist them during all of their operations.

SETTINGS, SALARIES, STATISTICS

Eighty-five percent of all surgical technologists work in hospitals—usually in the operating room but also in the emergency room and the delivery room. Surgical technologists also work in outpatient surgicenters as instructors and as private-duty scrubs for physicians.

At this time, there are approximately 38,000 surgical technologists in the United States. The average starting salary for surgical technologists is approximately $17,000 to $19,000 per year. Experienced surgical technologists average about $25,000 to $35,000 annually. Surgical technologists working on the East and West Coasts tend to earn more than average, and private scrubs also earn higher salaries. Surgical technologists usually work five-day, forty-hour workweeks and must spend some time on call.

Advancement to the positions of assistant operating room administrator (the manager of the operating room who orders supplies, arranges work schedules) or assistant operating room supervisor (the supervisor who directs the other surgical technologists in the operating room) is possible with experience. Other career options include materials manager, central service manager, educator, medical sales representative, and organ transplantation technician.

HOW TO BECOME A SURGICAL TECHNOLOGIST

There are several educational routes to a career as a surgical technologist. Most technologists today receive their education at vocational and technical schools and colleges. Surgical technologist educational programs offered by these institutions are typically nine months to one year in length. Some of the community college programs entail two years of study and award an associate's degree. All of these programs entail both classroom instruction and supervised clinical experience. Almost all require a high school diploma or its equivalent. In high school, courses in health and biology provide good background instruction. Surgical technologists are educated in asepsis and also study anatomy, physiology, medical terminology, microbiology, pathology, operating room procedure, environmental dangers, surgical complications, pharmacology, suturing, instrumentation, prosthetics, anesthesia, and transporting and positioning patients. In the supervised clinical phase of their educations, they will learn about the surgical procedures common to general surgery and to the surgical specialties (obstetric, gynecologic, plastic, thoracic, vascular, orthopedic, ophthalmologic, otorhinolaryngologic, pediatric, urologic, cardiovascular, oral, and neurosurgery).

Presently, more than 130 surgical technology educational programs are accredited by the Commission for the Accreditation of Allied Health Education Programs (CAAHEP), which, on July 1, 1994, succeeded the American Medical Association's Committee on Allied Health Education and Accreditation (CAHEA) in accrediting education programs for this and twenty-one other allied health professions. (CAAHEP is an independent body in which the AMA participates as one sponsor among many.) In 1993, approximately 2,200 men and women graduated from accredited programs. Students in these programs spend between 500 and 1,000 hours in clinical training in the operating room and a minimum of a high school diploma or its equivalent is required for acceptance.

Some surgical technologists are trained on the job over a period of six weeks to one year, depending on the institution and the student's previous experience. Often such trainees are nursing aides, practical nurses, or other hospital personnel who have transferred to their institution's department of surgery. However, surgical technologists who are trained on-the-job are not eligible to take the certification examination this profession offers.

The U.S. Army, Navy, and Air Force also train surgical technologists (designated as operating room specialists, OR technicians, and operating room specialists/technicians).

Personal qualities that are important for success as a surgical technologist include intelligence, stamina, manual dexterity, the ability to work as a member of a team, an orientation toward service to people, respect for the patient's privacy, the capacity for calm and reasoned judgment especially in stressful situations, attention to detail, and accuracy.

The Liaison Council on Certification, which is an independent certifying body affiliated with the Association of Surgical Technologists (AST), offers a certification examination for surgical technologists. To be eligible to sit for this examination, an applicant must be a graduate of a formal education program or its equivalent. On-the-job trained individuals are not eligible. This multiple choice examination, which is administered nationwide twice a year, tests the candidate's knowledge of the basic sciences, safe patient care, aseptic technique and environmental control, supplies and equipment, and surgical procedures. A passing score (which ranges from 65 percent to 75 percent, depending on the difficulty level of each exam) entitles the candidate to use the letters CST—for certified surgical technologist—after his or her name. Although not required for employment, certification is accepted by most employers as a measure of ability, and being certified definitely expands the number of job possibilities and enhances earnings. At this time, there are approximately 24,000 CSTs in the United States. To maintain certification, technologists must accumulate 72 continuing education credits every six years, or must retake the certifying examination. The Liaison Council on Certification of AST also offers an advanced certifying examination for certified surgical technologists who are practicing surgical first assistants. Upon passing this examination, a surgical technologist may use the letters CST/CFA—for CST certified first assistant—after his or her name.

Licensure for surgical technologists currently is not required anywhere in the United States.

THE FUTURE

The occupational outlook for surgical technologists—and especially for certified surgical technologists—is excellent, with growth in the field expected to be almost 40 percent in the next ten years. In fact, according to the U.S. Bureau of Labor Statistics, surgical technology will be the ninth fastest growing occupation in the U.S. Several factors should contribute to this strong demand. They include the growing American population; the aging American population; the fact that because of public and private health insurance plans, more Americans than ever before are able to afford surgery; greater health consciousness; the ever-increasing variety of surgical procedures available; and the expanded role of the surgical technologist. Cost containment considerations on the part of the hospitals and third-party insurers have resulted in the greater use of surgical technologists and their assignment to a wider range of responsibilities in the operating room, depending on the technologist's level of education and experience.

Surgical technologists do important work. Their days are fast paced, and both the technical and the human sides of their work are fascinating and rewarding.

For more information about surgical technologists, certification, and accredited programs write to the

> Association of Surgical Technologists, Inc.
> 7108-C South Alton Way
> Englewood, Colorado 80112

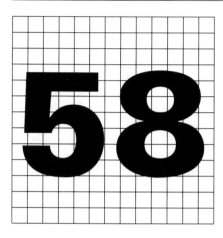

THERAPEUTIC RECREATION SPECIALIST

also known as
Recreation Therapist

A *therapeutic recreation therapist*, or TRS (also known as a *recreation therapist)* is a member of the mental health team who plans, organizes, directs, and monitors medically approved recreational programs that help patients having illnesses, mental or physical disabilities, or specific social problems to recover from or adjust to their disabilities. The goals of therapeutic recreation are resocialization, relief from anxiety and tension, improved self-image, and the development of important interpersonal relationships.

Whereas manual arts therapists (see Chapter 53) use vocational activities to evaluate the disabled patient, prevent anatomical and psychological deconditioning, and improve social and work skills and self-image; and educational therapists (see Chapter 53) use academic means to rehabilitate patients; the therapeutic recreation specialist uses adaptive sports, dancing, arts and crafts, music, gardening, camping, dramatics, and various social activities to bring the patient into the mainstream of life.

It is hoped that in the course of participating in a recreational activity the patient will not only experience the immediate excitement, fun, satisfaction, and social interaction of the activity, but that he or she will also gain the longer-range benefits of enhanced self-esteem, greater independence, and a sense of involvement, all leading, ideally, to a minimizing of symptoms and a maximizing of potential.

SETTINGS, SALARIES, STATISTICS

Nursing homes are the leading employers of therapeutic recreation specialists. In this setting, they are usually called activities directors. Therapeutic recreation specialists also work in public and private facilities for the mentally ill or mentally retarded; general, pediatric, and psychiatric hospitals;

senior centers; group homes; community recreation centers; correctional facilities; juvenile retention homes; orphanages; schools for the visually impaired; rehabilitation centers for the physically disabled; day-care centers; camps; and private community agencies. A few therapeutic recreation specialists are self-employed. Such therapists offer therapeutic recreation services on a contract basis to institutions or groups of institutions.

There are approximately 30,000 therapeutic recreation specialists in the United States. Among them are many individuals who themselves have overcome disabilities. Entry-level salaries for therapeutic recreation specialists range between $20,000 and $25,000 per year. Experienced therapeutic recreation specialists earned $29,500, on average, in 1993. Therapists working in small nursing homes had salaries at the low end of the scale, and experienced therapists working in large institutions had earnings at the high end.

HOW TO BECOME A THERAPEUTIC RECREATION SPECIALIST

Prospective therapeutic recreation specialists can enter the field at several different education levels. Students holding an associate's degree or certificate in therapeutic recreation from an accredited junior or community college may assume lower-level positions of limited responsibility (handling programming, assisting with one type of activity). To become a professional TRS, however, a student must have a minimum of a bachelor's degree in recreation, with a concentration of courses in rehabilitation or therapeutic recreation, and clinical training at an approved hospital. The National Recreation and Park Association/American Association of Leisure and Recreation (NRPA/AALR) accredits educational programs for therapeutic recreation specialists. At this time, there are approximately 50 NRPA/AALR-accredited programs offering a bachelor's degree in therapeutic education. Administrative, research, and teaching positions in this field usually require a master's degree in therapeutic recreation.

Certification in this field is offered by the National Council for Therapeutic Recreation Certification (NCTRC). While voluntary, certification is increasingly important because many states have already adopted or are considering adopting laws requiring certification for employment. The NCTRC offers two levels of certification: certified therapeutic recreation specialist (CTRS) and certified therapeutic recreation assistant (CTRA).

To become a CTRS, a candidate must hold a minimum of a baccalaureate degree with a major in therapeutic recreation or in recreation with an option in therapeutic recreation or have a minimum of a baccalaureate degree in art education, dance, drama, early childhood education, music education, physical education, psychology, rehabilitation, sociology, or special education plus five years of full-time, paid experience in the field of therapeutic recreation and 18 semester hours of graduate credit in therapeutic recreation. Upon successful completion of these educational and experience requirements, a candidate may sit for the 200 question NCTRC national certification examination.

To become a CTRA, a candidate must have a minimum of an associate's degree in therapeutic recreation or an associate's degree in recreation plus one year of full-time, paid experience in this field or the candidate must have an associate's degree in allied health, art education, dance, drama, gerontology, human services, mental health, music education, or physical education plus one year of full-time, paid experience. Two alternate routes to CTRA status also exist: a candidate may complete the NTRS 750-hour training program for therapeutic recreation assistant, or the candidate may have four years of full-time, paid work experience in an approved setting. At this time, there are approximately 12,500 certified therapeutic recreation specialists and about 1,000 certified therapeutic recreation assistants in the U.S.

Men and women who are interested in becoming therapeutic recreation specialists should be imaginative, enthusiastic, warm, and have a good speaking ability, sense of humor, and genuine desire to help.

THE FUTURE

Employment prospects for therapeutic recreation specialists should be very favorable in the coming decade. Recreation therapy is still a relatively new profession, and as rehabilitation programs and facilities expand to meet the demands of the growing and aging population and as recognition of the validity of this therapy grows, opportunities for therapeutic recreation specialists should increase. Unfortunately, however, as is the case with other support therapies, recreation therapy programs are very often subject to shifts in the economic picture.

For more information about therapeutic recreation specialists contact the:

National Therapeutic Recreation Society
2775 South Quincy Street, Suite 300
Arlington, Virginia 22206-2204

National Council for Therapeutic Recreation Certification
P.O. Box 479
Thiells, New York 10984-0479

INDEX

O

...OKS

CAREER DIRECTORIES
Careers Encyclopedia
Dicti...
Occ...

CA
Ani...
Boo...
Car...
Co...
Cra...
Cu...
Env...
Fas...
Filn...
For...
Go...
Go...
He...
His...
Kid...
Nat...
Nig...
Nu...
Pla...
Shu...
Spo...
Tra...
Wri...

CA...ERS IN
Acc...ting; Advertising, Business,
Child Care; Communications
Computers; Education;
Engineering,
the...ment; Finance,
Go... Health Care; High
Te...ion...
Jo...
M...
Re...

C
B
B
C...

Ca...
C...
Co...

C
(
I
E...

Guide to Basic Cover Letter
Writing

Business Majors
Psychology Majors

HOW TO
Apply to American Colleges and
  Universities
Approach an Advertising Agency and
  Walk Away with the Job You Want
Be...
...Quickly After
...ur Job
...Career
...Career
...un currículum vita
...ingles que tenga éxito
...d Your New Career Upon
...
Get & Keep Your First Job
  Today
Right Business Scho...
...ght Law School
...t Medical Schoo...
Things Your Way
...b Interview
...ning in Your
When You'...
...Skills
...d Career

Land a Better Job
Launch Your Career in TV News
...ke the Right Career Moves
...et Your College Degree
...e from College into a
  ...cure Job
...otiate the Raise You Deserve
...are Your Curriculum Vitae
...are for College
...Your Own Home Business
...ed in Advertising When all
  ...ou Have Is Talent
...ed in College
...ed in High School
...Charge of Your Child's Early
  ...ducation
...a Winning Résumé
...Successful Cover Letters
...Term Papers & Reports
...Your College Application Essay

...DE EASY
...r Letters
...ng a Raise
...Hunting
...Interviews
...més

O...ORTUNITIES IN
Th... extensive series provides
detailed information on nearly 150
individual career fields.

RÉSUMÉS FOR
Advertising Careers
Architecture and Related Careers
Banking and Financial Careers
Business Management Careers
College Students &
  Recent Graduates
Communications Careers
...cation Careers
...neering Careers
...onmental Careers
...Military Personnel
...0+ Job Hunters
...vernment Careers
...alth and Medical Careers
...h School Graduates
...h Tech Careers
...w Careers
...career Job Changes
...Entering the Job Market
Sales and Marketing Careers
Scientific and Technical Careers
Social Service Careers
...First-Time Job Hunter

VGM Career Horizons
a division of *NTC Publishing Group*
4255 West Touhy Avenue
Lincolnwood, Illinois 60646–1975